HIS ANGELS AT OUR SIDE

FR. JOHN HORGAN

HIS ANGELS

at OUR SIDE

✤

Understanding Their Power
in Our Souls and the World

EWTN PUBLISHING, INC.
Irondale, Alabama

EWTN Publishing, Inc.
5817 Old Leeds Road, Irondale, AL 35210

Distributed by Sophia Institute Press, Box 5284, Manchester, NH 03108.

Library of Congress Cataloging-in-Publication Data

Names: Horgan, John (EWTN Host), author.
Title: His angels at our side : understanding their power in our souls and
   the world / Fr. John Horgan.
Description: Irondale, Alabama : EWTN Publishing, Inc., 2018. | Includes
   bibliographical references.
Identifiers: LCCN 2018003459 | ISBN 9781682780305 (pbk. : alk. paper)
Subjects: LCSH: Angels—Catholic Church.
Classification: LCC BT966.3 .H67 2018 | DDC 235/.3—dc23 LC record available at
   https://lccn.loc.gov/2018003459

In memory of

Father François Crausaz, ICRSP
1958–1994

Sacerdos in Aeternum

CONTENTS

PREFACE

—————— ✛ ——————

One of the most beautiful and comforting elements of Catholic belief is the existence and ministry of angels. From early childhood, we learn that God has created "things visible and invisible," including those invisible but mighty servants, His messengers, who obey His commands and speak on His behalf. His angels watch over us, guide us on the path to holiness, and protect us from harm.

We picture them with shining faces, glorious wings that ascend on high, and strong arms that protect and surround us. Their images look back on us from the pages of Bibles and catechisms and the windows and walls of our churches. An angel announces the Incarnation of Jesus to Mary, and we echo his words in countless prayers each day. A host of angels sing Christ's Birth and proclaim His coming to the shepherds, and another moves the star to guide the Magi; they accompany the Lord throughout His life and Passion and even roll away the stone from the empty tomb. Angels work wonders in the lives of saints and prepare the way for the Mother of God in her apparitions to St. Catherine Labouré and the children of Fatima.

HIS ANGELS AT OUR SIDE

As guardian angels, they are sent by the Lord to stand by our side and to become our "personal patron saints," praying for us, protecting us from the terrors of darkness, and perhaps even prodding our consciences to bring us back from spiritual perils. We join our voices with theirs in Christmas carols and ask them to "light and guard, to rule and guide," long before we understand what those words mean for us. If we are fortunate, we are taught that they are the "invisible friends" whom we never outgrow, the inseparable companions whose unfailing love and loyalty to the saving mission of Jesus never allows them to desert us, even when we have deserted Him. They call us back, if we have not grown completely deaf to their voice, and they raise us from the dust and set us on the right road. And they continue their journey with us until we come home to our Father's house. There, they will always be by our side in the joys of Heaven.

This book is based on a television series that Mother Angelica invited me to film almost twenty years ago. That series, *Angels of God*, was the result of years of preaching retreats and days of recollection about devotion to the angels and their role in our spiritual lives. EWTN Global Catholic Network has broadcast the series around the world, and I have been delighted to hear from listeners in England, Australia, the Philippines, and South Korea who have found some benefit in it.

In preparing this book, I have retained some of the format and much of the substance of the original talks, with the addition of footnotes and references that will be useful for readers. I have also tried to add some more recent examples of angelic devotion from the Church's documents, the lives of saints and blesseds, and the teaching of our Holy Fathers. In my own formation, I owe much to the writings and spirituality of the Opus Angelorum, an international spiritual movement that has been a great blessing to me from my seminary years. I am particularly grateful to Father David

Dubois and Father William Wagner, ORC, who introduced me to this great work.

This book is meant to be not a treatise on the theology of angels (angelology) but an introduction to a unique friendship, a marvelous relationship, that is available to each person: the angel guardian whom God has chosen to be your companion on the journey of eternal life is a true spiritual "elder brother" and friend.

Spiritual friendships are remarkable things. The human experience of friendship, which is a true and lasting form of love, has a powerful role to play in our interior life. It links teacher and pupil, master and disciple, in a rapport characterized by respect, esteem, patience, and docility. It helps us to understand and live out the divine intimacy to which Jesus invites us: "I no longer call you servants, but friends" (see John 15:15).

When I was in college, I discovered a remarkable series of small books written in the 1920s by the American Jesuit Francis P. LeBuffe. *Our Changeless Friend* was made up of short, very practical meditations on the presence and friendship of Jesus in our lives, a presence that reveals its fullness in the Real Presence of the altar and the tabernacle. The meditations were but of a few pages each, but they were excellent introductions to prayer and adoration of Jesus, seen as our never-failing Friend.

As I was revising my notes from the television series, I thought that this book on the angels is meant to do the same thing: to prepare you to enter into prayer and communion with Christ our Savior through a growing friendship with your holy angel. The book can be read a chapter at a time, or picked up at a midpoint; it can be used as an introduction to an hour of adoration or simply read at leisure. The chapters are short and often repeat and reinforce certain fundamental ideas about the angelic world. I hope that it will make you eager to learn more of the Church's rich teachings about these great spirits.

HIS ANGELS AT OUR SIDE

May this little work bring blessings to all its readers! And please say a prayer for the author, who has a very patient guardian angel.

— *Father John Horgan*

HIS ANGELS AT OUR SIDE

Part 1

UNDERSTANDING THE ANGELS

Chapter 1

WHO ARE THE ANGELS?

———— ✤ ————

The angels are mighty spirits sent by God to bring us His message of life, grace, and peace. They are servants of Christ in the mystery of the Church who enlighten us, guide us, watch over us, defend us from harm, and lead us on the path of eternal life.

Every day, when the Church offers the Holy Sacrifice of the Mass, renewing the Sacrifice of the Cross that atones for our sins and gives the most perfect praise to God, the Preface of the Eucharistic prayer concludes with the Sanctus, which echoes the prayer of the angels recorded by the prophet Isaiah: "Holy, holy, holy is the Lord of hosts; the whole earth is full of his glory" (Isa. 6:3).

To prepare ourselves for the coming of Christ in the Eucharist, for this act of His redeeming love, the Church has us adopt the words of bodiless creatures, the angels, to praise the One Who took flesh for the life of the world. We ask to join our prayers to their adoration because we recognize their prayer as having a perfection that ours does not yet have, for they look on God face to face in the glory of Heaven, while we behold Him by faith.

Throughout the Old and New Testaments, we find the angels in constant adoration and praise of God in Heaven. While individual angels serve as messengers of God or accomplish particular tasks, whenever the angels are described as a group, it is as warriors ("hosts of angels") or choirs of singers and musicians. It is not so much that the angels *do* these things but that these actions are the deepest expression of their being. Angels do battle against evil simply by being so near to God and so rich in His likeness. The same is true of their praise and adoration. Their very being is adoration. If they were human, we would say that they are "adoration in the flesh." But angels do not have flesh. The great twentieth-century scholar Eric Peterson wrote:

> We are not saying that, in terms of human analogy, part of the angel-world is chosen for the task of always singing something before the Lord God. Indeed, that is an unbearable idea, and the desire to be doing such a thing for all eternity is plainly unthinkable. In reality we are concerned here with something totally different. [We are thinking here about] angels whose angelic nature consists precisely in their pouring forth, in the manner described, the praise of him who is Holy, holy, holy. This cry constitutes their ultimate nature; it is this effusion which makes them what they are—cherubim and seraphim.[1]

Yet, at the same time, mystics and saints and spiritual authors throughout the history of the Church have told us that if the angels, such remarkable and privileged creatures, could envy anyone or anything, they would envy us. They would envy us because we

---

[1] Eric Peterson, *The Angels and the Liturgy* (London: Darton, Longmans and Todd), p. 44.

have a likeness to Christ, the Son of God, that they do not have. We can be like Him in His sufferings; we can bear our crosses in union with the Cross of Jesus. We can love God the Father and accomplish His will in obedience and *in sacrifice*. Despite their communion with God, the angels cannot participate in His life in this way.

But there is something even grander about the human experience the angels would envy if they were capable of such a vice: the ability to receive Holy Communion — to be united to Jesus in His Eucharistic Body, Blood, Soul, and Divinity. We speak of the Blessed Sacrament in many beautiful hymns and prayers of the Church as being "the Bread of Angels," but, in fact, the angels do not receive the Eucharist. They adore Christ in the mysteries of the altar; they prostrate themselves before Him in wonder and praise and fascination; but because the angels do not have bodies, they cannot receive the Eucharistic Body of Christ. Because they do not share in our human nature, they cannot receive His Sacred Humanity — Body, Blood, and Soul joined to His Divinity in this most wonderful of sacraments. They are filled with wonder at the privilege that is ours, to be united to Christ in this way.

Long after we've left the church and gone on with the business of our day, however, the angels remain — adoring Him and surrounding us with their praise, their adoration, and their thanksgiving. In this way, the angels can teach us how to pray. They can share with us their spirit of adoring love, and they can strengthen us for the crosses of daily life — just like the angel whom God sent to the Garden of Gethsemane to console Jesus, Who had united His will to His Heavenly Father's. If we pray to the angels, our crosses will become lighter and our fidelity to God will increase. We will walk more surely in the way that Christ has traced out for us, following Him Who is our way, truth, and life.

Angels in the Order of Creation

The Church speaks about the holy angels in many documents, and these spiritual beings feature in the writings of innumerable saints and holy persons. But let's begin by turning to the Word of God—Holy Scripture. From Genesis to Revelation we find the angels mentioned more than 230 times, always accomplishing the same tripartite mission—adoring the Lord, carrying out His will, and bearing His message to men and women.

The Fourth Lateran Council in the year 1215 defined the existence of the angels as a truth of the Faith, a dogma that has been reaffirmed by the First Vatican Council in 1870, by the decrees of the Second Vatican Council in the early 1960s, and by Pope Paul VI in his apostolic letter *Solemni hac Liturgia* (Credo of the People of God) in 1968. The *Catechism of the Catholic Church* also speaks of the existence of the angels:

> The existence of the spiritual, non-corporeal beings that Sacred Scripture usually calls "angels" is a truth of faith.... As purely *spiritual* creatures, the angels have intelligence and will: they are personal and immortal creatures, surpassing in perfection all other visible creatures, as the splendor of their glory bears witness.[2] (328, 330)

The Old Testament does not, however, speak of the creation of the angels; we read only that they exist. Indeed, the Scriptures seem to take the existence of the angels almost for granted—but this should not surprise us, since neither do the Scriptures speak to us of God before the creation of the world. The existence of God and His heavenly court of servants would have been assumed by pre-Christian and early Christian readers.

---

[2] Cf. Pius XII, *Humani generis*: DS 3891; Luke 20:36; Dan. 10:9–12.

St. Paul fills this gap in his tremendous hymn of praise to Christ when he writes: "[Jesus] is the image of the invisible God, the first-born of all creation; for in him all things were created, in heaven and on earth, visible and invisible, whether thrones or dominions or principalities or authorities—all things were created through him and for him" (Col. 1:15–16). So, we see here that the angels, to whom the apostle refers when he mentions "thrones or dominions or principalities or authorities," have a beginning and have a purpose in Christ.

This passage led St. Augustine to suggest that the angels were included under the term "Heaven" or perhaps under "light" in the Genesis account of the first day of creation (1:1–5). The Church has adopted this understanding, teaching that the angels were created at the same time as the rest of creation:

> The Scriptural expression "heaven and earth" means all that exists, creation in its entirety. It also indicates the bond, deep within creation, that both unites heaven and earth and distinguishes the one from the other: "the earth" is the world of men, while "heaven" or "the heavens" can designate both the firmament and God's own "place"—"our Father in heaven" and consequently the "heaven" too which is eschatological glory. Finally, "heaven" refers to the saints and the "place" of the spiritual creatures, the angels, who surround God (Ps. 115:16; 19:2; Matt. 5:16). (CCC 326)

When we speak of the holy angels it is important to understand that they do not form a separate universe but rather are an integral part of our own universe. The *Catechism* continues:

> The profession of faith of the Fourth Lateran Council (1215) affirms that God "from the beginning of time made at once out of nothing both orders of creatures, the spiritual

and the corporeal, that is, the angelic and the earthly, and then the human creature, who as it were shares in both orders, being composed of spirit and body."[3] (CCC 327)

So, the angels are an integral part of *our world*. Their existence and their purpose are linked to our own. But in this universe there are *distinctions* made by the Holy Trinity to bring us together in one great chorus of praise—the praise of all creation made more beautiful by the unity that emerges from diversity.

Three's Company

Catholic tradition has identified three great divisions of creation, all directed to the Most Holy Trinity: the world of purely material creation, including the animal kingdom; the world of man, defined as beings of both matter and spirit, body and soul; and the world of the angels, who are spiritual persons of intellect, memory, and will, like ourselves, but have no material nature. Pope St. John Paul II alluded to this three-way division of creation in a catechesis on the angels in August, 1986: "We ... admire, struck dumb with wonder, the great mystery of the intelligence and love of God, in His *action of creation*, directed to the cosmos, to the human person, and to the world of pure spirits."

Often when we find the number three in Scripture or in Tradition, it points us to the Holy Trinity as the final point of reference, the center of all being and the source of all life. These triples or triptychs are what some ancient writers would have called *vesitgia Dei*, or "footprints of God"—signs of His *Trinitarian presence* in the design of the created world.

---

[3] Lateran Council IV (1215): DS 800; cf. DS 3002 and Paul VI, *Credo of the People of God*, § 8.

In this case, we might consider the cosmos itself to be a kind of reflection of God the Father, the Creator and Source of all life and the mind behind all the order, perfection, and harmony of our amazing world. Humanity, then, reflects the Word Made Flesh, the Son of God who became man for us and for our salvation; we are called to become like Him who is like us in all things but sin. And finally, the world of the angels reflects the Holy Spirit, for as the Spirit is the soul of the Church, so the angels are the ministers of the Spirit in our lives. The Holy Spirit, through the angels, continues to stir up in us the life that is the gift of Christ to His Church. As He is invisible, so are they. As He reminds us of all that Jesus has done and taught, so they make those teachings, truths, and examples present within us through enlightenments, inspirations, and intuitions. Now, while this is not a dogmatic interpretation but rather a spiritual one, it can be a way of thinking that can help us to be more aware of the Holy Trinity in our daily life.

The angels themselves seem to manifest this threefold reflection of the Holy Trinity in their very organization. There are nine names given to groupings of the angels in Holy Scripture; three come from the Old Testament and six from the New Testament: Seraphim (Isa. 6:2), Cherubim (Gen. 3:24; Exod. 25:18–20; Ps. 18:10; Ezek. 10:1–22; Heb. 9:5), Thrones (Col. 1:16), Dominions (Col. 1:16; Eph. 1:21; 1 Pet. 3:22), Powers (Col. 1:16; Eph. 1:21; Rom. 8:38; 1 Pet. 3:22), Principalities (Col. 1:16; Eph. 1:21; Rom. 8:38), Virtues (Eph. 1:21, Col. 1:16), Archangels (1 Thess. 4:16; Jude 9), and Angels (Rom. 8:38; 1 Pet. 3:22).[4] Although there are some variations in the ordering of the angels between the

---

[4] See "Commonly Asked Questions on the Angels," Q. 28, "What are the choirs of angels," Opus Sanctorum Angelorum, http://www. opusangelorum.org/membership/questions_answers.html.

Orthodox Churches and the Catholic Church, these are mainly due to nuances in translating certain Greek words in St. Paul's epistles.

The common teaching of the Church is that the nine choirs of angels draw us to the Holy Trinity so that we can experience the fullness of divine life—that is, grace—and the perfection of charity through complete love of God and neighbor. Scripture speaks to us using the image of a "ladder to Heaven," which the angels ascend and descend, as Jesus said to Nathanael (John 1:51), and so we should not be surprised that these holy friends and fellow servants help us to undergo the spiritual transformations that bring us from this world to the next.

In fact, there are three groups of three choirs each of the angels. The common task of all the choirs is our assimilation to the Triune God. The fact that we are created in the image and likeness of God, therefore, is the starting point of the angelic mission. St. Thomas points out that this triadic mission of assimilation deals with our sanctification and divinization by grace. This is threefold, as it were in a reverse image of the Trinity. The first transformation is according to the life of grace, and this is ordered to the Father. In the upper choir, this is the ministry of the Thrones. The second transformation is through contemplation of the Divine Word in wisdom, which is ordered to the Son, the Word of God; this ministry begins with the Cherubim. The third transformation is through the fire of Divine Love; this begins in the Choir of the Seraphim and is appropriated to the Holy Spirit. This is the ordering of the first and highest hierarchy.

The second and third hierarchies are modeled after this original grouping. Hence, the Dominations—in the suavity of the Holy Spirit—administer, for example, His Gifts under the Seraphim. The Powers carry the sword of battle under the Cherubim in the efficacy of the Word, which is sharper than any two-edged sword, and the Principalities watch over the discreet divisions of the Kingdom of God under the Thrones throughout the universe (in the Apocalypse the throne is the symbol of the power and stability of the Father).

In the third and lowest hierarchy which is focused upon our life in the Church on earth, the Virtues, under the Seraphim and Dominations, in the efficacy of the Holy Spirit order the living life within the Church to perfection in the beauty of the liturgy, in the great charism which manifests the love of God made man. The Archangels, bearing the sword beneath the Cherubim and Powers, defend the Church against her spiritual enemies. And the ninth choir of angels—under the Thrones and Principalities—look after the least units of God's Kingdom, the individual human heart and the family, where the life of faith needs to be consolidated and cultivated.[5]

What a marvelous help it is to remember that the holy angels are commissioned to draw us always closer to the Trinity. They are the "first created" by God—the first creatures to bear in themselves a reflection of the beauties and perfections of the All Holy. They can assist us to focus our attention and our free will on Him.

The mystery of the Holy Trinity is so great that it is sometimes difficult for us to hold it in our hearts and minds as we should when we pray. The Church in Her wisdom shows us in the prayers of the

[5] Ibid.

Mass that when we pray liturgically, we ordinarily address God the Father *through* His Son Jesus *by the power* of the Holy Spirit, who moves us to prayer. This truth is so central that the Church directs Her priests at the altar to bow their heads not only at the Holy Name of Jesus, but also whenever the names of the Three Persons are spoken together. At the end of the Divine Office, too, priests and religious bow their heads deeply at the end of each psalm when they pray the Glory Be.

These are small practices that all the faithful can adopt that help to put us into the company of the angels when we praise, pray, worship, and adore. If we adopt these physical gestures and make them part of our spiritual practice, we can better open ourselves to the angels' influence to help us turn away from sin and to practice the virtues as we ought.

The Praise of the Angels in the Old Testament

When we look at the psalms we can see this wonder and awe expressed in many contexts as the psalmist calls on all of creation to give glory and praise to God. In doing so, we join with the angels, whose praise has been offered from the very dawn of creation. As we unite ourselves to their hymns, their lauds, their wonder and fascination, our hearts are quickened with the grace of God.

For instance, in Psalm 148 we read, "Praise the LORD from the heavens, praise him in the heights! Praise him, all his angels, praise him, all his host! ... For he commanded and they were created" (Ps. 148:1–2, 5). As we have already seen, centuries later the Church Fathers would speak of the angels as being divided into choirs of song that last for all eternity.

The praise of the angels that is celebrated by the psalmist and the prophets culminates in one sense in the vision of the prophet Isaiah, who is privileged to enter into the very throne room of God. And though He cannot see the majesty of God, for no man can look on the face of God directly until He reveals Himself in His incarnate Son, nonetheless, in the midst of that splendor and glory he finds himself surrounded by the Seraphim, the fiery angels of God, who cry out from one to another: "Holy, holy, holy is the LORD of hosts; the whole earth is full of his glory" (Isa. 6:3).

This is the angelic song of praise that the Church has adopted for our Mass. For as Isaiah was called into the majesty and intimacy of the throne room of God and found himself sharing in the song of the angels, undergoing purification that he might undertake a mission, so when we come to Holy Mass we join in the praise of the angels so that we might be purified, sanctified, and divinized by the Flesh and Blood of Christ our Savior. Then we are sent out into the world to accomplish our mission: to do our part in the work of redemption and to cooperate with the Lord in the mystery of the Church so that all men and women might know the joy of love, the splendor of truth, and the beauty of holiness. The Seraphim, whose name means "burning ones," enflame us with this joyful love, and just as gold is purified in fire, they contribute to our progressive cleansing and purification. St. Francis of Assisi, who composed the Canticles of Creation and a profound "Office of the Passion" for his friars' prayer, is called the "Seraphic Saint" or "Seraphic Father" because he is thought to have a special affinity with this choir and its praise.

Do the angels have one mission or many? These passages of the Old Testament direct us toward the primary purpose of the spiritual beings: adoration of the Lord. They exist to praise God's splendor, a splendor that is manifest in all the works of His Hands. "The heavens are telling the glory of God; and the firmament proclaims his handiwork" (Ps. 19:1).

HIS ANGELS AT OUR SIDE

God's Messengers

We said above, though, that the angels' work is threefold: adoring the Lord, carrying out His will, and mediating His communication with His bodily creatures. Adoration is the *primary* end, or purpose, of angelic existence, but the other ends feature just as prominently in salvation history. In fact, our word for the spiritual beings evokes a different aspect of their work.

St. Augustine tells us in his Sermon on Psalm 103 that the name "angel," from the Greek *angelos*, means "messenger," a translation of the Hebrew *mal'ak*. Our word "angel," then, does not identify *who* these beings are so much as *what* they do, at least in part. Augustine goes on:

> The angels are spirits but it is not because they are spirits that they are angels. They become angels when they are sent. For the name angel refers to their office, not to their nature. You ask the name of this nature, it is spirit; you ask the office, it is that of an angel. Insofar as he exists, an angel is a spirit; insofar as he acts, he is an angel.

The *Catechism* quotes these words and then adds that angels announce God's will as his "servants and messengers" (329). In this role they are legates—ambassadors of God's power and authority. That is why in the book of Exodus the Lord spoke thus to His people:

> Behold, I send an angel before you, to guard you on the way and to bring you to the place which I have prepared. Give heed to him and hearken to his voice, do not rebel against him, for he will not pardon your transgression; for my name is in him. But if you hearken attentively to his voice and do all that I say, then I will be an enemy to your enemies and an adversary to your adversaries. (23:20–22)

The angels bear within themselves the power, the glory, and the authority of God. The inspirations they offer us must not be dismissed lightly; we should see the earthly assignments of the angels as a tremendous privilege God has given the world for our benefit. They speak to us in the name of the Lord. They become His "winds" and His "flames of fire" (Heb. 1:7). They even sometimes become visible to us in fulfilling their mission. Throughout the Old Testament we see how these great beings brought the message of the Lord to His servants, revealing His plan and disclosing His love.

> Angels have been present since creation and throughout the history of salvation, announcing this salvation from afar or near and serving the accomplishment of the divine plan: they closed the earthly paradise; protected Lot; saved Hagar and her child; stayed Abraham's hand; communicated the law by their ministry; led the People of God; announced births and callings; and assisted the prophets....[6] Finally, the angel Gabriel announced the birth of the Precursor and that of Jesus Himself (cf. Luke 1:11, 26). (CCC 332)

Ultimately, the mission of the angels is to assist the Lord Jesus Christ. For Jesus is the center of the angelic world. They are *His* angels, whom He has made messengers of His saving plan. "When the Son of man comes in his glory, and all the angels with him, then he will sit on his glorious throne" (Matt. 25:31).

It is the greatest hope of these ministering spirits that we will be there with them praising and adoring God for eternity. After all, they were sent forth to serve God and for the sake of our salvation — that unparalleled gift Christ entrusted to His Church and

---

[6] Cf. Job 38:7 (where angels are called "sons of God"); Gen. 3:24; 19; 21:17; 22:11; Acts 7:53; Exod. 23:20–23; Judges 13; 6:11–24; Isa. 6:6; 1 Kings 19:5.

intended for you and me. And so, if we want to live in the mystery of the Church—if we want to be filled with the riches that Christ lavishes upon Her day after day—let us turn to the holy angels and repeat often that simple but profound prayer, written some nine hundred years ago, that we learned as little children:

> Angel of God, my guardian dear,
> to whom God's love commits me here,
> ever this day be at my side to light,
> to guard, to rule, to guide. Amen.

Chapter 2

THE NINE CHOIRS OF ANGELS

✣

We know from Christian tradition and from the Holy Scriptures that there are different names given to groups of angels—nine "choirs" of angels in all. Over the centuries, many theologians and spiritual writers have considered the choirs from various perspectives.

In his introduction to the volume *Angelic Spirituality*, Steven Chase writes:

> The various angelic orders are like glass cathedral windows, each illuminating different hues, shapes, colors of holiness. The angels in a sense are co-workers with Christ and the Spirit in the work of sanctification. The angelic hues and colors represent the spectrum of light by which the Spirit unites us to Christ. Angelic spirituality thus belongs in the doctrine of sanctification.[7]

---

[7] Stephen Chase, ed., *Angelic Spirituality* (Mahwah, NJ: Paulist Press, 2002), p. 2.

This is a helpful spiritual truth to internalize as we grow in our love for God and progress along our spiritual journey: Whatever other purposes they may have, *the hierarchy of angels is meant to help us to understand the qualities of God and how we might grow in the ways of holiness*. It provides us with a sense of order, progress, and ascent in our understanding of how God's infinite knowledge establishes and maintains the order and beauty of creation through principles that we can grasp and through the ministry and oversight of His faithful servants, the angels.

These designations are not matters of dogma but rather spiritual tools to help us to appreciate the ways of holiness—the means by which God assists us through the mediation of the angels. The names themselves describe either a characteristic of these mighty spirits or an aspect of their mission in God's plan. Some of the most revered sources for our information about the angels (such as Pseudo-Dionysisus and St. Gregory the Great) have slight variations in their listing or ordering of the angelic names, usually based on nuances of translation. This should not bother us unduly. When we get to Heaven, all will be made clear.

The Angelic Hierarchy

In the fourth and fifth centuries, we begin to see an increasing interest in the role of the angels among the Fathers of the Church and other Christian writers and ascetics. One of these was an anonymous fifth-century monk who wrote under the name of St. Paul's famous convert, Dionysius the Areopagite. He is commonly known as "Pseudo-Dionysius" and is the person to whom we owe our common Christian understanding of the relationship between the ranks and choirs of the angels. His teachings have also profoundly affected and formed mystical and spiritual experience in the life of the Church. He wrote in his work *The Celestial Hierarchy*:

In my opinion, a hierarchy is a sacred order, a state of under-standing and an activity, approximating as closely as possible to the divine. And it is uplifted to the imitation of God in proportion to the enlightenments divinely given to it. . . . The goal of a hierarchy, then, is to enable beings to be as like as possible to God and to be at one with Him.[8]

The word "hierarchy" might sound rigid or even oppressive to some modern ears, but in the world of the angels the concept of hierarchy is a sacred ordering that makes knowledge and activity possible. St. Thomas Aquinas later took up this understanding and brought it to a new level. St. Thomas made intelligence the basis of the classification of the angels, who are themselves purely intellectual beings. The angels do not all have the same degree of likeness to the Lord, however; some participate in or reflect the divine perfections more than others. Therefore, according to the saint known at the "Angelic Doctor," angels belong to different choirs according to their intelligence and their place in God's plan.

The famous philosopher Étienne Gilson wrote, "In distributing the angelic hierarchies according to the progressive darkening of their intellectual illumination, [St. Thomas] is conferring a totally new organic structure upon the world of separates substances."[9] In speaking of the angels of little children, Jesus said that these angels "see the face of my Father who is in heaven" (Matt. 18:10). That means that even the humblest of angels contemplate God "face to face" and are united to Him without intermediaries. Each angel has a direct and immediate relationship with God, but they benefit

---

[8] Pseudo-Dionysius, *The Celestial Hierarchy*, chap. 3.
[9] Étienne Gilson, *Thomism: The Philosophy of Thomas Aquinas*, trans. Laurence K. Shook and Armand Maurer (Toronto: Pontifical Institute of Medieval Studies, 2002), p. 203.

from the understanding and love that higher angels are able to experience and communicate to the lower angels.[10]

The highest group of angels—the seraphim, the cherubim, and the thrones—not only contemplate God directly but are totally concerned with Him. In Him, they contemplate the source of all creation, the ultimate ideas and causes from which all creation flows. In other words, they contemplate God in His highest perfections. The second level, or sphere, of the angels—the dominations, the virtues, and the powers—do not possess the same kind of unified vision as the higher choirs. They see reality divided into the fundamental causes from which all things stem. And then the third group—the principalities, the archangels, and the angels—have a further devolved understanding of the truth of the universe, from the large and basic causes of all things into a multiplicity of particular causes.

But Pseudo-Dionysius also believed, as did St. Thomas, that the angels of the higher choirs enlighten those of the lower choirs, sharing their intelligence and understanding with them so that there is, in fact, true communication among the angels. And the angels in this way can cooperate with one another to fulfill the mission that God gives them.

The Arrangement of the Angels of the Lord according to Pseudo-Dionysius

Let's turn to the individual choirs so that we can examine the special powers each have, and how they relate with one another.

---

[10] Father Marcello Stanzione compares this to two people watching the same spectacle. The one with better eyesight may be able to describe and instruct his companion about things that the less visually gifted friend does not notice or cannot see. See Marcello Stanzione, *Gli Angeli: Guida essenziale* (Città del Vaticano: Libreria Editrice Vaticana, 2010), p. 65.

Seraphim

The seraphim are the angels closest to God. As such, they reflect most immediately the highest attribute of God manifest in creation: His love. They are on fire with the love of God; the very name means "incandescent ones" or "burning ones." Classical sacred art portrays them as entirely red and ablaze. They are usually depicted as having six wings but no faces—simply a sea or ring of flame around the Holy Trinity. Because of this burning love, more than any other angel they have the most perfect knowledge of God, which makes them the most perfect adorers. St. Jerome notes that they not only burn by themselves, but they also inflame others with the love of God.

According to the prophet Isaiah, the seraphim are the angels whom he hears crying out "Holy, holy, holy," as one of them purifies Isaiah's mouth with a coal from the altar so that he might serve as the Lord's messenger (Isa. 6:3–8). In the Extraordinary Form of the Roman Mass, the priest evokes this moment as he prays for worthiness in proclaiming the Gospel. We too should pray to the seraphim that we might be purified in our responsibilities as teachers and bearers of the Word to our families, our friends, and all those over whom we have responsibility. It was a seraph who appeared to St. Francis of Assisi when he received the stigmata. Later mystics, too, will speak of the seraphim as the Lord's messengers and intermediaries when they had extraordinary experiences of loving and transforming divine union.

Cherubim

The cherubim have a deep intellectual knowledge of divine secrets and of the ultimate causes of things; their name means "all-knowing one." As such, they constantly contemplate the wisdom and the love of God in His relationship with mankind. They reflect

His omniscience. The cherubim were the mighty adorers of the first covenant in its wisdom; images of the cherubim were the only images of beings that were permitted in the ancient Temple of Jerusalem. Their carved figures adorned the lid of the Ark of the Covenant, which prefigured both the Virgin Mary "tabernacling" the unborn Christ and the Eucharistic tabernacles of our churches, containing the new manna of Christ's sacramental Body and Blood. Embroideries of the cherubim also covered the beautiful drapery that separated the Holy of Holies from the outer court of the Temple. It was that veil that was ripped from top to bottom when Our Lord died on the Cross as the sign that He had passed into the Eternal Sanctuary and that the Temple of Jerusalem had fulfilled its purpose (Matt. 27:51). The cherubim are still considered protectors of the New Covenant and so are often depicted on tabernacles and Eucharistic vessels.

Thrones

The thrones, as their name suggests, can be thought of as beings raised up to form the seat of God's authority and mercy. A throne manifests the glory and authority of a king; it expresses stability and power. And since a throne is also a judgment seat, these angels are especially concerned with divine judgments and ordinances.

In the early Church, a common representation of God's glory in Heaven was a mosaic behind the altar and above the seat of the bishop that represented an empty throne with a radiant cross mounted above it. This image represented Christ the King, Lord of all and Judge of the living and the dead. But His judgment seat was also a throne of mercy, for Christ has redeemed the world by His Cross. His love has brought us to salvation. The thrones are never seen or experienced as "flying" but as "rolling" across the heavens, in keeping with their manifesting the Lord's stability.

* * *

The second hierarchy receives knowledge of divine secrets through the first three choirs—knowledge that they could not perceive by themselves. The ardor of the seraphim inflames their love; the wisdom of the cherubim reveals the depth of the mysteries; and the stability of the thrones draws them into constant adoration of God's majesty. In the *Summa Theologiae*, St. Thomas teaches that the names "domination," "power," and "principality" belong to government in different ways. The place of a lord is to prescribe what is to be done, and so Gregory says that "some companies of the angels, because others are subject to obedience to them, are called dominations."[11]

Dominations

The dominations are concerned with the government of the universe. They are the first of the three choirs in the second ring, which is the ring of the cosmos—the angels who are charged with great and universal stewardships. The dominations in particular are involved in the workings of divine power. They coordinate the ministries of all the angels who deal with creation. We see in the angelic world that the Church's teaching that God works through secondary causes is beautifully demonstrated. The angels mediate God's power just as the saints intercede for us with Him.

[11] *Homily 24 on the Gospels.* The translation and arrangement of the names of the choirs in the second and third spheres, or "rings," is not a matter of defined faith. Scholars continue to research the proper and best English translation of the Greek terms used in the New Testament. In the preceding chapter, I used the arrangement proposed by the Opus Angelorum. I am grateful to Father William Wagner, O.R.C., S.T.D. for his continuing research in these matters and await publication of his as-yet unfinished manuscript on this subject.

Virtues

St. Peter mentions the virtues in his first epistle (3:22), as does St. Paul in his Letter to the Colossians (1:16). The name is in some way a mistranslation or at least a "false cognate," since this choir of angels does not deal with acquired habits (virtues), but rather exercises innate, raw power over the physical universe. According to Pseudo-Dionysius, their name refers to "a certain powerful and unshakable virility welling forth into all their Godlike energies, ... mounting upwards in fullness of power to an assimilation with God; never falling away from the divine life through its own weakness, but ascending unwaveringly to the super-essential Virtue which is the Source of virtue."[12] They are the lords of causality and the principles of cosmic order in the material realm. They ensure the well-being of the world.

Powers

The powers (*dunameis*) form the third and last choir of the second angelic hierarchy, according to Pseudo-Dionysius, while other scholars and spiritual writers consider them to be the fifth choir. This choir is mentioned occasionally in the Old Testament, such as in the book of Daniel where we read, "Bless the Lord, all powers, sing praise to him and highly exalt him for ever" (Dan. 3:39). Some scholars maintain that the name "powers" is also used to indicate angels in general, since it is the Septuagint's translation of the Hebrew *sabaoth*. In the New Testament St. Paul writes that there are powers who have remained faithful to God and powers who have fallen away and become part of the empire of Satan (Eph. 6:12). The choir of powers is thought to introduce man to the higher mysteries while repressing the attacks of the "hostile powers" of Hell against the deepest laws of physical creation.

[12] Pseudo-Dionysius, *The Celestial Hierarchy*, chap. 8.

* * *

The third sphere of angels is concerned with Almighty God's plan of salvation for mankind. It receives from the highest sphere its focus on the immutability of God, which is manifested in creation by the harmonious principles and intelligent organization of the laws of nature, which are upheld by the angels of the second sphere. In turn, the angels of this third sphere pour out their influence on those who have the greatest interaction with us in the ordinary course of things established by God.

Princes or Principalities

The princes are also described as having members who have fallen away and others who have remained faithful. Principalities are the leading choir of the last hierarchy of angels. Their activities are described by Pseudo-Dionysius in this way, "The name of the Celestial Principalities signifies their Godlike *princeliness* and authoritativeness in an Order which is holy and most fitting to the princely Powers."[13] They are often seen as being the guardians of nations or peoples; this is why St. Michael is described in the book of Daniel as "the prince of Israel," who comes to the aid of Gabriel against the demonic prince of Persia. It seems fitting that this first choir in the "ring of salvation" should also look after the spiritual structure of the supernatural life of the Church.

Archangels

This choir is the most known and loved in popular devotion. Among the archangels we find St. Michael, St. Gabriel, and St. Raphael. It is traditionally believed, due to the statements of Raphael in the book of Tobit, that there are only seven archangels.

[13] Ibid., chap. 9.

Three of their names occur in Scripture, and so the Church uses these names in our worship—St. Michael, the prince of the heavenly host and the only one called "archangel" in the Scriptures; St. Gabriel, the messenger of the Incarnation; and St. Raphael, the angel of healing and of medicine. The names of the other four are not used in our Liturgy, though there are certain churches that preserve these names and make use of them in private devotion, including some Eastern Catholic Churches. Roman Catholics often refer to them as the seven archangels or the seven assisting spirits around the throne of God.

The seven archangels have been regarded from the very beginning as having a special place in God's plan; their number is often associated with the seven days of the week and the seven sacraments. It is thought that the archangels were outstanding in their fidelity to God, and so in the writings of the saints they are often called archangel princes, an appellation that connotes leadership and authority in the heavenly realm. Many spiritual authors and mystics speak of their special assistance and often attribute other "groups of seven" to their protection or patronage—virtues, gifts of the Holy Spirit, and so on. The archangels are also associated with the protection of nations, dioceses, religious communities, and the mission of the Church.

Angels

The ninth and final choir of angels is composed of those who are most involved with the doings of mankind. These angels are those who are sent out on missions from God and from whom the guardian angels are chosen. The angels who fill up this choir may be the lowest, but they are beloved because the Lord places them at our sides to watch over us and to care for us. They are the ministers of Christ's love and our protectors. They defend us against harm and temptation. They warn us of impending evil and inspire us to remain faithful to God in prayer.

The Angelic Hierarchy in Our Lives

The term "angel" can be used of each of the nine choirs inasmuch as they are all ministering spirits sent out from God. But tradition holds that only those of the ninth choir actually accomplish works involving individual persons. Certain saints and mystics throughout the history of the Church have believed that their guardian angels came from a higher choir. This has led some spiritual authors to believe that perhaps every angel has the opportunity to serve as an individual's guardian angel once. In this way, the angel shares in the redemptive mission of Christ in a particularly fruitful way, helping to guide one soul on its path of transformation and deification in Christ.

The nine choirs are often used in works of theology to understand the ways of God and the perfection of knowledge; but in our own prayer life, we can and should invoke all the choirs of angels so that we might grow in the love of God and advance in the ways of holiness.

One way we might invoke the angels is to pray the "Holy, holy, holy" of the Mass nine times in honor of the nine choirs. We can begin with our guardian angel and go all the way up to the seraphim, in that way asking all the angels of God to praise the Lord with us so that we might be strengthened and purified. Even if we do not know or understand all the responsibilities of the individual choirs, we are recognizing that God Most High has created them in their unity and variety for the glory of His Name. When we name them as individual choirs in our prayers, we are acknowledging His plan and, in effect, saying to Him:

> O Lord, my God, You have done all things worthily and well. Not only have You created Your holy angels with purpose, order, and mission, but You have revealed to Your Church a part of Your eternal plan for them and assured

us of their care and solicitude in our lives. I praise You and thank You for this gift of knowledge revealed to Your people. I glorify You for showing us the service of the holy angels to Your Divine Son, our Redeemer, Jesus Christ. I wish to benefit from their ministry in the fullest way possible, according to Your holy will. Grant, O Lord, that I may share in their understanding of the mystery of the Cross so that I can share in that mystery in the way Jesus my Savior desires for me. May Your holiness, Your wisdom, Your justice, and Your omnipotence lead me to everlasting life.

We need to ask the choirs of angels to intercede for us and to help us to understand the plan and the providence of God and to see all things in the light of His will and in the power of His grace. This can be a wonderful aid to our spiritual life, drawing us into the worship of the angels around the throne of God.

If we would praise God in union with these creatures, we must bow our heads before the incomprehensible majesty of God's creative powers. By our sides, the angels fall down in worship before the Lord and bid us to give all praise to God the Father, the Son, and the Holy Spirit. Authentic devotion to the angels will always lead us to the Trinity and to the Cross. For in the mystery of the death and the Resurrection of Christ, we find all truth, all beauty, and all salvation.

Chapter 3

THE FALL OF THE ANGELS

———————— ✤ ————————

Christian faith recognizes not only the good angels but also the
fallen angels and their leader, Satan. The fallen angels, also known
as demons, were created in goodness and beauty by God. Common
doctrine, moreover, holds that they were created in the state of
sanctifying grace. Nonetheless, they chose to turn away from God
and His will. How did this happen, even though they are so wise
and powerful?

The fall, or sin, of the angels is not described in the first pages
of the Old Testament; it is already assumed in the presence of the
Tempter in the form of a serpent in the Garden of Eden. In the
Catechism of the Catholic Church, we read:

> Behind the disobedient choice of our first parents lurks a
> seductive voice, opposed to God, which makes them fall
> into death out of envy (cf. Gen. 3:1–5; Wisd. 2:24.). Scrip-
> ture and the Church's Tradition see in this being a fallen
> angel, called "Satan" or the "devil" (cf. John 8:44; Rev.
> 12:9). The Church teaches that Satan was at first a good
> angel, made by God: "The devil and the other demons were

indeed created naturally good by God, but they became evil by their own doing."[14]

Scripture speaks of a *sin* of these angels (cf. 2 Pet. 2:4). This "fall" consists in the free choice of these created spirits, who radically and irrevocably *rejected* God and his reign. We find a reflection of that rebellion in the tempter's words to our first parents: "you will be like God" (Gen. 3:5). The devil "has sinned from the beginning": he is "a liar and the father of lies" (1 John 3:8; John 8:44). (391–392)

When the angels were first created, they did not "see God" in the way that the blessed in Heaven see Him now in what is called the Beatific Vision—the sight that fills us with endless joy. Instead, the angels knew God in a way similar to our knowing Him in faith. They understood that the Creator had made them in beauty, perfection, and order, and this attracted them to Him. They had gifts of grace analogous to our own as well as the virtues of faith, hope, and charity and the seven gifts of the Holy Spirit. God wanted them to love Him freely and to do so in a way that would engage their whole personality in His plan of creation and salvation. So He put them to a test, a trial of faith.

The Test

Servant of God Father John Hardon, SJ (1914–2000), wrote,

What was the angels' probation? We do not know exactly how the angels were tried. However, it could be only one of two conditions: obedience to the God Who created them and love of the God by Whom and for Whom they were made. And these two go together like condition and consequence.

[14] Lateran Council IV (1215): DS 800.

But the angels were to love God only in the measure they obeyed Him.[15]

Sacred Scripture has not told us what form this trial of faith took or what issue was at stake, but some early Fathers of the Church and many great theologians of later ages believed that the issue must have been the Incarnation of Christ, the center of history. Though the Church has not made a definitive statement on this matter, even the *Catechism* provides texts that could be used in its support:

> Christ is the center of the angelic world. They are *his* angels: "When the Son of man comes in His glory, and all the angels with Him ..." (Matt. 25:31). They belong to Him because they were created *through* and *for* him: "for in him all things were created in heaven and on earth, visible and invisible, whether thrones or dominions or principalities or authorities — all things were created through him and for him" (Col. 1:16). They belong to him still more because he has made them messengers of his saving plan: "Are they not all ministering spirits sent forth to serve, for the sake of those who are to obtain salvation?" (Heb. 1:14). (331)

If God revealed to the angels that His Son, the Eternal Word, would one day unite Himself in being to a human nature, a nature lower than the angels, that would mean that they would have to adore God in a form lowlier than their own. And by implication, they would not only bend the knee (so to speak) to the Word Made Flesh but would have to assist man, the as-yet-uncreated lower creature, in taking *his special place* in God's Kingdom. Their own intelligence, strength, and power would be directed to cooperating with God in this plan in which they did not have the highest

---

[15] Father John A. Hardon, SJ, *Meditations on the Angels* (Bardstown, KY: Eternal Life, 2006), pp. 7–8.

place, despite being the first created and despite many superior gifts in their angelic nature.

This, many theologians suggest, was the truth laid before them. Would they accept it? Would they be loyal to Him? This trial demanded faith from the angels, because the fullness of God's mysteries was not laid out before them, and hope (that is, trust) that the Lord God, from Whom they had received only love and perfection, would continue to be all good and all loving toward them. It also required them to be humble, which means—for them as it does for us—knowing who they were, who they were created to be, and who they were not.

Spiritual writers often speak of "dark nights" in which faith undergoes crisis and temptation. Human beings may undergo several in their ascent to God; they are progressive, and they purify, kindling the small flame of faith into a blazing fire of love. The trial of the angels was the prototype of all such trials, but it was experienced by creatures whose knowledge and ways of knowing were and are far beyond ours, and who therefore needed only one such test to elicit their final and irrevocable answer.

The Irish Benedictine abbot Blessed Columba Marmion (1858–1923), explains the way in which angels understood and chose in his beautiful volume *Christ in His Mysteries*:

> As you know, the angels are creatures exclusively spiritual. Their actions are not measured by time, as ours are. Further, those actions of theirs possess a power, a wideness of range, and a profundity, to which no human action can attain. Pure spirits, the angels do not reason at all. In us, the extreme excitability of our imagination, a sensitive faculty tied to the body's organism, presents a number of particular things to us for our choice as "good things," the variety of which slows up the action of our intellect and will. We go from

one "good thing" to another; we afterwards return to one of them that perhaps at first we had decided to reject. It is not the same as this for the angels. In an angel, wholly spiritual by nature, hesitation has no place. In an angel, acts of intellect and of will take on a character of fullness, of fixity, of irrevocability, that confers on those acts an incomparable strength.

No human existence, however prolonged, will attain, through the whole of its operations put together, either the power or the amplitude of the intensity of that one single act by which the angels, put to the test, made and fixed their choice.[16]

So when God revealed His will to the Angels, they not only understood Him, but they also understood the ramifications and consequences of their choice. And choose they did: Those whose pride would not accept the place that God had decreed for them in His plan banded behind Lucifer, formerly the most magnificent of all the angels, whose rejection and refusal are summed up in the words "I will not serve." How awful those words sound when we think of them being shouted out for the first time by an angel whose nature was a masterpiece of God's primordial creation!

Order of Battle

Lucifer, whose name means "light bearer" of God, refused God's plan, turning his gaze inward on his own created beauty and perfections as ends in themselves. He did not choose a positive good in which he could be happy; he knew his happiness could be only in God and in and through obedient love. In so doing he *became*

---

[16] Blessed Columba Marmion, *Christ in His Mysteries*, trans. Alan Bancroft (Bethesda, MD: Zaccheus Press, 2008), pp. 213–214.

darkness because he no longer *reflected* the divine light of God; he *excluded* God in his being, his intellect, and his will; he *chose* only himself. Henceforth, his trinity has been egotism, pride, and selfishness: "I, Me, and Myself" take the place of Father, Son, and Holy Spirit. And with him, there fell a great multitude of other angels as well: "His tail swept down a third of the stars of heaven, and cast them to the earth" (Rev. 12:4).

But in the midst of the upheaval in the orders of angels, among those who had chosen against God and His will, another shout arose from an angel who was placed in one of the lower ranks, an archangel who cried out with an intensity of love that overcomes all personal pride: *God is all perfect. God is all good. Who is equal to Him in wisdom or power? Who is like unto God?*

These words, the first rhetorical question in the history of creation, were formed in perfect truth, love, and humility. They identify and name the angel who spoke them: Michael, who becomes the leader of the heavenly hosts in the first clash of wills between God's angels and those who had become His adversaries:

> Now war arose in heaven, Michael and his angels fighting against the dragon; and the dragon and his angels fought, but they were defeated and there was no longer any place for them in heaven. And the great dragon was thrown down, that ancient serpent, who is called the Devil and Satan, the deceiver of the whole world—he was thrown down to the earth, and his angels were thrown down with him. (Rev. 12:7–9)

This passage from the book of Revelation describes St. John's vision in which the whole breadth of God's plan of salvific love was laid out before him. But it has also been traditionally and rightly used as the description of the very first warfare in creation, when Michael and his angels did battle against their former brothers.

We know this to be true because St. John declares that their place was "no longer" found in heaven, so he is actually describing the original rebellion and battle that started at the revelation of the Woman with Child. This is the reference used by many theologians to identify the trial of the angels and the nature of their sin: It is the rejection of the Incarnation (see 1 John). The scene goes on to reveal Satan's ongoing battle against the Word Made Flesh and His Immaculate Mother, from the first moment in which God revealed His plan to its final consummation at the end of days. St. Michael's work of casting the Evil One out of God's presence continues in the unfolding of His plan for the Church and for each one of us.

When Lucifer and his angels were driven out of heaven by Michael and his armies (see 2 Pet. 2:4), God confirmed the good and faithful angels in grace and granted them the Beatific Vision (see Matt. 18:10). Now they look upon God in all His beauty, perfection, and goodness; they love even as they are loved. Nothing can turn them away from beauty, truth, and goodness revealed in all their fullness.

Devil's Advocates

But what about the fallen ones? Why did they not repent? Why were they not redeemed, as we are? We have to remember that since the angelic way of "thinking" is so different from ours, so is the quality of their choosing. We are often influenced by passions, circumstances, incomplete knowledge, conflicting motivations, and so on; we can reevaluate our choices and reasoning, alter our conclusions, and even repent of our malice. But angelic malice is of a different order. The choice the angels made was not influenced by emotions, conditioned by circumstances, fostered by bad education, or formed in partial knowledge of the consequences of the choice. Their will is unchanging; and so is their decision to rebel. The *Catechism* states:

> It is the *irrevocable* character of their choice, and not a defect in the infinite divine mercy, that makes the angels' sin unforgiveable. "There is no repentance for the angels after their fall, just as there is no repentance for men after their death."[17] (393)

In his catechetical talks about the angels, St. John Paul II said:

> When, by an act of his own free will, he rejected the truth that he knew about God, Satan became the cosmic "liar and the father of lies" (John 8:44). For this reason, he lives in radical and irreversible denial of God, and seeks to impose on creation — on the other beings created in the image of God, and in particular on people — his own tragic "lie about the good" that is God....
>
> In this condition of existential falsehood, Satan — according to St. John — also becomes a "murderer", that is one who destroys the supernatural life which God had made to dwell from the beginning in him and in the creatures made "in the likeness of God": the other pure spirits and men; Satan wishes to destroy life lived in accordance with the truth, life in the fullness of good, the supernatural life of grace and love. The author of the Book of Wisdom writes: "... death has entered the world through the envy of the devil, and those who belong to him experience it" (Wisd. 2:24). And Jesus Christ warns in the Gospel: "... fear rather him who has the power to destroy both soul and body in Gehenna" (Matt. 10:28).[18]

[17] St. John Damascene, *De Fide orth.* 2, 4: PG 94, 877.
[18] St. John Paul II, General Audience, August 13, 1986.

The *Catechism* reassures us of the limitations of the Devil's power:

> The power of Satan is, nonetheless, not infinite. He is only a creature, powerful from the fact that he is pure spirit, but still a creature. He cannot prevent the building up of God's reign. Although Satan may act in the world out of hatred for God and his kingdom in Christ Jesus, and although his action may cause grave injuries—of a spiritual nature and, indirectly, even of a physical nature—to each man and to society, the action is permitted by divine providence which with strength and gentleness guides human and cosmic history. It is a great mystery that providence should permit diabolical activity, but "we know that in everything God works for good with those who love him" (Rom. 8:25). (395)

The Angels and Atonement

In his *Meditations on the Angels*, Father Hardon traces the basis for the theology of atonement and expiation—the meaning and significance of human suffering—in the differences between human sins and the sin of the angels. By God's mercy and design, we can repent of our sins and be restored to God's friendship; we can learn from the consequences and results of our sins and be moved by His goodness to repentance and even to a deeper love than we had known before. This is part of the deep mystery of the Cross, which not only gives purpose to the crosses we bear in life but invites us to atone for our sins and the sins of others—healing and repairing the damage done by sin, healing and atoning for the sufferings of Christ Jesus.

Father Hardon writes:

> The cross is a grace providing us with the opportunity not just to atone for our past sins, but by embracing the cross

we can become holier than we could humanly have done had we not sinned.[19] It is not just that by having sinned, we can therefore atone for our past misdeeds, but we can also obtain expiation in God's mercy for the sins of others.

What are we saying? We are saying that as sinners we owe God the price not only of atoning for our past misdeeds but the privileged opportunity of expiating the sins of others. Our suffering is a divinely granted opportunity to expiate the sins of other people: to expiate the anger of other people by our own patience; to expiate the lust of others by our own chastity; to expiate the greed of others by our own generosity; to expiate the envy of others by our own selfless charity; to expiate the sloth of others by our untiring labor; and to expiate the gluttony of others by our practice of abstinence.

All this is locked up in the lessons of the angels. They sinned and were punished. We have sinned, and we have the privilege not only of expiating our own sins but the sins of others, and we thus have the privilege of becoming holier because we have sinned.…

Love builds on gratitude. If there is one gift of God for which we should be eternally grateful, it is that we sinners have been spared the punishment of hell.[20]

Deeply formed in Ignatian spirituality, Father Hardon has given us a wonderful insight into the mission of the guardian angels and,

---

[19] This is not meant to be an absolute statement, but a *limited one*, referring only to *individual cases*. Father Hardon's point is that after sinning we *can* achieve a higher degree of perfection through the mercy of God causing in us a deeper conversion of heart than we had experienced before.

[20] Hardon, *Meditations*, p. 11.

indeed, of all the angels: They want us to grow in love rooted in gratitude through the contemplation of the Savior's Cross and the practice of atoning, repairing, and healing love. We atone and make reparation not only by the patient and generous "bearing up" of sufferings and trials, but by the loving practice of virtue, service, and mission. We not only console the Pierced Heart of Jesus by our holy hours, sacrifices, and renunciations, but we also heal the wounds of His Mystical Body, the Church, when we reach out in charity, kindness, and service to others.

When we seek to do the perfect will of God *as completely and lovingly as we can today, in whatever circumstances present themselves,* we are entering into a new and deeper way of prayerful union and faithfulness that will make even the heaviest burdens bearable and the darkest nights no longer frightening. Our holy angel will be by our side, a pillar of fire, to go before us and to guide us along the way. He will teach us the way of humility and faithfulness, which will be our greatest safeguard against all the attacks of the adversary.

Father Hardon concludes his meditation with this beautiful prayer, which we can use often:

> Lord Jesus, we thank You for the lesson that the fall of the angels should teach us: the lesson that sin is most displeasing to Your Divine Majesty; that suffering is a grace by which we can expiate our own sins and the sins of others; that having sinned in the past, You want us to become holier than we have ever been. Lord, have mercy on me, a sinner. We beg You, dear Jesus, to give us the grace to die rather than ever to offend You by a single mortal sin. Help us to learn from the fall of the bad angels. Help us to follow the example of the good angels and remain obedient to Your Divine Will so that, like them, we may join You in that

everlasting happiness that is reserved for the angels and to human beings who use their free will to submit themselves to your Divine Will. Amen.[21]

---

[21] Ibid., p. 12.

Chapter 4

INTERACTING WITH THE ANGELS

If we were to summarize the activities of the angels in the pages of Scripture, we might say that their duties relate to God, to the created and material world, and to man and his place in God's plan of covenant and salvation.

These activities may seem to be extraordinarily broad, especially when we think of the angels directing every aspect of the material world *and* participating in the work of salvation. And yet, when we consider that the scientific principles that guide our world—the laws of gravity and so on—are not just created but sustained by God, then it shouldn't seem to be so far-fetched that He might delegate some part of the management of the universe to His ministering spirits.

Indeed, in the ancient world, philosophers such as Aristotle and Plato believed that this was so—and they did not have the benefit of revelation. They knew nothing of Scripture or of what God had revealed to the Jewish people. In the early Church, St. Augustine believed that every visible thing in the world has an angelic power placed over it, and later on Cardinal Newman, the great convert who wrote in the nineteenth century, went as far as to say in a sermon that, when it comes to the mysteries of existence, "we have more real knowledge about the Angels than about the brutes [animals]."[22]

How Many Angels Can You Fit ...?

Holy Scripture speaks to us on many occasions of the great number of angels that exist, a number that is impossible for our minds to calculate or even to estimate. In the book of Daniel, we read that the prophet saw the Lord as "the Ancient of Days"—an image of God's eternity—and saw that "a thousand thousands served him, and ten thousand times ten thousand stood before him" (Dan. 7:10, 22). These massive numbers of angels are meant to communicate to us a numberless multitude far too great for our minds to understand. And in the New Testament, St. Luke tells us that "a multitude of the heavenly host" appeared to the shepherds in Bethlehem on the night the Savior was born. St. Thomas Aquinas taught that the number of angels was far greater than that of any of the material creatures. He wrote in the same article of the *Summa Theologiae* that the more perfect creatures were made in greater numbers because God's creation is primarily ordered toward the perfection of the universe (I, q. 50, art. 3).

The Scriptures really do not reveal anything to us about the number of fallen angels or demons, though some theologians argue that a proportion of good angels to bad can be found in the book of Revelation, which says that a dragon's tail sweeps a third of the stars out of the heavens (12:3). "Stars of heaven" may be a metaphor for the angels, and the dragon a metaphor for the Devil. In

---

[22] John Henry Newman, Sermon 13, "The Invisible World," in *Plain and Parochial Sermons.*

any case, we can safely assume that the number of faithful angels far exceeds those who fell away.

Our Lord Himself alludes to the great number of angels during His arrest when He tells Peter, "Do you think that I cannot appeal to my Father, and he will at once send me more than twelve legions of angels?" (Matt. 26:53). In the time of Our Lord, a legion of Roman soldiers consisted of nearly seven thousand men, so Our Lord here seems to be impressing upon Peter — and upon us — the truth that He has all the hosts of Heaven, "a great multitude," at His command.

One of those angels had appeared a moment before, comforting Jesus in Gethsemane after He had accepted the *chalice of suffering* for us and for our salvation (Luke 22:43). Popular devotion has identified that angel as a special comforter of the sick and those who care for them. Catholic nurses, particularly after the 1940s, often recited prayers to the angel of the Garden of Gethsemane so that they could be strong in tending to the patients entrusted to their care, particularly during the long and lonely hours of the night. For those who take care of suffering relatives or sick children, and for those who work in health care, devotion to this angel may be a source of great grace and wisdom to help them find the right words to say to those who suffer. It is in Christ and His Sacrifice that we find significance and meaning for our human pains. If we are called to be angels of consolation for the sick, we can call down the grace of God through the intercession of that angel who was chosen by the Lord to bring comfort to His Divine Son on the night of His Passion.

O Angel of Gethsemane, chosen by the Father to bring strength and consolation to Jesus during His agony, I ask you to be with me now as I keep watch over my loved one who is sick and suffering. Help me to offer my best care, love, and protection to this child of God. May my words and my touch be filled with gentleness, my presence bring comfort, and my prayers bring rest and healing sleep. Do what I cannot do, O loving Angel, to bring healing and strength to soul and body, according to the Father's will. Amen.

The Angelic Nature

When we say that angels are pure spirits, it means that there is nothing material about them at all. They lack a permanent body and even a physical shape. Nonetheless, we often have very definite ideas of what angels should look like, ideas that have come down to us from paintings and sculpture, Christmas cards and pop culture. Although these representations are often charming and attractive, we have to remember that they are all the product of imagination—robes and wings and swords and chubby little faces may have symbolic or emotional value, but they can also mislead us about the real nature of the angels.

We human beings are formed with and limited by matter; that is, we have a certain size, a certain shape, a certain weight, and so on, and we move from one place to another at a certain speed. Our material self binds us to a definite framework—the laws of the material world, including time and space. But angels have none of the limitations—nor the capacities—that come with a material body. Touch, taste, sight, smell, hearing, passions, emotions—these are all tied to the physical nature of human persons but are totally foreign to the angelic experience. These capacities affect us in many ways, allowing us to experience pleasure and mirth, suffering and death. But the angels are subject to none of these.

So, when we see depictions of angels as winged humans, we have to remember that this has very little in common with the presentation of the angels in the Holy Scriptures, the Tradition of the Church, or the lives and experiences of the saints. Holy men and women of all ages always described angels in terms of light, power, and majesty. Even when they appear in "gentle form," like the angel in the form of a child who appeared to St. Catherine Labouré, there is something unworldly about them that fills the soul with awe and reverence. They have been sent to us with a message, and their purpose is to communicate it to us in words and signs.

The powers and faculties of the angels are purely spiritual ones. This means that angels have an intellect, a mind, and a free will. Angels can know and can love. But the ways in which angels arrive at knowledge and love are very different from the ways in which we do.

Our way of getting information and ideas into our minds is through the senses—for instance, through hearing when we converse or through sight when we read, as you are doing right now; then our intellect works through the information and processes it. We observe the world around us and our observations are carried to our mind, which sorts and analyzes and forms conclusions. We eventually reach the truth, but sometimes only after errors have crept in, due to misperceptions, misunderstandings, and so on. The human intellectual process is one of trial and error.

The angels don't have to go through this process. With them, there are no trials because there are no errors.

Learning from the Angels

Studying the nature of the spiritual beings can help us to purify the aspect of our nature that corresponds to theirs: the soul. The soul is usually thought of as having three faculties: (1) memory, the sum total of the experiences of our lives with which we construct our identity; (2) intellect or mind, by which we reason and understand and grow in knowledge; and (3) will, by which we love and choose what is good and true and beautiful. These spiritual faculties are "who we are" after we die; when we come into the Lord's presence for the particular judgment, they are flooded with His light. When we enter Paradise, we experience the Beatific Vision and the Communion of Saints through them.

Here on earth, we can be attracted to and choose what is sinful because our intellect is clouded and our will is weak. As part of the spiritual life, we must progress in purifying our memory, our will, and our intellect so that Christ may reign in us, ruling all these powers of our soul. That is how we become holy.

The angels can help us in this task by leading us to and teaching us about prayer and adoration. Further, they lead us to see comprehensively God's plan for us. The example and prayers of the angels can help us to cease cultivating the memory of past sins and nursing past hurts; to direct our mind to the truth of God; and to strengthen our will so that we might choose what is good and right day after day.

Cardinal Newman points out the difference between the way human beings and angels think and understand. This is his description of human learning:

> We know, not by a direct and simple vision, not at a glance, but, as it were, by piecemeal and accumulation, by a mental process, by going round an object, by the comparison, the combination, the mutual correction, the continual adaptation, of many partial notions, by the employment, concentration, and joint action of many faculties and exercises of mind.[23]

Angels don't do any of these things. An angel's intellectual knowledge starts about where ours leaves off. His knowledge of the world

---

[23] John Henry Newman, *The Idea of a University*, discourse 7.

is part of his very nature; it is innate and total. He starts off with the complete picture that you and I, with time and hard work, have to piece together. The turn-of-the-century theologian Cardinal Alexis-Henri-Marie Lépicier wrote this about the angelic intellect:

> Although an angel's intellect is not his own substance, just as our intellects are not our own substances, yet he possesses such penetration, that he is able, by a single glance, to take in the whole field of science lying open to his perception, just as we, at a glance, can take in the entire field of vision lying exposed to our view.[24]

Now, angels *do* grow in knowledge because they have participated in the history of salvation and in the revelation of Christ. As Christ has progressively disclosed Himself through the course of salvation history, the angels, too, have added to their understanding and experience of God. We might say, too, that an angel grows in knowledge and understanding through his ministry on our behalf. As an angel accompanies a man or woman as guardian and sees how the grace of God grows in that person, and how he or she experiences fulfillment through the love of God and the life of the sacraments, the angel comes to know the ways of God in a new and powerful way.

And what does that knowledge serve in the angels? What is its purpose? Well, it must be for the increase of their love and adoration because, as we have said, the angels were created for adoration. They constantly behold the face of God in Heaven (Matt. 18:10). They live to proclaim His glory. Their entire being, all of their activities, and all that they experience in their relationship with us

---

[24] Alexis-Henri-Marie Lépicier, *The Unseen World* (London: Kegan Paul, Trench, Trubner, 1906), pp. 27–28.

contributes to this praise and magnifies in them a happiness that is beyond the comprehension of anyone who has not experienced it.

Even while they are watching over us, even while they are declaring their dominion over all creation as servants of the Lord, they are at the same time gazing on the face of God in Heaven. It is this loving and adoring union with God that is the source, not only of their praise, but also of all the help and clarity they offer to us — that is, the grace they communicate to us that flows from God Himself.

Praying with the Angels

If we want to benefit from the companionship and guardianship of the angels — if we want our minds, our hearts, and our memories to be purified and sanctified — we must look to the angelic way of adoration. Remember: Mankind, too, was created to adore and to love God above all else. We can adore Him here with these bodies on this earth, but we can view Him only with the eyes of faith; as St. Paul wrote, "For now we see in a mirror dimly, but then face to face" (1 Cor. 13:12). Even so, our worship is, by the grace of God, true and good and worthy.

The angels, though, can amplify our praise by reflecting it directly to God, "face to face." This is what we call upon them to do in every Mass when we pray the Gloria, adapted from the angelic praise the Shepherds heard on Christmas night and found again in the book of Revelation: "Blessing and glory and wisdom and thanksgiving and honor and power and might be to our God forever and ever!" (Rev. 7:12).

It is precisely because the angels never turn their faces from the Lord that they can carry out His missions for them on earth. In the same way, if we want to grow in the spiritual life; if we want to become holy; if we want to be *divinized*, as the Fathers of the Church describe the life of grace, then we should ask the angels to help us never to turn our faces away from the face of God and to be mindful of Him always and in everything, just as they are. In loving our neighbor, we love God; in loving our God, we learn to love our neighbor. Let us ask the angels, therefore, for three gifts: First, to pray always; second, never to withdraw our face from the face of God; and third, to live, to act, to move, and to choose always in the presence of God. Whenever we pray the Sanctus (Holy, Holy, Holy), we can remember these three angelic characteristics and order our prayer of petition in union with their praise.

We learn how to pray always by remaining united to the will of God, by asking that the Lord's will be done in us and through us in our every action. One way to make this possible is to offer up short prayers throughout the day. Every time we finish something—whether it's writing a work memo, finishing class preparations, correcting a law brief, washing the dishes, or changing a diaper—we can offer up our efforts to the Lord with a little prayer: "For the love of You, my God." Or: "Jesus, I offer You this work for Your glory and that I may be transformed and changed." And when we have this spirit of prayer, addressing the Lord with little aspirations throughout the day, we will also learn to offer up to the Lord the crosses and the hardships of daily life.

One of the most powerful and thought-provoking prayers that we can say is the very simple, "Jesus, I want what You want for me." It is a prayer that little children can learn in just a moment and that we can pray until the very last moment of our lives. To say these words means that we believe and trust that Jesus not only wills what is the best for us but that He knows better than we do *what* is best for us. It is a prayer that expresses dogmatic faith and personal loving trust.

Of course, in a very real sense it is no different from repeating the words of the Our Father, "Thy will be done," or the Blessed Mother's reply to St. Gabriel, "Behold the handmaid (or, for a man, *servant*) of the Lord. Be it done unto me according to thy word." However, sometimes we need to take the words of Scripture or the formal prayers of others and make them our own by repeating them in simple, short, and direct language that is adapted to our needs and our stage in the spiritual life. Even the saints did this; for example, one holy Italian priest and famous spiritual writer, Father Dolindo Ruotolo (1882–1970), used to say in moments of anxiety or frustration, "O Jesus, I surrender myself to you; take care of everything!"

"I want" is an expression that we hear our children say constantly; but if we are honest, it is even more often repeated, even if silently or subtly, by adults. We grown-ups also mistake wants for needs and are thus drawn to things that may satisfy us for a moment but soon leave us empty and hurting. Overcoming our selfishness, bending our pride, submitting our will to that of another out of love—these are lessons that we must learn and live in our family life, in our human loves, and in our friendships as well as in our relationship with Almighty God. Yet, because we do not always realize the full consequences of our actions for ourselves and others and because our previous sins (even if they are forgiven) and our unexamined emotions often influence our decisions, such learning may take an entire lifetime.

The holy angels, unlike ourselves, have an intelligence and a way of understanding that sees a decision in all its dimensions, as well as the potential consequences of each possible choice. They are not influenced by past sins, since they remained faithful to the Lord in their moment of trial, and they are not subject to emotions as we experience them. If we turn to them in our moments of choice and decision, asking for their clarity, strength of purpose, and obedience to the will of God, our minds will become ever clearer and our wills shall become ever freer as we pray, "Jesus, I want what You want for me."

There will be times when it will be difficult to say this little prayer because it is not always easy to let go and to let God act. And there may be moments when we clearly know that what we want is not what Jesus wants for us or from us. Love and obedience begin in the will before they are expressed in our actions. If we do our best to will what He wills and to ask for His grace with humble and trusting hearts, He will not refuse us. And our little prayer, however weak, will be magnified by our angel's presence and his joyful shout, "Here I am Lord, I come to do Your will."

The angels will always watch over us with wonder and awe if we give ourselves to Our Lord, remaining in His presence and uniting our daily crosses to His. As we do so, we'll find that we will make Him present to others. Other people will find in us a magnetically attractive beauty—the beauty of holiness, the beauty of Christ shining through us. And we will find that the Lord makes use of us to be messengers to others, to collaborate with His holy angels, and to bring our brothers and sisters closer to Him, the Source of love and life.

Chapter 5

GROWING WITH YOUR ANGEL

———————— ✠ ————————

In the Old Testament's book of Tobit, we meet the angel Raphael, whose name means "God has healed." When he reveals himself to Tobit, the archangel says, "And so, when you . . . prayed, I brought a reminder of your prayer before the Holy One; and when you buried the dead, I was likewise present with you. When you did not hesitate to rise and leave your dinner in order to go and lay out the dead, your good deed was not hidden from me, but I was with you" (Tob. 12:12–13). This demonstrates that the angels rejoice in our good works and present them to the Lord as offerings of worship and prayer.

And in the book of Revelation, at the end of the New Testament, we also read that the angels of God participate in our prayers being lifted up to the Most High. In Revelation 5:8 we meet the four angels who fall down before the Lamb, each with a harp and golden bowls full of incense, "which are the prayers of the saints." Later, in chapter 8, we see a similar instance: "And another angel came and stood at the altar with a golden censer; and he was given much incense to mingle with the prayers of all the saints upon the golden altar before the throne; and the smoke of the incense rose with the prayers of the saints from the hand of the angel before God" (8:3–4). The meaning of these images is unmistakable: The angels offer our prayers to God. They join their praise and worship to ours.

Every day at Mass, when priests pray the Roman Canon (also known as Eucharistic Prayer I), we ask that the Lord's angel may come and take this sacrifice to God's altar of Heaven, so that in turn we might receive Christ's blessings and graces. The prayer of an angel is like a flame; he is consumed by it, not in the sense that he is *destroyed* by it, but in the sense that his entire being *becomes* prayer. And so, if we want to grow in the life of prayer, we do well to turn to the angels and ask them to pray with us and for us, taking our prayers up into theirs, so that our prayer becomes richer in charity and our obedience to the Father's will becomes more complete.

In their ministry, the angels are conscientious and faithful. When they stand by our side, God sees us joined to them. And so, we can hardly do better than to ask the Lord to help us to draw closer and closer into the fidelity that characterizes the life of the angels.

Echoing the many instances of the symbolic groupings of seven angels or spirits in the book of Revelation, we may infer that there are seven habits and seven "spirits" we can nurture that will bring us closer to the Lord through His angels.

Respect for Truth

The most basic first step to growing in relationship with God and His angels is to cultivate a great respect and love for all the truths of our Faith. The Lord wants to reveal more and more of His richness to us, but we must first be open to it. Uniquely among the bodily creatures (but in common with the angels), we have the ability to ponder the absolute sovereignty of God and the place of Christ as the center of all creation—and so to place Him at the center of our hearts. In exercising this capacity in ways great and small, such as through spiritual reading and prayers for understanding God's truth, we predispose ourselves for the Holy Spirit's gift of understanding, one of the seven gifts poured out on us in the sacrament of Confirmation.

We waste so much time each day letting ourselves be bombarded by information, imagery, and entertainment of all kinds that has no lasting value, and may even be harmful to our faith. We can easily let our minds and our souls become desensitized and coarsened, weakening our free will and losing our appreciation for spiritual truths as well as our ability to examine and to process the experiences of our lives in the light of faith and eternal truths. Critical thinking (in the positive sense), our sense of humor, and even our sense of music can all become debased and isolated from who we think ourselves to be. We must look within ourselves honestly and bravely in order to purify our minds and hearts.

Regular Sacrifice

Respect for the truth is just the beginning. It is also necessary for us to make sacrifices—to offer our work, our labor, our challenges, our daily crises, big and small—in union with the sacrifice of Christ. To do this, we have to live in the presence of God and be aware of Him so that we can act *intentionally*. This supernatural awareness gives us a sense of inner peace and gives meaning to all our actions. When the Angel of Peace appeared to the children at Fatima to prepare them for the coming apparition of the Mother of God, he said, "Make of everything you do a sacrifice."

All too often, we think that we can offer only painful or unpleasant things to God as sacrifices; but God is the giver of all our blessings and happiness, too. When we remember this truth, we can lift these things up as a spiritual gift that is very pleasing to Him. We offer our joys to the Lord as well as our sorrows, as what is called a sacrifice of praise. When we give Him such an offering, we not only sanctify that moment, that particular happiness, but also transform the capacity that we have for happiness so that we can indeed become a constant sacrifice of praise and thanksgiving to God and prepare ourselves for the endless joy of His presence in Heaven. When we practice this way of sacrifice *and* praise — concepts that seem contradictory but are essential to one another in the Christian life — we dispose ourselves for God's gift of wisdom.

Purifying Our Conscience

We must also consciously train ourselves to be faithful to the Lord. The good habits of mind and body that form us in virtue don't just happen: We have to purify our conscience with the intention that all that we do might be for God's greatest glory, and therefore for our highest good. In this way, again, we can act in imitation of and in collaboration with the angels.

We accomplish this purification by submitting ourselves to the guiding light of the Magisterium — that is, the teaching authority of the Church. We look to the Church to help us and to guide us so that we can live our lives as God intended. So many people today, and even many Catholics, wander in darkness and confusion because they do not look to the living Magisterium of the Church for guidance on issues that determine their happiness in this life and in the next. The angels possess all this knowledge perfectly; we can grow in it through our efforts and the grace of the Holy Spirit's gifts of understanding, counsel, and wisdom.

If we are going to overcome the culture of sin and death that so dominates our world, we have to steep ourselves in the culture of life that is the Church. The resources at our disposal are nearly endless: the encyclicals and other instructions of the popes, the guidance of our local bishops, the writings of the saints, the commentaries of the great Catholic scholars through the ages, and so on. We need to reflect upon these treasures and ponder them prayerfully so that we can acknowledge and be faithful to the truth about God and about our own selves. This is how our conscience is formed and reformed—how we become informed practically and how we grow in grace. It is only by doing these things that we can learn to accept and to embrace God's will in our own lives and in the lives of others. It is only in this way that we can accept and do good with the experience of suffering, illness, and aging here on earth. This is how we come closer to the mystery of Jesus' Cross and experience its saving power. This is the school of the gift of knowledge, also called the "science of the Cross."

Choosing the Good

Knowing what to do is one thing; choosing it is quite another. The next step to growing in Christ through the angels is in the choices we make every day. Quite simply, we need to pattern our lives on Jesus. This is important to remember: We do not imitate the angels as an end in itself; rather, we ask the angels to assist us in imitating Christ Jesus. We imitate the angels to become more like Christ—true God and true man, the perfect fullness of spirit and matter.

Mother Alexandra, a famous Romanian Orthodox nun, wrote these beautiful words in her book *The Holy Angels*:

The choirs each successively reflect and channel the perfection flowing from the Godhead. The angelic orders impart the holy light one to another and it reaches us and enlightens us according to our several capacities. One could then liken the choirs to a threefold waterfall falling in three consecutive cascades, bringing clear mountain water to the thirsting plain below. At the same time they can be likened to an ascending ladder by which we may reach ever higher, even unto "Deification."[25]

That is our goal: to be so conformed to Christ that we can be called "deified." The holy angels assist in this work, so that we can drink of the "living Water" and ascend by the ladder of their choirs. And so, by looking to the Lord, by turning to Scripture each day, and by pondering the Word of God that is given to us in the Bible and the Church's Sacred Tradition, we come to grow strong in the ways and the means of fidelity. Through following Christ day after day, denying ourselves, and imitating Him in the little things of life as well as in the great, we ascend step by step. Even when we find the climb demanding, we find ourselves at peace — at peace with God and at peace with ourselves, for our angel is by our side, encouraging us along the way.

Acts of Kindness

Every day our imitation of Christ should express itself in the practice of kindness. Kindness is an expression of generous love that goes beyond and exceeds the duties of justice. In the words that we speak and the smiles that we offer to others, we express the peace of God within us and give a gift whose impact cannot be measured. In these little things, we show the delicacy of our spiritual life and our attention to the will of God. As the Letter to the Hebrews notes,

[25] Mother Alexandra, *The Holy Angels* (Minneapolis: Light and Life, 1989), p. 159.

"Do not neglect to show hospitality to strangers, for thereby some have entertained angels unawares" (Heb. 13:2).

Many of the saints demonstrated such acts of kindness by their words and their example. St. Camillus de Lellis, the reformed mercenary soldier and gambler, founded his Ministers of the Sick as an army of nursing priests and brothers in service to the suffering. As he went through the wards, seeing needs that others could not see, he would invoke the guardian angels of his patients and frequently whisper into the ear of one of his eager but maladroit disciples, "*Più cuore nelle mani!*" (Put more heart into what your hands are doing!) The same spirit filled the heart of the Spanish Blessed Speranza (+1983), foundress of the Sanctuary and Congregations of Merciful Love. This mystic, who lived in great intimacy with the angels, would often tell her Sisters, "Before you do any work of kindness for anyone, look at them with love. That is the most important thing you can do."

A kind word of charity overcomes many temptations and actually banishes the Devil. Every act of kindness that we perform is like a little exorcism moving away the power of darkness, pushing back the shadows of our pride and establishing the reign of light in our world. Remember: The saints and angels show themselves in the little things as well as in the great. Most people experience the help and presence of their guardian angels in the "small services" they offer us in day-to-day life that simply make things easier. As Jesus taught us in the Gospels, "He who is faithful in a very little is faithful also in much" (Luke 16:10). So, if we can practice kindness in the ordinary encounters of daily life, we will be ready for those difficult moments when we are tested and find ourselves having to call upon the love of God and to implore the graces of the Holy Spirit. But we will possess that love of God already through the fire of divine charity within. "Jesus, I want what You want for me."

The Way of Prayer

To walk constantly in the presence of God and in the company of
the holy angels, we must also cultivate a spirit of prayer, consis-
tently and patiently lifting up our mind and our heart in dialogue
with the Lord. One of the ways we can do this is by adopting the
prayers of the Mass that are associated with the angels in everyday
life. If we pray the Sanctus (Holy, Holy, Holy), for example, at
the beginning of a time of mental prayer, we will unite ourselves
with the praise of all creation, and our prayer will begin on a firm
foundation. For people who do well with calmly repeated prayers,
we can say the Sanctus nine times, thinking one by one of each of
the choirs of angels and "climbing their ladder" to the very presence of God Himself. This reminds us that prayer takes effort; it
is a journey and an ascent to God. And so on the pilgrim way, we
will be praying not only with our guardian angel but with all the
hosts of Heaven.

In his book *The Angels and the Liturgy*, Eric Peterson speaks in
great depth of the importance of this triple cry, "Holy, Holy, Holy,"
in the book of Revelation. He points out that it is not only the
seraphim of the prophet Isaiah who shout forth this hymn, but also
the Four Living Creatures—angels who represent the Gospels and
the life of the Church—whom John hears.

> The whole description of the heavenly court culminates in
> the Sanctus cry of the living creatures. The eternal world
> blossoms out in the praise of God.... Because the eternal
> world is utterly imbued with the praise of God, (the four
> living creatures) cry day and night without ceasing: "Holy,
> holy, holy, is the Lord God ..." In Isaias 6 we do not yet hear
> about the ceaselessness of the cry of praise. If the Apocalypse
> emphasizes that the cry of "Holy" goes on day and night,
> this is connected with the fact that here it is the divine

throne-bearing angels and not the seraphim who utter the Sanctus, so that it is as representatives, as it were, of that eternal world in which God Himself sits enthroned, that they send up their cry of "Holy" forever without interruption.[26]

Our prayer opens us to the Lord's will, to the enlightenment and the encouragement that God wants to give us. When we leave our prayer, then, we can go back to our daily life refreshed and renewed, strengthened for what lies ahead, better able to give witness in our actions, in our choices, in our words, and in our works to the presence of Christ within us — His abiding love and His constant grace.

Ceaseless Rejoicing

Finally, if we would be faithful to the Lord and to the mission of the holy angels — to their work, to the presence in our lives, to their guardianship — it is important for us to rejoice in our loving God. St. Teresa of Avila is said to have quipped, "From silly devotions and sour-faced saints, good Lord, deliver us." We are to radiate joy — the joy that is ours in recognizing that we are children of God, the joy of realizing that Christ has won the victory, the joy of knowing that every day is not simply a day of bearing a cross but of bearing witness to the Resurrection.

Many of the saints were known particularly for their joy. St. Philip Neri, who was called "Philip of the Joyful Heart," drew many to Christ through his radiant personality. He even had a special gift of healing those suffering from depression. What was his secret? Certainly, he had particular personality traits that made him a lovable friend. But above all, it was his trust in Christ Jesus our Savior that filled him with peace and overflowed from his heart.

[26] Eric Peterson, *The Angels and the Liturgy* (London: Darton, Longman, and Todd, 1964), pp. 3–4.

Another outstanding example of such "joy in the Lord" is Blessed Edward Poppe, a diocesan priest from Belgium who died in 1924 at the age of thirty-three. After a very active first few years of ministry, he developed a heart condition that would lead to his early death. While convalescing at a village convent, he became known to the children as "the priest who smiles when he prays." Father Edward would spend his holy hours before the Blessed Sacrament renewing his acceptance of God's plan for him, often smiling silently at the invisible Friend who dwells in the Tabernacle. His days and nights were heavy with all the burdens of illness and infirmity; but deep within, he was at peace. Deep within, he knew that he possessed a joy that would not be taken away from him. This is the kind of truth we must all learn, usually over time; it is vitally important for our spiritual lives, for our life of prayer, and for our discipleship.

Let your heart always be joined to the Heart of Mary—Mary who rejoiced in the Lord and magnified Him by her words and by her works. Mary *stood* beneath the Cross of her Son; she did not swoon or faint. She is an icon of strength and quiet courage, sharing our pains and showing us how to remain constant, asking us always to say, "I am the servant of the Lord. Be it done unto me according to Your word" (see Luke 1:38). In this way, you will be not only enriched with the presence of Christ but filled with the joy of the Holy Spirit and able to give that joy to all whom you meet.

These steps unite us to the angels and bring us to God's love. But there are also seven essential traits of character, seven habits of virtue, that we should develop in the company of the holy angels if we want to imitate these great servants of God and, with their help, deepen our discipleship of the Lord.[27]

[27] These seven characteristics are found in the spirituality of the Opus Sanctorum Angelorum, which means "Work of the Holy Angels." The meditations that follow are my own composition for this introduction to the spiritual life.

Spirit of Fidelity

The only trial the angels went through was one of faithfulness. There were those who remained constant in their love of God and their obedience to His will. And there were those who turned away, who cast themselves out of God's presence and focused their attention and their love only on themselves and their idiosyncratic idea of goodness and happiness.

For ourselves, fidelity is expressed in our obedient and loving trust in God and in our confidence in the Church as our mother. This begins in our thoughts. We must guard ourselves against temptations against the Faith. Sometimes, these temptations cannot be dismissed simply by reasoning them away; we can become confused or just unable to access the information we need at the moment. Sometimes it's better just to flee from them, as we would from temptations of the flesh, offering a prayer and putting down or turning off whatever is troubling us. (Occasions of sin can just as easily be intellectual as physical.) In all things we want to express that loyalty to God that is essential to our happiness and our salvation.

That is why I recommend that every day, when we begin our time of prayer, especially mental prayer, we should renew our acts of faith, hope, and charity. These simple prayers that many of us learned in our first catechism classes are often overlooked today, but they are very important because each day brings with it objections and temptations against the Faith, whether in media and pop culture or among colleagues, friends, and even family members.

So, let us resolve to begin our prayer by saying, "My God, I believe in all that You teach, in all that You have revealed through Your Church because You are the source of all truth and Your Church can neither deceive nor be deceived." If we do so, we will receive a special gift from God to remain open to wisdom, to understanding, to counsel — indeed, to all the gifts of all the Holy

Spirit. And we will be steeled in our resolve to choose fidelity every day, as the angels did during their trial of faith.

Our fidelity must also extend to the way in which we live out the other virtues of life: loyalty to our family and friends, patriotism toward our nation, and responsibility to our word, to our work, and to our other obligations and duties. To have an interior life means that we strive to be constant, long-suffering, and true. Fidelity is the foundation of all these qualities, and therefore of true character.

The Spirit of Humility

This fidelity then expresses itself in humility. Humility is one of the most misunderstood of the virtues. All too often, it is mistaken for a lack of self-confidence or a negative self-image. Humble people are easily ignored but may, on the other hand, attract bullies and others who seek to prey on their goodness. When we are confronted with true humility, we realize that there is a winsomeness and a graciousness about it. If we are not prepared to encounter this virtue, it can make us very uncomfortable. And yet, we all recognize its absence—at least in others. The proud or arrogant person is always talking about himself—when it would be much more interesting if he talked about us!

So, what is humility all about? The word comes from the Latin *humus*, which refers to "soil" or "earth." The humble person recognizes that, like everybody else, he or she has been created from the dust of the earth, but also from the breath of God's mouth. In other words, all creation is made up of the same microns and subatomic particles, but we have been given a human soul with its human endowments by God Himself. Indeed, all we have that is good comes from God. God is the source of all life, all truth, all beauty, and all goodness in the universe and in each of us. And even if we have developed these original God-given gifts and capacities through our own efforts, nonetheless we must give God the glory that is due to Him.

Jesus Himself spoke of this virtue, which so characterized His incarnate life on earth, when He said, "Learn from me, for I am meek and humble of heart" (Matt. 11:29). These words are the key to understanding humility as the virtue that prepares for and protects all the other virtues that we strive to acquire and to practice here on earth. Even the virtues of faith, hope, and charity require humility: We cannot believe in God and His Holy Church if our pride and self-importance blind us to His truth and will. We can only hope and trust in the Lord's promises by recognizing that He is infinitely good and that He loves us more truly and more effectively than we love ourselves. Humility is absolutely necessary for divine charity, for it makes it possible for us to love God above all things and in all things, to choose Him for Himself because He is "all good and deserving of all our love."

Humility is also essential to our faithful and growing love for our neighbor, which involves the overcoming of selfishness and the sacrifice of our ego for the sake of another person. It helps us to overcome what I sometimes call the "unholy trinity": I, Me, and Myself. It is this "triune ego" that locks us up in the little hell of our own making, the isolation and loneliness of pride and self(ish)-sufficiency. When humility and fraternal charity are united, we can practice Christlike forgiveness in an ever-fuller way.

To speak about the saints "excelling at humility" may seem to be a strange turn of phrase, but it is unquestionably true. Examples from their lives abound and are often among the things we remember most clearly from their biographies: Consider St. Francis, who gave up wealth, family, and station to serve the poor and the forgotten, and St. Thérèse of Lisieux, who wrote the magnificent doctrine of her "little way" with a pencil and a few schoolgirl's notebooks. Think of the simplicity of the Curé d'Ars—St. John

Vianney—the man all France talked about; the heroic service of Mother Teresa; or the strange and charming lives of St. André Bessette or Blessed Solanus Casey, both of whom answered doors, swept floors, and worked miracles with an almost routine regularity.

We can be grateful too for the refreshingly dry humor of St. Bernadette Soubirous, whose patience was often tried by visitors to her convent. When confronted by a lady who marveled at her modest responsibilities, the saint answered with a humility rooted in realism, "What do you do with a broom, madam, after you have finished sweeping? You put it behind a door until it is useful again, no? And that is exactly what the Most Blessed Virgin did with me!"

My own favorite teacher of spiritual humility is not yet beatified, though we may certainly hope for that day to come: Cardinal Rafael Merry del Val (1865–1930), an extraordinary man of exceptional gifts. The son of the Spanish ambassador to England, he was brought up in English public schools (what we would call private schools), entered the Diplomatic Corps while still a seminarian, and was made a Monsignor before even being ordained! Handsome, multilingual, and a talented horseman (and a fine dancer, before the seminary!), he seemed destined for great things. At age thirty-eight, he was secretary to the conclave that elected St. Pius X as pope in 1903. The new pope recognized all his talents and made him his secretary of state and cardinal. For eleven years, he worked at the side of a saint who became a second and beloved father to him, and so he became the second most powerful man in the Church.

Even after the death of Pius X, Merry del Val retained important positions as the archpriest of St. Peter's and secretary of the Holy Office. But he also poured all his money into an orphanage and boys' club in the poorest neighborhood of Rome, wore a hair shirt, and frequently used the discipline on Fridays in memory of the Passion. Why did he do all this? The cardinal was acutely aware of the temptations to pride and selfishness that were constantly around him. He knew his own talents, gifts, and responsibilities—and he knew that if he did not live entirely for Christ, he would be the unhappiest of men. He composed the Litany of Humility[28] as his own profound expression of prayer as he did battle against what is fleeting in order to win what is eternal.

The invocations in this litany are the words of someone who is very aware of the temptations of power and influence, as even a few lines demonstrate:

> From the desire of being honored, *Deliver me, Jesus.*
> From the desire of being consulted, *Deliver me, Jesus.*
> From the fear of being forgotten, *Deliver me, Jesus.*
> From the fear of being suspected, *Deliver me, Jesus.*

> That in the opinion of the world, others may increase,
>   and I may decrease,
> *Jesus, grant me the grace to desire it.*

> That others may be praised and I unnoticed,
> *Jesus, grant me the grace to desire it.*

> That others may become holier than I, provided that
>   I become as holy as I should,
> *Jesus, grant me the grace to desire it.*

The cardinal made this litany a part of his daily private prayers; it was discovered only after his sudden death at the age of sixty-five. When first published, it made a profound impression on people

---

[28] See the appendix in this book for the full version of the Litany of Humility. I am happy to note that Nicolas Diat, who collaborated with Cardinal Sarah on his book *The Power of Silence*, has included the litany in his introduction to the book. Silence bears fruit in humility.

around the world. You have only to read it through to have some sense of how much it meant to the man who wrote it, and what it cost him to come to such a place in his own spiritual life. What courage he had to put the thoughts of his mind and heart down on paper in these words! After you have read it, try to *pray* it according to your needs and your vocation. You may not be able to pray the whole litany at once, but it will bring you to a different place in your prayer and in your relationship to Our Lord.

You can ask your guardian angel to help you to understand this litany in relation to your life, for here again the angels go before us as models and examples. They are spiritual beings with nearly unimaginable power, and yet they use that power solely to glorify the Lord and to cooperate in His will — all with perfect joy. Their trial of faith involved the willingness to look beyond their own perfections and marvel before the infinite perfections of God — to choose His will for them rather than create a false world out of their own vanity. Ultimately, they would find their greatest likeness to the Word and participate in the mystery of His Incarnation by *serving* — think what that word means — as our guardians here on earth. This plan of God cannot help but amaze us, whenever we think of it. Surely we, with much more mundane talents, can aspire to do the same.

The Spirit of Magnanimity

St. Thomas Aquinas and many of the great teachers of the Middle Ages said that the virtue of humility must be paired with another virtue called magnanimity, or liberality of heart. The virtue of magnanimity expresses the desire to do great things for God and neighbor because God has done so much for us. To respond to the Lord with generosity means to give back to Him, in whatever ways our circumstances will allow, for all that He has given us. If we live in this way, practicing magnanimity together with the virtue of humility, then our offering to God will be whole and complete and our lives will be lived with a special joy—the joy of serving the Lord in truth and in goodness, with unity of heart and a spirit of wholehearted trust in His providence for each one of us.

Magnanimity is often associated with philanthropists and others who give generously to charities or projects to help those in need. But in fact, magnanimity is most often found among the poor, among those who share the little they have with a truly generous heart, who give "without counting the cost." We ought to practice this virtue not only toward the Lord directly by our worship or through works for the Church, but also and especially toward our neighbor, whom He commands us to love even as we love ourselves. This generosity is expressed in compliments and kind words, in praising others rather than blaming, in finding something good to say about even the most frustrating people. Generosity in forgiving others disposes us to receive the merciful forgiveness of Christ. Jesus taught, "The measure with which you measure will be measured back to you" (Matt. 7:2; Mark 4:24, NABRE). Even more important are the words Jesus teaches as part of the Our Father: "Forgive us our trespasses *as* we forgive those who trespass against us." That small word, which indicates degree or amount, may be critical to our salvation.

The Spirit of Obedience

As we grow in the practice of humility and magnanimity, we realize that there is no room for pride or for envy. Pride and envy would be foolishness. They would not fulfill us; rather, they would destroy the works of God within our hearts because humility and magnanimity lead us toward wholehearted obedience to God. The obedience Jesus practiced so perfectly to His Father's will is not simply an exterior obedience—an obedience of activity or of "doing"—but an interior obedience—an obedience of mind and of will. To practice this kind of obedience, we need to see it as an expression of justice to God, Who is the All-Mighty One Who sustains us and to Whom we owe everything; and of the virtue of religion, which moves us to reverence and worship. These virtues gradually move us toward an ever-more-perfect charity (love) for God in Himself. We do what He wills out of love, a love that increases in power and in its embrace of all that He loves. As we love more and more perfectly, so we practice obedience ever more joyfully. We do not obey out of fear or subjection: as St. John teaches in his first epistle, "Perfect love casts out fear" (1 John 4:18). Like Edward Poppe, we learn how "to smile at the will of God," and to fulfill it in peace.

We ought to obey when we are sure of the Lord's will, even when it goes against our own insights and preferences. When we do this, the grace of humility will join itself with the grace of obedience to bring the matter to the good end that God desires. St. Teresa of Calcutta, for example, found it easy to offer all kinds of difficult personal services and care to the most outcast among the poor, but she found it very difficult to allow herself to be photographed over and over wherever she went. She spoke about this to various priests and bishops, who all told her that she had to allow the photography. Finally, she made a deal with Our Lord: for every photo she had taken, He had to release a soul from Purgatory! With this thought in mind, she became remarkably patient with all her photographers, professional and amateur—and she must have tens of thousands of heavenly friends who were former poor souls! Though I am sure that only Mother Teresa could cut that kind of deal with Our Lord, we can advance in patience and grace in our own ways.

In our practicing obedience, the Lord certainly does not want us to be robots; rather, He wants us to dedicate our free will totally to Him—and that can take place only when and to the degree that *we trust that God loves us more than we love ourselves* and that He cares for us and desires our happiness, and the happiness of those whom we love, more perfectly than we do. Then we can be obedient to the Lord, handing over to Him the cares and concerns that lie upon our heart.

The practice of obedience, therefore, requires us to purify our will and our memory. To do this, we must learn to eliminate criticism, rebellious thoughts, indignation, spitefulness, bitterness, and so on from our memories and our way of thinking. As we get older, we realize how much of our memory is devoted to "bad memories." We retain all the thoughts of past hurts, disappointments, and wounds we have suffered from others. We may also spend too much time thinking of our past sins. We brood over them consciously, and all too often they unconsciously influence our ways of thinking and of judging others, diminishing our love for Our Lord.

It is vitally important to work through all these memories, entrusting them to Our Lord and leaving them in His Sacred Heart—a heart that was wounded so that we could find understanding and healing in Him. Each of us has memories of hurts and wounds over the years that we cannot ever seem to understand, no matter how much we try. We remain baffled at how things happened the way they did or why someone treated us in such a cruel way. The angel who walks by our side has seen all these things more clearly than we have, but it may not be in God's plan that He reveal his knowledge to us in this world. We may simply have to turn them over to Our Lord, trusting that He will explain all things to us in Heaven. That is something that we can do in prayer, formally willing not to give ourselves over to such endless considerations and reconsiderations.

Lord Jesus, here in Your Presence, with my angel at my side,
I turn over to You these memories, hurts, and confusions

from my life. I entrust them to Your infinite wisdom and Your loving Heart. I do not want to become lost in their entanglements any longer. I believe that You will one day explain all things to me in Your Heavenly Kingdom and that I will be at peace in the truth. When such memories return to me, I ask You to help me to be strong by remembering this act of trust I have made. Give me Your grace to break away from the power of such memories, to eliminate all bitterness in my thoughts, and to do Your Holy will in that moment and always. Amen.

In learning to forgive those who have hurt us or who have made themselves our enemies by their actions, we must follow the same path. Forgiveness can be very, very difficult, especially when we have been hurt by someone whom we loved, and may still love. In today's world, there are few among us who do not belong to broken families or who have not known the pain of a broken heart. Forgiveness is a process that has many steps, and most of them are painful—like peeling an onion, which brings new tears with every layer exposed.

We have to remember that forgiveness is a matter not of our emotions but of our will. What has happened to us was real, and it may hurt us for a long time to come when we remember or think about it. But forgiveness is a choice we make. *We have to will to forgive. We do so because it is the right and best thing for us to do: That is why Jesus asks it of us.* It is right and best for us because it restores our freedom, liberating us from the domination of another's evil, expressing our self-determination and free will, and affirming our faith in the justice and mercy of God.

There are times, on the other hand, when others who are ready to be forgiven desire and seek out our forgiveness. These are sweet moments and consolations that penetrate our souls, though there may still be hard times to come. But all too often, the person who has hurt us is not ready to be forgiven, nor even ready to change or to repent. There may be real physical or emotional danger involved; psychological illness, addictions, and substance abuse can seem to split one person into two (or more). Situations like these may require a spouse to flee in the night, to take the children away to safety, or to exclude a family member from the home. And even when these grave dangers are not present, a long-suffering person may know that trust is lost, and there will always be the real and present danger that this once-beloved, still-loved person will repeat the same or worse actions — if not to oneself, then to other innocent victims.

Forgiveness does not mean that the person is restored to the same level of trust or friendship that was once enjoyed. We may have to accept the painful but real truth that the relationship is now forever changed, and that we have to maintain a safe distance in the future. St. Aelred of Rievaulx, a great English Cistercian monk, spoke of this as "unstitching a friendship."

So, how do we forgive in these situations? How do we obey the Lord, Who asks us to forgive not seven times but seventy times seven times (see Matt. 18:22)? To listen to the words of Jesus is to find peace and freedom, and so we come back to that same difficult but necessary first prayer:

> Lord Jesus, I will what You will. I want to will it with all my heart. Hear me and heal me, help me to let go of the hurt that N. has done to me. Let me leave them in Your arms and in Your heart. In Your time, in Your wise and perfect ways, make them understand what they have done and give them the grace of repentance, change and conversion. Help me to be strong now, to go forward in my life as Your friend, Your faithful disciple. Free me from bitterness and be with me in

my solitude. Fill the empty places in my heart and my days with Your divine love. Amen.

If possible, it is good to speak about this forgiveness to a priest in confession or perhaps during a retreat, particularly if we believe we have to limit access to or end all contact with a person. This does not mean that our forgiveness was not real, only that the harm done still requires a "separation in peace."

The Spirit of Love

Any book on the spiritual life—and certainly any book on the angels—must repeat the word "love" again and again. Love is always in the center of our life of faith. The goal of everything we do is to be united to God in eternal love.

First of all, we must remember that love is not just a feeling that comes and goes, but, like forgiveness, it is an act of the will—a choice. Whereas the angels now spend eternity loving God, we have both the challenge and the privilege of being able to *choose* that love. But that relationship of love, just like any relationship, must be regularly renewed. We can't declare our love for God and then go on as if nothing has changed any more than we can say "I do" at our wedding and then ignore our spouse.

Every day we are challenged with decision points when we can choose to love God and our neighbor, or choose to love ourselves with a disordered love that looks only to our own needs, wants, and demands. True love sees excellence, goodness, beauty, and truth in the other person and delights in these qualities. We want that relationship to continue and to expand forever. We want to share in these delights, not by taking them into ourselves but *by giving ourselves* to the other person. This is "gift love."

Perfect love of God recognizes that we have been created for absolute truth, utter goodness, and happiness without end; all human beings by our very nature seek these goods, even if we cannot name them. We learn, however, that even the happiest of lives cannot supply these ultimate, transcendent goods because they are to be found only in God. He is absolute truth, perfect goodness, and infinite beauty. Only He can make us completely, eternally happy. Frustration comes when we look for these goods in all the wrong places here on earth, especially by means of sin. Sin always deceives, disappoints, and frustrates.

The Son of God was born into this world to strip away the lies and deceptions of sin, to take away the guilt of the world, and to be for us the God who never fails. He reveals the face of the Father as all merciful and all loving, overthrowing the falsehoods of the Demon and his fallen ones. He reveals the truth about man, about us men and women created in the image and likeness of God and called to an eternal inheritance. He breathes forth the Holy Spirit upon the Church and into our souls so that we can cooperate and collaborate in lifting up our world to the Holy Trinity.

How do we live such truths? How do we respond to such an extraordinary plan of grace? We must do so according to our own personalities and gifts, our own strengths and capacities, our own attractions and circumstances—healed by His wounds, washed by His blood, enlivened by His Spirit. We seek to love God as much as we can at every minute of the day, doing our duties, working at our jobs, caring for our families, reaching out to our neighbors. We must not wait for great opportunities to love God; we have to begin with "the heroically humble" moments of daily life: Give the first moment of your day to Christ (a heroic act!) and make your own bed! It sounds deceptively simple, perhaps even annoyingly so, but that is the case with many of the lessons that our holy angel tries to communicate to us day after day.

Blessed John Henry Newman, that great intellectual and convert, wrote something similar when asked for a plan of how to be perfect. Though he himself was a great scholar and theologian, he remarked one day that he would be very content in Heaven to shine his beloved St. Philip Neri's shoes. The image might seem to be an odd one, but its meaning is clear: Nothing is too little or too great for the sake of the one we love. In a similar way, we must learn how to practice a love of God that expresses itself in *delighted obedience* in words, thoughts, and deeds. St. Gerard Majella kept a sign on his door that read, "Here the will of God is done as God wills and as long as God wills." Though he was a simple Redemptorist lay brother, he helped many of his more learned confreres reach the perfection of charity and the heights of prayer—which should be our goal, too.

The Spirit of Silence

There are many kinds of silence. Silence may be calming or healing; it can be restful at the end of a day or expectant as we wait for the first note of an orchestra or the sound of a loved one's voice. Silence may also be cold and foreboding, vast and empty, mocking and rebuking. It can be as poignant and uplifting as the pause following a well-spoken address before applause breaks forth or as crushing as stillness following a cry for help or the confession "I love you" that receives no reply.

But the silence that I am thinking about here is different from all of these. A holy silence—a supernatural silence—is a dimension of the soul's response to God. It is made up of humility, wonder, and gratitude joined to memory, delight, and longing. This is a deeper kind of silence than we usually experience—a silence that is not simply the absence of words or of noise but one that prepares us and empties us out so that we might be ready to hear the word of God and keep it in our hearts.

Cardinal Robert Sarah has written an extraordinarily beautiful book on this subject, *The Power of Silence: Against the Dictatorship of Noise*. His profound analysis of the deep meaning of silence expresses this mysterious reality:

> At the heart of man there is an innate silence, for God abides in the innermost part of every person. God is silence, and this divine silence dwells in man. In God we are inseparably bound up with silence. The Church can affirm that mankind is the daughter of a silent God; for men are the sons of silence.[29]

St. Joseph is perhaps the best model of this silence. There is not a single word recorded of St. Joseph in the pages of the Gospels, but that is not because he had nothing to say. It is rather because Joseph had so much to listen to. He lived in the presence of the Word Made Flesh. He felt the beating of the Sacred Heart of Jesus as he held the Christ Child against his chest. He dwelt with the Immaculate Conception. Joseph, then, shows us that silence is not wordlessness; silence is the preparation for God's speaking and for our understanding our mission and vocation. These words speak to me of what St. Joseph might have felt whenever he bent down to pick up the Christ Child:

> God carries us, and we live with him at every moment by keeping silence. Nothing will make us discover God better than his silence inscribed in the center of our being. If we do not cultivate this silence, how can we find God? Man likes to travel, create, make great discoveries. But he remains outside of himself, far from God, who is silently in his soul.

---

[29] Robert Cardinal Sarah with Nicolas Diat, *The Power of Silence: Against the Dictatorship of Noise* (San Francisco: Ignatius Press, 2017), p. 22.

I want to recall how important it is to cultivate silence in order to be truly with God.[30]

Silence is the preparation for action, as active people soon come to realize:

Every day it is important to be silent so as to determine the outlines of one's future action. The contemplative life is not the only state in which man must make the effort to leave his heart in silence. In everyday life, whether secular, civil, or religious, exterior silence is necessary.[31]

Cardinal Sarah also distinguishes the role of silence in spiritual transformation, the growth of our interior life:

The episode of Jesus' visit to the home of Martha and Mary, related by Saint Luke (Lk 10:38–42), eloquently illustrates the priceless character of silence in everyday life: "Martha, Martha, you are anxious and troubled about many things" (Lk 10:41). Jesus rebukes Martha, not for being busy in the kitchen—after all, she did have to prepare the meal—but for her inattentive interior attitude, betrayed by her annoyance with her sister. Since the days of Origen, some commentators have tended to heighten the contrast between the two women, to the point of seeing in them respectively the example of an active life that is too scattered and the model of the contemplative life that is lived out in silence, listening, and interior prayer. In reality, Jesus seems to sketch the outlines of a spiritual pedagogy: we should always make sure to be Mary before becoming Martha. Otherwise, we run the risk of becoming literally bogged down in activism and

[30] Ibid.
[31] Ibid, p. 31.

agitation, the unpleasant consequences of which emerge in the Gospel account: panic, fear of working without help, an inattentive interior attitude, annoyance like Martha's toward her sister, the feeling that God is leaving us alone without intervening effectively. Thus, in speaking to Martha, Jesus says: "Mary has chosen the good portion" (Lk 10:42). He reminds her of the importance of "calming and quieting the soul" (see Ps 131:2) so as to listen to one's heart. Christ tenderly invites her to stop so as to return to her heart, the place of true welcome and the dwelling place of God's silent tenderness, from which she had been led away by the activity to which she was devoting herself so noisily. All activity must be preceded by an intense life of prayer, contemplation, seeking and listening to God's will.[32]

In Heaven, we will delight in the conversation of St. Joseph, the memories of Martha and Mary, and the voice of Our Lady singing an everlasting *Magnificat*. But to prepare ourselves for that day, let us ask for the gift of their attentive silence.

The Spirit of Temperance

From such an experience of inner silence, then, we learn to practice temperance in all our actions. Like the other cardinal virtues, temperance is what I like to call a "structural virtue"—one that is not usually seen or recognized in distinct acts, but is hidden behind many. It is an essential element of the skeletal structure of character and integrity. Temperance affects the ordering of our interior and exterior lives so that we grow in holiness, *striving for the things that are above* (see Col. 3:2), according to our state of life (vocation),

---

[32] Ibid., pp. 27–28.

in our particular circumstances (relationships and responsibilities), and in fidelity to our personality, *united to and transformed by Christ Jesus*. Just as practical experience is the "fertile ground" in which we cultivate the virtue of prudence, so too is temperance developed over time as we mature and integrate our experience with self-knowledge and the understanding of faith. Temperance brings rationality and measured judgment to our desires, wants, and needs. It involves not only renunciation but also abstinence, fasting, and judicious patience in making our choices. Temperance grows out of silence because it requires self-awareness and self-reflection.

As one of the cardinal virtues, temperance gives order, harmony, and measure to our desires for pleasure, especially the powerful natural bodily pleasures such as food, drink, comfort, and physical love. It also has a role in our acceptance of sadness and sorrows, assisting us to keep our eyes and hearts on the goal without being shattered by life's blows, but rather strengthened by them. Temperance is not a "negative" virtue, but a conscious and conscientious practice of restraint and moderation that allows us to live lives of harmonious purpose, tending toward our goal—union with God—through the perfection of charity (love of God and neighbor), realized through habits of strength (virtues) that allow us to do what is good *promptly, habitually, and joyfully*. Temperance allows us to control impulses and dominate our own selves. It is both sword and shield against selfishness, gluttony, lust in all its forms, undue curiosity, and a host of other evils.

In an essay on this theme, Father William Wagner, ORC, has written:

> The virtue of temperance, strictly speaking, deals with the dominion of the most basic emotions of joy (pleasure) and sadness, insofar as they are related to the sense of touch, including the sense of taste. Temperance tames man's

non-rational, sensual appetites for food, drink and sexual activity. It has the humble but important task of moderating and bringing these appetites under the sway of reason. How wisely God has so created and ordered the universe and man's nature that the more natural an action is, the more pleasurable it is. Moreover, among the natural actions, those which are most necessary are simultaneously those which include the greatest pleasure. And by contrast, the more an action deviates from nature, the more it brings sadness. As temperance increases, pleasure is better and more easily ordered by the intellect and integrated into the divine plan. Under the guidance of temperance, delights become moral goods that are proper and fitting to the well-being of man. Sadness, too, is moderated and virtuously integrated into one's life. The emotional life is more than ever humanized and ennobled.[33]

You may be picturing the image of *tempered or fire-tried steel* when thinking of this virtue. The image has merit since it calls to mind the hammer blows of the blacksmith, who creates a strong, powerful metal that can withstand stress and pressure. In a similar way our souls too must be strengthened to withstand sudden blows and the corrosion of vice and the violence of sin. However, we must remember that temperance is a living virtue, and, as such, it must grow in us throughout our lifetime; it is not something that is simply achieved, once and for all. Furthermore, temperance involves flexibility as well as resistance; for a virtuous and reasonable person makes use of prudence and grace in judging the situations and choices that present themselves. Our daily life should lead us

---

[33] Father William Wagner, ORC, "Temperance: Restraining Strength that Beautifies the Soul," Opus Sanctorum Angelorum, http://opus angelorum.org/oa_spirituality/seven_char_docs/Temperanc.html.

not to insipidity but rather to strength in purity of heart, tranquility of conscience, clarity of mind, and sanctity of soul.

The Imitation of Mary

The model of faith and discipleship for the Church and for every individual is Our Lady, the Blessed Virgin. Throughout the pages of Scripture, she is presented to us as the all-holy and ever-obedient Woman who tabernacles the Child in her womb, ponders the unfolding of the divine plan in the events of His birth and infancy, and accompanies Him in the consummation of His mission as she stands at the foot of the Cross. She does not need the sign of water changed into wine in order to believe in Him, like his other disciples at Cana: She knows that He is flesh of her flesh and yet "True God from True God, consubstantial with the Father, by Whom all things were made." She is present at prayer in the Upper Room when the Holy Spirit descends upon the Apostles and the others in tongues of flame and rushing wind (Acts 1:14; 2:1–3). She is the Mother and image of the Church, as the Second Vatican Council proclaimed her, the archetypal handmaid of the Lord, to whom all men and women must look if they would seek Christ and adore Him.

We come to know the virtues and perfections of our Mother Mary as we contemplate her in relationship to God's plan: She is truly Daughter of God the Father, Mother of God the Son, and Bride of God the Holy Spirit. And yet, even as we come to understand more deeply her sublime privileges and singular gifts, she calls us closer to her so that we can know her as pure maiden and loving mother. She is Queen of Angels, but Mother to us, no matter how little we are. She is near to us in our joys and in our sorrows; she knows what it is to be a widow, what it is to lose a child, and what it is to go on with a pierced heart. She is Mediatrix, Advocate, and Refuge because she is Mother. She comforts, heals, and teaches.

"Do whatever He tells you" (John 2:5). Sometimes I think that that one word, "whatever," is among the most important words in the Fourth Gospel. And when I reflect on the love with which the Blessed Mother spoke it, I understand that it must be one of the most important words I ever listen to.

Part 2

THE ANGELS IN SCRIPTURE

Chapter 6

THE ANNUNCIATION
ENTRUSTED TO ST. GABRIEL,
BEARER OF THE GOOD NEWS

✦

We meet St. Gabriel for the first time in the book of Daniel (8:15–17; 9:20–22). Daniel is one of the four major prophets of the Old Testament. He shared in the sufferings of the deportation to Babylon and saw the fall of the Babylonian Empire. His visions not only had an immediate meaning for his own life and time and that of his people, but they also looked forward to the time of Jesus, for Daniel described "one like a son of man," riding on the clouds of heaven, presented to the Most High, "and to him was given dominion and glory and kingdom, that all peoples, nations, and languages should serve him (7:13–14).

The book of Daniel is filled with the presence of angels who act as messengers, protectors, warriors, and worshippers. They are presented in a new manner: They each have individual characteristics and manifest a concern and care for human beings that point to an ongoing relationship between the heavenly beings and

God's creation here on earth. Two of the great angels of Heaven are revealed by name: Michael and Gabriel. The prophet describes Gabriel as "one having the appearance of a man" and calls him by a personal name, which means "Strength of God," before the angel fulfills the command to explain the vision that Daniel has just seen. A second time, too, Gabriel appears to Daniel to explain the vision of the "seventy weeks." Though he appears with such divine authority that Daniel prostrates himself when he sees him the first time, there is something gentle and reassuring in the manner in which the Lord sends his heavenly messenger. Daniel describes the second appearance in these words:

> While I was speaking and praying, confessing my sin and the sin of my people Israel and presenting my supplication before the Lord, my God for the holy hill of my God; while I was speaking in prayer, the man Gabriel, whom I had seen in the vison at the first, came to me in swift flight at the time of the evening sacrifice. He came and he said to me, "O Daniel, I have now come out to give you wisdom and understanding. At the beginning of your supplications a word went forth, and I have come to tell it to you, for you are greatly beloved: therefore consider the word and understand the vision." (9:20–23)

When God is about to bring all things to completion in the coming of His Son, it is this same angel who is chosen as the bearer of the good news — good news that never loses its freshness or power. In his Apostolic Letter *Tertio Millennio Adveniente*, "On the Beginning of the Third Millennium," Pope St. John Paul II called us to a new evangelization — a new proclamation of the good news of salvation. The first time we find the term "evangelization" or "to evangelize" in Scripture is in the Gospel of St. Luke, and the first evangelizer is the same angel who appeared to

Daniel: the archangel Gabriel. Gabriel appears as the messenger of the Most High, bearing the good news of salvation in two annunciations — one to Zechariah, fulfilling the hopes of Israel, and the second to Mary, the Mother of the Savior, surpassing them beyond all hope.

The Annunciation

In the Gospel of Luke (1:5ff.), we read that the priest Zechariah was called to serve his term in the Temple at Jerusalem, and by lot he was chosen to offer incense before the Holy of Holies. This was the highest of honors for a Jewish priest and occurred only once in a lifetime. And it was at that moment that the Lord God determined to send His holy angel to speak to Zechariah to reveal to him His plan for the unfolding of the history of salvation and the part he would play in the coming of the Messiah.

The incense that Zechariah offered was placed before the Holy of Holies and the great purple curtain on which the cherubim were embroidered, the only beings whose images were permitted within the Jerusalem Temple. There, as he was watching the smoke of the incense rise to God, an angel of the Lord appeared, standing at the right side of the altar. Zechariah was filled with awe at the sight, and the angel spoke to him, his words and tone echoing both the power and the kindness with which he had spoken to Daniel: "Do not be afraid, Zechariah, for your prayer is heard, and your wife Elizabeth will bear you a son, and you will call his name John" (Luke 1:13). As the angel continued his message, his words revealed not only the fulfillment of the divine plan but also the healing of the human family:

> And he will turn many of the sons of Israel to the Lord their God, and he will go before him in the spirit and power of

Elijah, to turn the hearts of the fathers to the children, and the disobedient to the wisdom of the just, to make ready for the Lord a people prepared. (Luke 1:16–17)

Despite his own knowledge as a priest and the majesty of the angel's appearance, the old man gave in to doubt and answered, "How shall I know this? For I am an old man, and my wife is advanced in years" (Luke 1:18). The reply of the angel left no doubt that this was a divine message:

I am Gabriel, who stand in the presence of God: and I was sent to speak to you, and to bring you this good news. And behold, you will be silent and unable to speak until the day that these things come to pass, because you did not believe my words, which will be fulfilled in their time. (Luke 1:19–20)

It was customary for the priest to give a blessing to the bystanders upon coming out of the holy place, but Zechariah could speak no words. The message of salvation remained within his heart and only by signs was he able to communicate to those around him that something great had happened. For the angel of the Lord had brought the good news of the coming of salvation to Israel.

In order to appreciate more deeply the message given to Mary at Nazareth by the angel Gabriel and ponder it in our prayer, we have to note the differences between these two apparitions, these two annunciations. Though St. Luke describes the angel as appearing to Zechariah in the Temple of the Lord, his description of the same angel's coming to Mary is quite different. In fact, the Evangelist simply tells us:

In the sixth month the angel Gabriel was sent from God to a city of Galilee named Nazareth, to a virgin betrothed to a man whose name was Joseph, of the house of David; and the virgin's name was Mary. And he came to her and said, "Hail, full of grace, the Lord is with you!" (Luke 1:26–28)

Though Zechariah is frightened by the appearance of the angel, Luke does not tell us that Mary is frightened at all by the angel coming to her. The Gospel does point out twice, however, that Mary is "troubled" by his words—when he addresses her as "full of grace" and then later when he reveals to her the mission for which she has been chosen by God.

We must pause to consider this greeting, "full of grace," which is one of the most repeated phrases in Christian prayer. For centuries scholars and spiritual writers have pondered its beauty and meaning. *Kecharitoméne* is the Greek word used by Luke, a phrase that appears only this once in all of Scripture. Its significance is in this uniqueness, as Father Giacinto Marie Dagesse, FI, points out in a recently published and very remarkable study.[34] Many scholars have found in this phrase the biblical evidence for the Immaculate Conception because grammatically it is a past participle, signifying grace *that Mary already possessed at the time of the archangel's greeting.*[35] It identifies who Mary is, as fully graced, and, because it is an "angel of the Lord" who greets Mary, God Himself is doing so through His messenger (CCC 2676). Father Dagesse then goes on to explain how the same term, *kecharitoméne*, may also provide the scriptural basis for Mary's role as Mediatrix of Grace. Gabriel's greeting, therefore, expresses both Mary's identity and her mission.

---

[34] Father Giacinto Marie Dagesse, FI. "The Marian Commentaries: Word Study: Kecharitoméne" in Fr. Peter Damian M. Fehlner, FI, ed., *Mariological Studies in Honor of Our Lady of Guadalupe 3* (New Bedford, MA: Academy of the Immaculate, 2016), p. 96.

[35] Ibid., p. 99.

Praying with Gabriel

There are several things we should study in this account that we may not have noticed before, no matter how many times we've meditated upon the words and prayed the Hail Mary and the Angelus. The dating ("sixth month") may refer to Elizabeth's pregnancy: it is in the sixth month since Elizabeth became pregnant with John the Baptist that Gabriel goes to Nazareth. Some commentators, though, think this also has a symbolic meaning. The prophet Haggai tells us that under the reign of King Darius, it was in the sixth month that the people of Israel began to rebuild the Temple of Jerusalem, "the house of the Lord" (Hag. 1:14–15). The Temple was the sign and symbol of God's presence among His people. Now the angel has come to announce that the Lord Most High is preparing a new Ark for a New Covenant.

First of all, Mary is not afraid of the appearance of the angel. Throughout the Old Testament, when someone sees an angel for the first time, he or she is always struck with awe and reverent wonder and fear because the angel bears about him the authority and the glory of God. But Mary has no such reaction. The description of Gabriel's visitation seems very ordinary. The angel comes into the house — not into a sacred and mysterious Holy of Holies, but into an ordinary home. He enters almost as if he were accustomed to doing so, a practice not commonly associated with the angels of the Most High God.

Could it be that Mary was prepared for this day by earlier appearances of the same angel? The Scriptures do not tell us this, though certain saints and holy writers throughout the centuries have conjectured that this was the case — that Mary was gradually prepared for the Annunciation by Gabriel. Perhaps her own sinlessness and the purity of her trust in God made her simply recognize the heavenly being with delight, her perfect love casting out all fear. And, in fact, we can deduce from the text of the conversation that will follow that our Blessed Lady had already been apprised by God in some unmistakable way of her special vocation to virginity in marriage.

It is, however, that same sinlessness and humility that prompts her reaction to Gabriel's greeting: "But she was greatly troubled with his word and considered what sort of greeting this might be" (Luke 1:29). Gabriel sees before him the all-pure Daughter of Zion chosen by God.

> And the angel said to her, "Do not fear, Mary; for you have found favor before God. And behold, you will conceive in your womb and bear a son, and you shall call his name Jesus. He will be great, and will be called the Son of the Most High; and the Lord God will give to him the throne of his father David, and he will reign over the house of Jacob forever; and of his kingdom there will be no end. (Luke 1:31–33)

This is the most glorious message an angel has ever been given to deliver! It is the revelation of the Incarnation, the enfleshing of the Eternal Son of God, the joining of Creator and creation in a union of *body, blood, soul, and divinity*. It signifies the nuptials of Heaven and earth, the dawn of the everlasting wedding feast. It weaves together the essence of Who this Child-to-be-born is from all eternity and how He will be seen and known by generations yet unborn. Reread these words and think about how St. Gabriel felt when he spoke them for the first time, in the clarity of his angelic intellect and the purity of his free will, unswerving in his loyalty to and faith in Almighty God from the moment of the angels' creation through the darkness of their testing and now arriving at this moment of stillness in the history of salvation. He awaits with angelic anticipation the response of the Woman at whom all Heaven marveled.

Her response may at first seem to be like that of Zechariah—
"How can this be, since I have no husband?"—but it is actually
spoken in faith (Luke 1:34). Far from doubting the angel's words,
Mary is asking for deeper understanding: But why does she ask this
question? Mary is formally espoused to Joseph, which signified the
first stage of marriage under Jewish law. She would not have been
ignorant of "the facts of life." So, what prompts Mary's statement
and question? Catholic scholars through the centuries have seen in
these words a clear indication that Mary and Joseph had vowed a
virginal marriage. Such an arrangement was unknown in Israel and
so could have been made only if the couple had been convinced
that this was God's will for them. The cause of this conviction must
have been as strong in Mary's heart and mind as the appearance
of Gabriel was real before her. Her question is a sincere searching
in faith, as if she were saying, "How can I understand what you
are telling me now in the Lord's Name in the light of what He has
told me before?"

And so she is not struck dumb, as was Zechariah, but rather
the angel answers her succinctly, "The Holy Spirit will come upon
you, and the power of the Most High will overshadow you; therefore the child to be born will be called holy, the Son of God"
(Luke 1:35). He goes on to tell her that her cousin Elizabeth,
Zechariah's wife, is also with child, "for with God nothing will
be impossible" (Luke 1:36–37). He gives Mary a sign that she had
not asked for and in the face of his words—harmonizing all that
she had understood of God's will for herself and Joseph,[36] and so
clear, so rich with the authority of God—Mary replies, "Behold,
I am the handmaid of the Lord; let it be to me according to your
word" (Luke 1:38).

---

[36] In the next chapter, we will see how the Lord confirms His plan
for St. Joseph.

In this act of loving, trusting faith, the Church has found a "word" that is ever fruitful for our spiritual lives. Whether we are male or female, young or old, we must learn to repeat this perfect Marian response to the divine will: "I am the servant of the Lord; may His will be done in me, through me, by me; now and always and forever." Two Latin words are often used to sum up the Immaculata's response and our "adoption" of them in our own spiritual life: *Ecce* (Behold) and *Fiat* (Be it done). Together with the word *Magnificat*, the opening phrase of Our Lady's canticle to Elizabeth ("My soul doth *magnify* the Lord"), these three words form the inner structure of our imitation of Mary—obedience, trust, and thanksgiving.

When the Blessed Mother speaks these words, the Holy Spirit does indeed overshadow her and the Word is made Flesh in the tabernacle of her body. She becomes in that moment the Ark and Tabernacle of the New Covenant, the Bearer of God's love. He would be Emmanuel, God Among Us, fulfilling the sign of the ancient Temple in His own flesh.

Gabriel falls down before her to adore God made man. He now sees the fulfillment of the angelic trial, for it is believed that the angels' trial was precisely with regard to the coming of the Word as man—that the angels, and indeed all creation, would have to kneel in worship of Almighty God, God the Son in the form of man. The humility and fidelity of the angels was in view of this moment, and now it takes place, as the Word is made flesh within Mary—and Gabriel humbles himself before Him. Gabriel, therefore, is not only the first announcer of the good news of salvation when he speaks to Zechariah, but now he becomes the first adorer of Jesus Christ, God made man, living in Mary. This is a profound moment, not only for the history of salvation, but also for each of us. In fact, in many European churches built in the Middle Ages have images of the archangel Gabriel and of

Our Lady on either side of the main doors. To enter the church, therefore, you must pass through the mystery of the Incarnation and be spiritually aware of the words of Gabriel and the loving response of Mary. And by so doing, you enter into the mystery of Christ's life, expressed symbolically by the church building itself, and come at last to the altar of the glorified Christ, the Lord who reigns now in Heaven.

When we pray the Hail Mary or the Angelus, then, we are not simply reciting a prayer but are entering deeply into the mystery of God's love. God stoops down to us through the humility and trust of Mary, the handmaid of the Lord. Meditating on the Annunciation can fill our hearts with a tremendous desire to love and to serve God so that Christ may take flesh in us. The accompaniment of the angels, especially our guardian angel, helps us to understand how the Word can take flesh in us.

This does not happen through incarnation, as happened with the Blessed Mother. That is a once-and-for-all-time occurrence. Rather, each of us must learn to give to Christ our lives, our bodies, the talents of our minds and hearts, the works of our hands—all of ourselves. We must become like Mary, the servant of the Lord, and consecrate ourselves to Him. If we ask the archangel Gabriel, who bore this joyful news to the Blessed Mother, to assist us, particularly when we are in adoration of the Lord in the Eucharist or contemplating His mysteries in Our Lady's Rosary, he can inspire us with some of the sentiments that he experienced—the wonder and awe, the fascination and the reverence toward God's plan.

Let us ask the holy angel, then, to be with us and to exercise in us the same ministry that he showed to Mary—to announce the will of God to us clearly and to remove the obstacles that would impede God's will from bearing fruit in us. Let us ask Gabriel to teach us how to accept the signs of God's love, the indications of His power, and the fullness of the reality of Jesus' Incarnation.

St. Joan of Valois

Throughout her life, Our Blessed Lady must have thought often about the message of the angel Gabriel. And certainly in her prayer and her faithfulness to the will of God, she repeated over and over that oblation that she had first expressed at Nazareth: "Behold the handmaid of the Lord. Be it done unto me according to thy word." She repeated it at Cana when she let her Son know of the needs of the young couple: "They have no wine" (John 2:3). And she must have repeated it over and over on Calvary in the silence of her heart as she looked up into her Son's face and heard His words: "Behold your son.... Behold your children" (see John 19:26, 27). The Annunciation was for Our Lady the beginning of her new life of acceptance of God's will in all its fullness so that she might truly become Mother of the Savior—and Mother of each one of us.

Throughout the history of the Church, many saints and holy people have written about the Annunciation. One of the less well-known of these spiritual giants is St. Joan of Valois, who left to the Church a profound spirituality of the Annunciation. She based her insights on her own meditations on the angel Gabriel's words and Mary's response—a response that continued throughout Her life, a response that continues to echo now throughout the ages of the Church's life.

St. Joan was born into the French royal family in 1464. At the age of twelve she was betrothed to the future King Louis XII, but later the king rejected her, and her marriage was annulled. Through these sorrows, Joan meditated on the life of Mary and her acceptance of God's will, and this gave her a profound peace. Her trust in the Blessed Mother led her to add the name Maryann (a portmanteau of the names of the Blessed Mother and her mother, St. Anne) to her own baptismal name. And so, throughout her later life, she always signed her name "Jeanne Maryann."

After the annulment of her marriage, St. Joan founded a community of sisters dedicated to the Annunciation. These religious contemplatives were to ponder not simply the words of Gabriel to Mary but also the virtues of Mary that grew of that great acceptance of God's plan.

St. Joan proposed to her nuns ten virtues of the Blessed Mother that we would do very well to bring into our regular prayer, so that, in understanding Mary's faithfulness to God, we might discover how to be faithful in the joys and sorrows that we experience.[37]

The Ten Virtues of Mary

† Purity: "How can this be, since I have no husband?" (Luke 1:34)

† Prudence: "But she was greatly troubled at the saying, and considered in her mind what sort of greeting this might be." (Luke 1:29)

† Humility: "Behold, I am the handmaid of the Lord." (Luke 1:38)

† Faithfulness: "And blessed is she who believed that there would be a fulfilment of what was spoken to her from the Lord." (from Elizabeth's greeting of Mary, Luke 1:45)

---

[37] The Ten Virtues of Mary were also an important part of the spirituality of St. Stanislaus Papczynski (1631–1701), the founder of the first male community explicitly dedicated to promoting the doctrine of the Immaculate Conception: the Marians of the Immaculate Conception (MIC). In the twentieth century, his congregation became the leading apostles of St. Faustina's message of Divine Mercy, particularly in the English-speaking world. Is there not a deep significance in the community's charism of the Immaculate Conception finding its renewed "spiritual fruitfulness" in the devotion to the Merciful Jesus? As always, Mary leads us to discover her Son.

† Devotion: "My soul magnifies the Lord." (from Mary's response to Saint Elizabeth, the Magnificat, Luke 1:46)

† Obedience: "And when the time came for their purification according to the law of Moses, they brought him up to Jerusalem to present him to the Lord." (Luke 2:22)

† Poverty. "And she gave birth to her first-born son and wrapped him in swaddling cloths, and laid him in a manger, because there was no place for them in the inn." (Luke 2:7)

† Patience: "Son, why have you treated us so? Behold, your father and I have been looking for you anxiously." (upon finding Jesus in the Temple, Luke 2:48)

† Charity: "They have no wine.... Do whatever He tells you." (John 2:3, 5)

† Compassion: "And a sword will pierce through your own soul also, that thoughts out of many hearts may be revealed." (from Simeon's prophecy at the Presentation of Jesus, Luke 2:35)

These ten virtues that St. Joan of Valois entrusted to her daughters and to the whole Church were the hallmark of her order, which she called "the Order of Peace." Once again we see that in the spiritual understanding of the Church, peace comes from the wholehearted acceptance of God's will. Mary is Queen of Peace because she is totally obedient to the will of God. She is filled with trust and with submission of mind and heart; the Holy Spirit moves her to place herself before the Lord as handmaid, ready to accept and unite herself to His will in all things.

The Sign of the Woman

As we ponder these virtues, we return again to the Wedding Feast of Cana for a moment to revisit the final word that Mary speaks in the Gospels. Of course, this is not the last time that Our Lady appears in the Gospels, but it is the last time that she speaks. Her words are simple: "Do whatever He tells you" (John 2:5). That is the message that Mary brings to the Church. In every shrine, in every apparition, in the charism of any saint devoted to the Blessed Mother, we find expressed again and again this one instruction.

Mary places herself always at the side of Christ as ministering servant; for this reason she is Queen of His *ministering angels*. We always speak of Mary as being Queen rather than Mother of the angels because Mary doesn't share the angelic nature. She is *our* Mother — the Mother of humanity, the Mother of men and women. This is our privilege.

To the angels, however, she is Queen, and this is a title of intimacy, affection, and chivalrous devotion — the most beautiful human person ever created, the perfect exemplar of God's plan for His creation, raised above them as a tabernacle of the Most High God. She is the delight of the good angels and the everlasting confusion of the fallen ones. She crushes Satan's head through her innocence and obedience to the will of God, manifest in her Son: "Do whatever He tells you." We have seen and will continue to see Mary repeat this message in all of her apparitions, whether at Lourdes, at Fatima, or in those other shrines around the world where the Mother of God has come to share with us the good news of salvation as once Gabriel brought the good news to her. When she hears our prayers, dries our tears, and saves us from dangers, both moral and physical, she always seeks to leave that message with us. If we do not hear it, it is perhaps because we are not yet sensitive enough to who she really is. If that is the case, she will patiently wait — as mothers do — to teach us "the missing lesson" and open our hearts up to her Son.

But, dear reader, you have heard these words and so are ready to take the next good steps on the journey of faith: Let us, then, ask the Blessed Mother to open our minds and our hearts to her prayer, her contemplation, and her obedience to God. Let us ask that the angel Gabriel—who brought this joyful news of salvation; who had once disclosed the secrets of Heaven to the prophet Daniel; who spoke to the priest Zechariah at the right hand of the altar of incense; who bowed low before Mary—to inspire us so that our words may always be words of truth and that they might bring joy and peace to others. Let us ask him who is now invoked as the patron of radio and television communication (angels are always receiving new missions!) to help us to communicate clearly, sincerely, and charitably with all whom the Lord places on our path, whether we are face to face or linked only by the mechanics of telephone, e-mail, text, and social media.

No matter how often we pray the Hail Mary and the Angelus, let us pronounce, as if for the first time, those words that Gabriel spoke in awe and in wonder—the words that Mary repeated with wholehearted trust and obedience. Let us learn to imitate Mary in her virtues so that we might share in the reward of her children—those who have been faithful to her Son, the Word Made Flesh.

> Mary, Mother of God and Mother of the Church, obtain for us something of your deep faith in what the angel told you two thousand years ago. Help us to believe more deeply that your Son Jesus is the Son of the Most High God. Help us believe more deeply that His kingdom will endure until the end of time as the Church Militant on earth, and will endure as the Church Triumphant into the endless ages of eternity. Amen.[38]

---

[38] Hardon, *Meditations on the Angels*, p. 50.

Chapter 7

ST. JOSEPH AND THE ANGELS

In serving the Lord's plan and purpose, Mary of Nazareth had a special companion: St. Joseph. St. Joseph was also chosen by God from all eternity, chosen to be the foster father of Christ, to be *the shadow of the eternal Father* on earth, and to present to the boy Jesus, as He grew up, the human image of the fatherhood of God.

St. Joseph, whom theologians call the *virginal father of Christ*, is patron of the Universal Church and patron of our interior life. He is the patron of workers and artisans, and indeed the protector of all families, but he has a special, in fact singular, relationship with the angels. We can learn from this relationship about how the angels help us to discover our vocation and to overcome impediments to God's plan—not just impediments that come from sin but those that come from our human limitations and our lack of trust in God, and perhaps in ourselves.

Doubting Joseph

When angels appear to people, they adapt themselves to the conditions and the personality of the persons to whom they come;

therefore, St. Gabriel appeared to Mary in corporeal form, both reassuring her and presaging the message that he had come to give her. He entered her home and spoke to her, and when he did so, he sanctified the world and all human homes with his message.

When the All-Holy took flesh in the body of Mary, she became the Ark of the New Covenant and Joseph her betrothed was called by God to support and to share in her mission through a new obedience, a new trust, and a new vocation.

Now, there are many Scripture scholars and modern translations that make it appear that St. Matthew is telling us that Joseph doubted Mary's virtue when he writes that Joseph planned to separate himself from her quietly (Matt. 1:19). Some translations even use the term "divorce." But this is not the tradition of the Catholic Church. In fact, in the writings of saints and the declarations of theologians, Joseph's response to Mary's mysterious pregnancy is explained very differently. The great English theologian Father John Saward provides a marvelous summary of the Church's understanding of Joseph's interior dilemma in his work *Redeemer in the Womb*. He defines Joseph's response as one of "reverence and religious fear" before this tremendous mystery.[39] He would translate the Gospel passage in this way:

> Before they came together, she was found with child by the power of the Holy Spirit; and her husband Joseph, being a holy man and not wanting to reveal her mystery, resolved to withdraw from her quietly.[40]

Father Saward demonstrates very clearly that the tradition of the West, against modern and often secular reevaluations, is that Joseph's

[39] John Saward, *Redeemer in the Womb* (San Francisco: Ignatius Press, 1993), p. 38.
[40] Ibid.

doubt was not so much about the purity of Mary but about himself. Joseph accepted with his trust in God that this mysterious pregnancy was divinely willed, but he doubted his own purity, his own holiness, and his own worthiness to be part of this unfolding plan of God.

He and Mary had pledged themselves to a virginal marriage, because of some form of divine inspiration that Scripture does not reveal to us. Now, this form of consecration, which some of the Essenian Jews evidently practiced in later years of married life, was to be transformed through this unexpected, supernatural pregnancy. Joseph must have felt that he was completely in over his head, unable to see how he could be part of such a divine occurrence.

Father Saward cites the teaching of St. Bernard of Clairvaux (1090–1153), who saw himself continuing the tradition of the Fathers of the Church, when he wrote:

> Joseph wanted to leave her for the same reason Peter begged the Lord to leave him, when he said, "Depart from me, O Lord, for I am a sinful man," and for the same reason the Centurion kept him from his house, "Lord, I am not worthy that thou shouldst come under my roof."
>
> Thus Joseph, considering himself unworthy and a sinner, said to himself that a man like him ought not to live under the same roof with a woman so great and exalted, whose wonderful and superior dignity filled him with awe. He saw with fear and trembling that she bore the surest signs of the divine presence, and, since he could not fathom the mystery, he wanted to depart from her. Peter was frightened by the greatness of the power; the Centurion feared the majesty of the presence. Joseph, too, as a human being, was afraid of the newness of the great miracle, the profundity of the mystery, and so he decided to leave her quietly. Are you surprised that Joseph judged himself unworthy of the

pregnant Virgin's company? After all, have you not heard that St. Elizabeth, too, could not endure her presence without fear and awe? As she says, "Whence is this to me that the Mother of my Lord should come to me?" this then is why Joseph decided to leave her.[41]

This presents a very different image of St. Joseph from the one many Catholics have today. We tend to think that Joseph wanted to depart from the possibly sinful Mary. But in fact, Joseph anticipates in his own heart the words that Peter would one day speak to Jesus, "Depart from me, for I am a sinful man, O Lord" (Luke 5:8). And, as Father Saward points out, this reading is not the opinion of St. Bernard alone. He quotes St. Thomas Aquinas:

> Joseph wanted to give the Virgin her freedom, not because he suspected her of adultery, but out of respect for holiness; he was afraid to go and live with her.[42]

Among the modern Catholic Scripture scholars who have upheld this tradition, Father Saward notes the great French Mariologist Canon Rene Laurentin (+2017), whose books and conferences are widely known, and the widely respected Belgian Jesuit Father Ignace de la Potterie, SJ (+2003), who taught for decades at Rome's Pontifical Biblical Institute. Both of these men were known for their deep Marian devotion and their Christ-centered spirituality, as well as for their academic gifts.

But this interpretation of St. Joseph's dilemma is not simply restricted to a few biblical scholars or even the ancient Fathers of the Church. There is evidence that it was also part of the Church's

---

[41] St. Bernard of Clairvaux, *In Laudibus Virginis Matris*, Sermo II 14; quoted by Saward, *Redeemer in the Womb*, p. 40.

[42] St. Thomas Aquinas, *Summa Theologiae*, Supplement, q. 62, art. 3, ad 2.; quoted by Saward, *Redeemer in the Womb*, p. 40.

St. Joseph and the Angels

liturgical life in the East. St. Romanos the Melodist, a sixth-century
deacon and hymn writer, composed a magnificent hymn, filled with
Old Testament imagery, in which St. Joseph addresses the Virgin
and reveals his own fears:

> Then Joseph, who never knew the Virgin, stopped,
> Stunned by her glory,
> And, gazing on the brilliance of her form, said:
> "O shining one, I see that a flame and hot coals
>   encircle you.
> It frightens me, Mary. Protect me, do not consume me!
> Your spotless womb has suddenly become a fiery furnace.
> Let it not melt me, I beg you. Spare me!
> Do you wish me, like Moses of old, to take off my shoes,
> That I may draw nigh and listen to you, and taught by
>   you say:
> Hail, Bride unbrided!"[43]

This hymn evokes the image of the burning bush on Mount
Sinai and, perhaps, the fiery furnace mentioned in the book of
Daniel. Joseph is overwhelmed by the Divine Power present in
Mary—as was Elizabeth at the Visitation (Luke 1:41–45)—and
feels the interior compulsion to show his reverence outwardly. He
wants to approach her, to draw near, but he is afraid. Therefore,
when we look at St. Joseph, we should see someone who is marveling at the power of God, but doubting his own self.

So when St. Matthew tells us that an angel of the Lord appeared
to Joseph as he slept to reassure him, the reassurance is not about
the virginity of Mary, but about his own goodness and readiness
to take up his mission:

---

[43] St. Romanos the Melodist, *Canticum in Annuntiatione* 15; quoted
by Saward, *Redeemer in the Womb*, p. 41.

But as he considered this, behold, an angel of the Lord appeared to him in a dream, saying, "Joseph, son of David, do not fear to take Mary [as] your wife, for that which is conceived in her is of the Holy Spirit; she will bear a son, and you shall call his name Jesus, for he will save his people from their sins." (1:20–21)

It is in these final words of the angel that we find the key to understanding the true meaning of this scene: In addition to being words of reassurance, these words also confirm Joseph's God-given vocation to fatherhood, because, according to Jewish tradition, it was the father who named the child. We can see how the Gospels of Matthew and Luke harmonize to give us this insight: When Elizabeth told her family and neighbors that her child was to be called John, they wondered at this, because there was no one in the family who bore that name. So they surmised that Elizabeth was taking advantage of Zechariah's muteness, and they asked him what name he wanted his son to be given. When Zechariah wrote, "His name is John," his speech was restored to him because he had fulfilled all that was required of him by God's plan and the angel's command (Luke 1:57–66).

Now we find Joseph being given the honor of naming Jesus. He not only receives a mission and a responsibility, but also an authority by which to carry them out. In other words, God is confirming through the angel's message that Joseph is to be in everything but procreation the earthly father to this Divine Child. It is for this reason that we sometimes see Joseph described as "the virginal father of Christ," a term meant to indicate that he is *more* than a foster father, *more* than an adoptive father.[44]

---

[44] As St. John Paul II notes in his 1989 Encyclical Letter *Redemptoris Custos*, "The Son of Mary is also Joseph's Son by virtue of the marriage bond that unites them: 'By reason of their faithful marriage

When Joseph awoke from his sleep, he fulfilled the angel's command and took the expectant Virgin into his house, the second stage of the Jewish marriage ritual (Matt. 1:24). Even here, Scripture scholars have begun to note a detail in the language that may point to a deep truth of Faith: As Father Giacinto Dagesse argues very persuasively in his Marian Commentaries, the verb used twice in the Greek is *paralambano*, a word that is never used for marriage anywhere else in Scripture. The Septuagint uses *lambano* 103 times for "taking a wife," and the Greek New Testament uses it 8 times. Only the union of Joseph and Mary is described with the word *paralambano*, which is a term related to kinship in the Scriptures, but apparently not *consummated marriage*. Is this, then, a discrete allusion to the perpetual virginity of Mary and Joseph?[45]

The perpetual virginity of Our Lady is a dogma of the Church, a teaching that must be held by all Catholics, an integral and defining element of Catholic Faith. This virginity continued after the Incarnation of the Savior; that is why Our Lady is often referred to in the Church's prayers, such as the *Confiteor*, as "blessed Mary, ever-Virgin." Rarely do we consider what this meant from Joseph's perspective. The relationship between Joseph and Mary was a true marriage, based in interpersonal love, but it was lived out in an intentional and consecrated virginal manner. Theologians have always believed that Joseph and Mary made this gift prior to their espousals. With the revelation of the Incarnation, Joseph would have come to understand his virginal marriage in the sacred tradition of reverent awe in which the Ark of the Covenant was held

----

both of them deserve to be called Christ's parents, not only his mother, but also his father, who was a parent in the same way that he was the mother's spouse: in mind, not in the flesh'" (quoting St. Augustine).

[45] Dagesse, "The Marian Commentaries," pp. 110–120.

by the Jews: Mary was "set apart," consecrated to the service of the Lord alone. Joseph would never lay claim to the bride who tabernacled the Most High. Just as Moses had taken off his sandals and prostrated himself before the bush filled with the Fiery Presence, so would Mary ever remain in Joseph's eyes and heart: his bride touched by Divine Fire. He would be the protector of the Mystery within her and guardian of the Child and the Immaculate Mother as long as he lived.

Joseph's Vocation and Ours

Is this just a matter of sacred history, or are there other lessons in St. Matthew's account of St. Joseph's crisis? What does his doubt teach us? Many times we too are afraid to do the Lord's will, not because of a disobedient attitude, but because we are mindful of our weaknesses, especially our past sins, even those sins that have been forgiven. How much good goes undone because the memory of past sins binds us in a way that God doesn't intend? How much good goes undone because we are afraid that in standing up for the truth, someone may accuse us of hypocrisy? And so time and again, the Lord's missions for us — opportunities to proclaim the Gospel, to defend the Faith, to stand up for the truth, to bear witness to God's goodness, or even to protect the innocent and the needy — go unfulfilled. These we fail to accomplish because of the power of past sins or the feeling of weakness and inadequacy.

Therefore the angel appeared to St. Joseph by night and counseled him, like a friend at the end of a hard day, reassuring him in the intimacy of sleep. Pope Paul VI pointed out that angels counsel Joseph in his sleep three times in the Gospels, demonstrating that he had an ongoing experience of heavenly counsel and a profound relationship with the angels. Although St. Matthew doesn't name the angel who appeared to Joseph, many of the saints and Fathers of the Church who have commented on this passage believe that it was indeed St. Gabriel. Gabriel, who brought the good news to Mary, then continued his mission as a protector of the Holy Family so that the good news of salvation might take root both in the heart of Mary and in the heart of Joseph and so bring forth much fruit. St. Joseph listened to the voice of the angel, and Gabriel strengthened him to fulfill his calling. The angel reassured him that in God's plan he was the right man for the job—that it was his vocation to be foster father to the Christ Child. Joseph was to be the model of masculine human nature for his Son; he would love Him, sacrifice for Him, defend and risk everything for Him with a father's brave and manly love.

We do not know whether the angel Gabriel continued to appear to Joseph in his dreams, but we can be sure that the angels continued to surround him, to strengthen him, and to enlighten him in the life and home he provided for Mary and Jesus. Our guardian angels also strengthen us. They remind us of God's power, a power that shows its perfection in our weakness, our littleness, and our infirmities. The angels strengthen our minds and our hearts, so that we might do the will of God and not be overcome by the past.

St. Teresa of Avila, that marvelous Doctor of the Church and patron of common sense, is said to have quipped, "In times of trial I remember that with God and five cents I can do anything." We should pray to St. Joseph for this same gift of acceptance of our vocation from God —the plan that God, from all eternity, has determined for us—because each of us has a unique mission to accomplish. We carry out this mission not only for ourselves and in ourselves but through our influence over other people.

Joseph was to be privileged to hold the Christ Child in his arms, to listen to the beating of the Sacred Heart in that helpless infant, to hear the first syllables of the Word Made Flesh, and to help guide His feet to walk, those feet that would one day be pierced by nails.

Joseph taught Jesus the satisfaction and the joy of work. The Word, by which all things were created, learned how to handle a hammer and nails, a saw, and a plane through Joseph's guidance. Joseph listened to the heartbeat of the whole world when he lifted the Child in his arms, but Jesus also listened to the heart of Joseph. As He grew and increased in His human intelligence and understanding, He knew that Joseph's heart beat for Him—He and His Mother were Joseph's whole world—and in that humble, just man He saw the providence of His Heavenly Father at work. In Joseph, Jesus saw and loved and understood all the simple, hardworking folk of the earth; He blessed all family life by sharing in it Himself.

Let us ask this great saint to be with us and to guide us in the ways in which our vocation can give praise to God.

Hope and Trust

The mission of St. Joseph was unique, but from the way he lived that mission we can see the virtues by which God prepared him for this great role in the life of His Son.

St. Joseph possessed a remarkable interior docility. He was open to the teaching of the Lord, specifically to the word that was spoken by the angel in sleep, and he showed an exceptional promptness in responding, with a spirit of obedience and a wholehearted desire to do all that the Lord demanded. Joseph didn't argue; he didn't hesitate; he didn't speak of his own rights, hopes, or aspirations. He left everything to the plan of God.

These are virtues that you and I have to develop also in our own spiritual lives. We must learn to trust God above all else and to base our hopes and our desires in His will with the conviction that God wants the very best for us. He will give us every grace necessary for us to accomplish His work and to persevere in the ways of holiness.

The virtue of hope is easy to forget in our prayer life. We pray for faith: "Lord, I believe. Increase my faith." That's an excellent prayer to make. And we pray for love: "Lord, I love You, but not yet enough. Lord, increase my love. Help me to love You in others, especially in the people in whom I find it difficult to see You." Again, what a beautiful prayer this is. But we must also remember to pray an act of hope:

> Lord, I hope in You. I am convinced that You will give me today and tomorrow and the day after everything that I need, every grace and every blessing, so that the promises of Christ may be fulfilled in me. Lord, I know that I do not have to give in to temptation, that I do not have to turn my face away from Your will or to take back my hand from the plow. Lord, I trust in You that everything in my life You will arrange and order to bring about Your will. Your providence is enough for me. Lord, let me trust in You more and more, like St. Joseph and the Blessed Mother. Be always by my side, holy angel, and make me silent within so that I may listen to your voice and fulfill the mission and responsibilities that the Lord has given me.

St. Joseph abounded in trust. But remember that Joseph did not live to see the fulfillment of his Son's mission; he died, we believe, before Christ's public life began, perhaps before the Wedding Feast at Cana, when Jesus accompanied His Mother. Joseph never had the opportunity to see Jesus' miracles or His preaching. He did not see the acceptance of Jesus by great crowds or hear Him acclaimed as King. He did not witness the Cross, nor did he ever receive Jesus in Holy Communion. But it was given to him to whisper the Holy Name for the first time. It was given to him to see the first blood shed for the salvation of the world at the Circumcision. It was given to him to hear, day and night, the breath of the Word who sustains the universe. And this was enough for Joseph.

St. Joseph is the model of contemplative prayer because in his works and his labors he was ever united to Jesus and Mary. As we have seen, there are no words of St. Joseph recorded in the Gospels, but Joseph, by his presence, was in constant dialogue with God Almighty, with the Son of God made Man, and with the Immaculate Conception, who was His spouse.

We should turn to St. Joseph in all the needs of our life and ask him to make us open and docile to the inspirations of our angels, whether they come to us when we are asleep or when we are awake. It's important to note that St. Matthew is extremely precise when he speaks about the visits of the angel. He doesn't say that Joseph *dreamed of* an angel; he says that the angel *appeared to* Joseph in a dream—in other words, while he was asleep. It was at the end of the day, when his mind was quiet and calm, that God's word could be received. And it must mean too that Joseph ended his day in a spirit of prayer and recollection, so that he was ready for this communication from Almighty God.

Saint Joseph: The Patron of Daily Life

How do we discover Joseph's gifts of simplicity in our own lives? For Joseph is also the patron of a simple life; simplicity of heart is the way in which he responded to God's love. Our world may be very different from the world of Joseph and Mary, but we can look to the life of the Holy Family as an example for us, and we can see in their unity and harmony the model to which our families should aspire.

We must begin each day by rising with joy, ready to serve the Lord, ready to begin the day in the blessings and the grace of God. The first thing we should do is to think not of our work, or of our troubles, or of our plans, but rather of the Lord, Who has given us the new day: "Good morning, dear God. How beautiful You have made this world, and how beautiful You have made this day. I thank You for all Your blessings." When we greet the Lord in this way, we express our gratitude for His love for us.

Blessed Solanus Casey, the American Capuchin friar who died in 1957, used to counsel people who came to see him to thank God ahead of time for the favors they were requesting. That would be a wise idea for our morning prayers too: Thank God for the food you will eat and the presence of family and friends around you. Thank Him for the work you will accomplish and the good that you will try to do. Thank Him for the beauties of His world and for the lessons that He wants to teach you this day. Begin your day with loving confidence in Our Lord and in the maternal care of His Blessed Mother. Thank your angel for being at your side and for all he will do on your behalf.

If it's possible, there is no better way to praise God than through morning Mass and Holy Communion. This is absolutely the most powerful means of sanctification that we have available to us. Even if we cannot do anything else during the day, due to infirmity or other circumstances, and even if we have no other interaction with anyone else, we will have participated in something of infinite value. We will have shared in the renewal of Calvary and offered the Son back to His Father, joining our will to His in the most perfect and powerful act of love. That changes us; indeed, it transforms us. Daily Mass creates an intimacy between the Triune God and ourselves—and between us and our neighbor. We begin to look at others with different eyes and different hearts. Daily Mass is the greatest act of praise we can offer, the greatest means of atonement we can make; it is the greatest means of petition of which we can avail ourselves and the most perfect hymn of thanksgiving we can sing.

That is why the priest speaks in the words of the psalmist as he receives Communion, "What can I return to the Lord for all that He has given me? The cup of salvation shall I raise and I shall call upon the name of the Lord" (Psalm 116:12–13). If Mass is not possible for us, nonetheless we should begin our day with prayer by offering all that we do to the Lord, in union with the Masses celebrated throughout the world. The morning offering is an extremely powerful spiritual tool that lifts us up and changes the day.

Although offering our morning prayers is the most important thing we do to begin the day in the sight of the Lord, there are also practical virtues we should practice, virtues that discipline us and make us ready for the day. We can make our bed, straighten our room, and do other little but important things that make life easier for other members of our family. Then, when we leave our room or our house, we should endeavor to speak good words to as many people as possible, to say thank you, to greet others warmly, to wish them a good morning and a good day. In this way we will offer to others the joy of God reflected in our faces and our souls.

Blessed Angela of the Cross (1846–1932), the Spanish foundress of the Society of the Cross, a nursing community in service to the poor in their homes, understood this spiritual practice very well. When her Sisters go out in pairs to do home care, one is assigned to pray while the other has the special mission of smiling and greeting people along the way. She told them, "If you do not show joy in belonging to Jesus, who will teach the people this?" But you don't have to be a habited religious to do good. A pleasant face, a polite nod, or a small greeting can change a person's day and perhaps his life. Your greeting may dispose someone to receiving an inspiration from his or her angel later in the day. If the presence of the angels has become important to your spiritual life, you might also find yourself greeting the holy angel who walks silently at each person's side. He will be grateful for your efforts on behalf of his charge.

Throughout the day we should try to be conscientious in doing our work as an offering to God, and we should always try to render good service, doing the best that is possible at the time. Both at work and at home we must avoid quarreling, disagreement, and dissension. Rather, we must try to understand why others speak to us in the way they do, entering into their trials and difficulties and empathizing with them. And if we cannot offer any words of counsel or material help, we can certainly offer a prayer asking the Lord to be merciful.

Finally, when the day has been long and toilsome, let us go to the Lord — if possible, to the Real Presence in the Blessed Sacrament, or, failing that, perhaps before a crucifix in our home — and lay before Him all the burdens of our day. We can entrust them to Him, like St. Joseph, thanking Him for the good that we have been able to do, offering Him those things that are unfinished, and asking His pardon for those things that have gone badly or the times we have failed. And then, at the end of this offering of ourselves to God, we can entrust ourselves to the care of the holy angels and ask them to watch over us.

Let us ask St. Joseph, the patron of our daily life, to open our hearts to the promptings and encouragement of the angels so that we might find Christ in all things.

Chapter 8

ANGELS IN THE LIFE OF CHRIST

— �֍ —

When I was a little boy, one of the parish churches near my home had beautiful representations of the choirs of angels. The holy angels were painted in a semicircle around the apse surrounding the altar of the church, bordering groups of saints painted near the ceiling. And in almost all the images of the life of Our Lord around the church, there were angels in the background. They were not just in the scenes of Bethlehem but also at His baptism, throughout His public ministry, and at His agony in the garden. In fact, the angels were shown in scenes in which the Gospel did not mention them at all.

When I was a little older, I thought for a time that the artist was simply fond of angels and had looked for any opportunity to paint them. But when I began to read the Gospels and to study theology, I realized that the holy angels always surrounded and assisted Jesus, ministering to Him but also contemplating with wonder the unfolding of God's plan. Then I began to understand why my old church had depicted the angels in every scene. Many saints, mystics, and theologians have written about the angels' loving contemplation of the life of Jesus. Seeing them contemplating the Lord's life disposes us to do the same. And the angels are able to share their contemplations with us, as they inspire and guide us in the ordinary paths of the spiritual life.

As we become more open to the inspirations and support of our guardian angels, we will discover new riches in the familiar stories of Our Lord's life and teachings. We will go beyond being familiar only with the narrative details we hear at Mass as the angels help draw us into intimacy with these great mysteries and truths; we will begin to fathom the deep meaning of Our Lord's words and actions and to desire that profound relationship with the Father that He has come to reveal to us. We will find the Lord in His Word, in the Cross, and in the Bread of Life. And so we will live in the company of the angels.

Angels at the Birth of Christ

We have already considered how the angels were privileged to announce the birth of John the Baptist to Zechariah and to bring the message of the Incarnation to Our Lady and St. Joseph. We can also deduce from the Gospels that angels were responsible for the star that beckoned the Wise Men and, certainly, the messenger spirits who warned them in a dream not to go back to Herod but to return to their own home by another route. And as we have just seen, the angels spoke to St. Joseph, too, reassuring him about his vocation to be the spouse of the Virgin Mary and the foster father of the Word Made Flesh.

Just as Mary Magdalene would be chosen to be the first witness of the Risen Christ (John 20:14–18) even though women were not allowed to bear witness in Jewish courts, so too the first witnesses of the miracle of Christmas were not considered to be respectable and reliable. Shepherds were considered by the Talmud to be impure in virtue of their profession and dishonest in their dealings with others.[46] Jewish proverbs warned families against letting their sons grow up to be shepherds. They were not only poor but also socially marginalized, as Pope Francis noted in his Christmas Mass of 2013. And yet it was to these men, keeping night watch over their flock, that the angels were sent:

> And an angel of the Lord appeared to them, and the glory of the Lord shone around them, and they were filled with fear. And the angel said to them, "Be not afraid, for behold, I bring you good news of a great joy which will come to all the people; for to you is born this day in the city of David a Savior, who is Christ the Lord. And this will be a sign for you: you will find a babe wrapped in swaddling cloths and lying in a manger. And suddenly there was with the angel a multitude of the heavenly host praising God and saying, Glory to God in the highest, and on earth peace among men with whom He is pleased. (Luke 2:9–14)

The shepherds dwelled in tents, moving themselves and their families from pasture to pasture. They usually had no other home. When the angel appeared to them, they were overwhelmed with fear; he appeared alone and delivered his message before allowing the other "pillars of fire" to join him. The angel took away dread and gave them the greatest reason for hope: "For to you is born … a Savior, who is Christ the Lord" (Luke 2:11). This highest of gifts had come down first to the very poor to give joy: The Child will be recognized in rags, lying in a trough, as St. Luke's Greek states it plainly.

---

[46] Marcello Stanzione, *Gli Angeli della Natività* (Milano: Sugarco Edizioni, 2015), pp. 80–81.

Perhaps there is even more to this message than we have previously understood: Certain Christian scholars believe that the shepherds of Bethlehem were Levitical shepherds, who raised sheep for the Temple sacrifices and the celebration of Passover. How fitting it is, then, that the angels should reveal their message to these men, identifying the "Lamb of God" who had come down to earth "to take away the sins of the world" to the guardians of the sacrificial lambs of the Old Covenant.

Then the angels showed themselves, "a multitude of the heavenly host" (Luke 2:13). Now, what constitutes a multitude? It would have been an uncountable number that the shepherds saw in the Bethlehem skies—all the heavenly hosts were rejoicing that night as the Savior came forth into His world. All of heaven was silent to hear the first breath of the One through whom all things were made (see John 1:3). Then they burst into the song of praise that has echoed throughout the silent universe ever since.

Glory to God in the highest, and on earth peace among men with whom he is pleased! (Luke 2:14)

Father Marcello Stanzione, one of the world's leading angelologists, tells us that this angelic hymn is designed with three couplets that stand in a certain opposition to one another "glory—peace," "to God—among men," and "the highest (heavens)—earth." What the angels offer was not a wish—"May it come true!"—but a proclamation: "It is *now* come!" What they were saying is, "By the Birth of this Child, God is glorified! By the Birth of this Child, Peace has come to the earth!"[47] In a very real sense, the angels had been waiting to sing this song of praise since the moment they passed through their trial of faith; for now,

[47] Ibid., pp. 83–84.

the Father's plan reached yet another moment of fulfillment as God the Son looked upon His creation through human eyes, and creation looked back at Him through the love-filled eyes of His Immaculate Mother.

Doctors tell us that when a newborn's eyes are able to focus, the first thing he sees is the face of his mother, at the distance of the nursing baby's face to his mother's. That means that the first sight that the Christ Child saw was the face of Mary Immaculate—and in seeing and loving her, He saw and loved all of us.

The communion of love that was established as Mary tabernacled her Child within her womb now took on a new dimension of sacrifice and atonement as she lifted Him in her arms and offered Him to the Father. Once again Mary spoke her *Fiat* to the Father's will as she accepted with love the Child and all that His coming signified. When the shepherds arrived, their eyes filled with joy and their hearts with wonder, she listened, delighted but unsurprised, to their story of the angels' song. Why shouldn't the angels fill the night sky with their songs, just as they were filling her heart with their joy?

We Three Kings

Was the visit of the Magi guided by an angel or simply by a star? St. Matthew's account (2:1–12) does not resolve the question, but it would not have occurred to anyone in the first century to make such a distinction. Were not all the stars of the heavens under the direction and care of the angels? Perhaps the angels moved a star into place or, having appeared in human form to the shepherds, they now manifested themselves in a truly "heavenly" manner to the Magi astrologers? Both Sts. John Chrysostom and Thomas Aquinas noted that the star behaved with the intelligence of "an invisible power," and the earliest Christian representations of the

Magi's visit show not only a comet-like star, but also a guiding angel.[48]

Since the time of the early Christians, the Magi have come to represent the great and the good—learned seekers who humbly persisted in their search for truth until they discovered more than they expected: a Child in His Mother's arms, not an idea enclosed in parchment scrolls. He was a King to be acknowledged, a God to be worshipped, but also a Child to be loved without fear. These men fell down before Him in adoration without hesitation or argument, offering gifts that mysteriously symbolized all that the Child would be: King, God, and Sacrifice.

Warned in a dream not to return by way of Jerusalem, the Magi left Bethlehem but carried the Child with them in their hearts. They were to become symbols of seekers and gift-givers. Catholic devotion has attributed to them names, ages, and origins—bearing witness perhaps to the truth that Christ may be found in our youth, our middle years, or even in great age; by men and women of any race; and by people in every place and time. A star will appear; an angel will guide. We must simply have the courage to follow and, when we find, to adore.

As the Magi departed on their way, the Lord's angel returned to Joseph in his sleep and commanded him: "Rise, take the child and His mother, and flee to Egypt, and remain there till I tell you: for Herod is about to search for the child, to destroy Him" (Matt. 2:13). And so he rose immediately and returned with his family to the land of slavery. On the road, did they hear of the massacre of the Innocents in Bethlehem? In our Catholic devotion to the Seven Sorrows of Mary, the first mystery is the Flight into Egypt, but that sorrow of flight must be linked to the news of Herod's murderous soldiers attacking the homes of his own citizens. The

---

[48] Ibid., pp. 168–169.

Holy Family would have settled with other Jewish families who lived in Egypt, and news would have been carried across the desert. Surely, this was the first of the many swords that pierced the Heart of Mary and opened her soul to our sorrows and pains. Her heart must have wept for the other mothers who lost their sons to the brutality of evil and sin.

But time passed and once again the angel returned, saying, "Rise, take the child and his mother, and go to the land of Israel, for those who sought the child's life are dead (Matt. 2:20). And so the Holy Family returned to Israel — not to Bethlehem, but to Nazareth — where Jesus remained in the "hidden life" of His family and grew to manhood. The angel who had been the protector of the Holy Family had completed his missions of intervention. Now it was Joseph and Mary who were to guide and to watch over the Child until it was time for Him to go forth from them and to begin His public ministry. The angels were always to be present and ready to do His will: Did He not say later that He had "more than twelve legions of angels" at His command? (Matt. 26:53). But they manifested themselves only once before His Passion.

Calling Us to Him

We find the angels next in the accounts of the temptation of Christ in the wilderness (see Matt. 4:1–11; Mark 1:12–13; Luke 4:1–13), when Satan offered Him three temptations that corresponded in a real yet mysterious way to the names given to the Devil in Scripture: murderer, liar, and accuser. Each of these "names" reveals the Devil as the adversary of God. The Evil One strikes out at God as the Author of life, the Source of all truth, and the Paraclete-Advocate who speaks on our behalf.

We are told that after the Lord had answered Satan and routed him, the angels came and ministered to Him (Matt. 4:11; Mark

1:13). We do not know what form this ministry took, but it evokes the journey of the Chosen People in the desert—the Exodus journey. For there, too, the angels comforted and ministered to God's chosen and provided them with bread from Heaven. But now the angels were ministering to the Living Bread come down from Heaven as Jesus began His ministry, already taking upon Himself the burden of the sins of the world.

Following these forty days in the desert—this time of trial and preparation for all the hardships that would be part of Our Lord's ministry—Jesus began to preach and to call His apostles. In the Gospel of Saint John (1:45ff.), the sixth disciple whom the Lord calls is Nathanael, who is also known by his father's name, *Bar Tolomei* or Bartholomew, the son of Ptolomey. Nathanael is reluctant to believe that "anything good" can come out of Nazareth, but when Jesus indicates that He has seen Nathanael "under the fig tree," Nathanael is convinced that Jesus is all that his friends have claimed. We do not know what was happening "under the fig tree." The Gospel does not provide details; whatever it was, it seems to have been a moment of personal victory and grace for Nathanael, something witnessed by no other human being, yet so profound and joyful that Jesus' acknowledgment of it was enough to convince Nathanael of Jesus' mission and perhaps even His divine identity. Yet Jesus still chooses to invoke the testimony of the angels to confirm His identity: "Truly, truly, I say to you, you will see heaven opened, and the angels of God ascending and descending upon the Son of man" (John 1:51). The image both recalls Jacob's Ladder (Gen. 28:10–17) and surpasses its meaning. As once the Old Covenant and Law were entrusted to the angels themselves, now Christ the One Mediator between Heaven and earth receives the angels as *His* servants and ministers.

On another occasion recorded by St. Matthew, Our Lord says of little children, "See that you do not despise one of these little ones; for I tell you that in heaven their angels always behold the face of my Father who is in heaven" (Matt. 18:10). This passage has been adopted from the earliest days of the Church as evidence for the existence of a personal guardian angel. In the Old Testament, angels were seen as guardians of nations, but by the time of Jesus, people were ready to believe that the all-generous God would place an angel by the side of even His littlest ones. And yet, even when an angel is serving as a guardian for a human being, the angel is still in the presence of God, as Jesus clearly says. The ministry of guardianship does not detract from the angel's vocation to adore the Lord. Remember that the angels do not have bodies that are bounded by the space they occupy; the angels come into a place simply by thinking of it. So, as the angel adores God, he is also always thinking about the one over whom he has charge. And vice versa: As the angel serves us, so he is also always praying for us to the Lord God.

Earlier in that same chapter of Matthew, we find this teaching: "And calling to him a child, he put him in the midst of them, and said, 'Truly, I say to you, unless you turn and become like children, you will never enter the kingdom of heaven'" (18:2–3). Note that Our Lord does not tell us to become *childish* but *childlike*. And what are the childlike virtues? Simplicity, perseverance, innocence, trust, wonder, awe — these pure qualities distinguish children from cynical adults. In little children there is neither false pride nor false humility. A child's soul is translucent, and we might even say transparent. An angel could "look through" a child's soul and see God unhindered. Perhaps this is why the Blessed Virgin usually chooses little ones, such as St. Bernadette and the seers of Fatima, to be her messengers on earth. They repeated her words simply and directly, without "interpretations."

We would do well to ask our guardian angels to increase these qualities in us, so that we too may be childlike in our maturity, so

that our littleness might make us capable of bearing within our-
selves the Infinity of God Himself. Which saints have displayed
these characteristics? In modern times we can look to St. Thérèse
of Lisieux, known as "the Doctor of the Little Way of Spiritual
Childhood," and to St. Gemma Galgani. Among the male saints,
St. Francis of Assisi and many of his Franciscan sons stand out.
In the New World, St. Juan Diego, St. Rose of Lima, St. Brother
André, and Blessed Solanus Casey of the Capuchins come to mind.
These holy persons lived lives of simple, trusting faith and generous
service to their neighbor; each did so in the varying circumstances
of life and duty.

There is a lesson for us in this: The angels manifest these qualities and gifts of transparency, awe, and purity according to their
angelic nature, but we must learn to do so in ways proper to our
human nature. Christ Jesus is *enthroned* upon the angels, but He
wants *to dwell within us*. The indwelling of Christ through grace
and the sacramental life make the simplest and most ordinary life
wondrous and wonder-filled. The angels surely rejoice when they
find that childlike reverence in us.

That's why the saints who have been most linked to the angels
have retained and radiated this childlike trust, wonder, and innocence. There is a winsomeness, an attractive beauty about such
personalities. St. Thérèse of Lisieux was marvelously devoted to
her guardian angel and wrote poems to him to express her praise.
St. Francis of Assisi, the *poverello* (poor man), who had converted
from a life of thoughtless pleasures and sin to a life of innocence
and concerned love for all, saw the seraphim bearing the crucified
Christ when he received the stigmata; he is called the "Seraphic
Saint" because he burns with love for God, a love that enflames
others. The intellectuals among the saints display the same qualities, if we know how to find them: Thomas Aquinas's theology
could not contain the depth or breadth of his love of God, so he

wrote hymns and prayers in poetry; Blessed John Henry Newman composed songs and poems to explain his understanding of the angels' missions and their gracious courtesy toward us.

The Lord's words about the guardianship of the angels and the virtues of childhood should impress themselves on us so that we may accept their aid and care with docility, as did the saints of every age.

Ministers of Justice

Jesus also spoke of the angels when He taught his disciples about judgment and justice. In the parable of the wheat and the weeds, for instance, He described the angels going out at harvest time. (They are the reapers in Matthew 13:30: "Let both grow together until the harvest; and at harvest time I will tell the reapers, Gather the weeds first and bind them in bundles to be burned, but gather the wheat into my barn.") This imagery is found in the book of Enoch, a Jewish text that was not included in the canon of the Old Testament but it is quoted by St. Jude in his epistle.

It was of these also that Enoch in the seventh generation from Adam prophesied, saying, "Behold, the Lord came with his holy myriads, to execute judgment on all, and to convict all the ungodly of all their deeds of ungodliness which they have committed in such an ungodly way, and of all the harsh things which ungodly sinners have spoken against him" (Jude 14–15).

In speaking of His Second Coming, Jesus once again depicted the angels as heralds of His justice and ministers of His judgment: "And he will send out his angels with a loud trumpet call, and they will gather his elect from the four winds, from one end of heaven to the other" (Matt. 24:31).

Now, the angels themselves, though ministers of God's judgment, have no foreknowledge of events; their commitment is simply to carry out God's will and to fulfill their service to the Lord. And that is why, when describing the events of the last day, Jesus said, "But of that day and hour no one knows, not even the angels of heaven, nor the Son, but the Father only" (Matt. 24:36). At that hour, it is Jesus Himself who will stand before the Father on our behalf. "And I tell you, every one who acknowledges me before men, the Son of Man also will acknowledge before the angels of God" (Luke 12:8). Our Lord's words are not simply information for us; they are formation for our lives of obedient faith. Now, therefore, the angels wait to see our response to the Lord. They expect us to be faithful, and faithful without compromise; it is only by our loyalty that we can grow into friendship with the Lord and enter into intimacy of mind, will, and mission with the angels.

The passage from Luke's Gospel continues ominously: "But he who denies me before men will be denied before the angels of God" (Luke 12:9). What an awful thought! That is why the Lord gives us a lifetime on earth in the presence of the angels—in their company and under their guidance—to grow in faithful and loving friendship with Our Savior. This may require heroism on our part—the heroism of daily duty, responsibility, renunciation, and sacrifice. The trials we pass through may demand that we risk everything for Christ and His Name. It is in these moments that the angel draws near and reminds us, "Fear not! The Lord is with you. He has already won the victory."

St. Peter refers to the Devil as "a roaring lion, seeking someone to devour" (1 Pet. 5:8). The angels are our protectors against that roaring lion. As once an angel stopped the mouths of the lions when Daniel was cast into their den (Dan. 6:22), so our guardian angels alert us to the spiritual dangers that surround us; they shield us from many evils and help us to see the Light of Christ burning brightly in the darkness.

Jesus also speaks of the joy of the angels in reference to repentant sinners, which should give us great hope: "I tell you, there is joy before the angels of God over one sinner who repents" (Luke 15:10). The angels want to see us benefit from the power of the Cross and experience the salvation of the Lord. And while they may be shocked by our sins, since they have never committed sin themselves, they never turn away from us. Instead, they seek to inspire us to turn back to the Lord, to repent of our sins, to grasp the Cross, and to come to the fullness of salvation. The angels who have witnessed the repentance of Peter and the conversion of Paul find their delight in our conversions, our confessions, and the little victories of daily life.

Angels at the Passion and Resurrection

As Our Lord's Passion drew near, the angels gazed with loving awe at the unfolding of the Father's plan and the obedience of the Word Made Flesh. The angels were present in the Garden of Gethsemane, unseen by the Apostles. They watched the Lord pray in agony. They saw Him weep and sweat blood as the weight of the world's sins pressed down upon Him. Even His own disciples and closest friends failed Him in these moments of supreme struggle. The angels heard the Lord speak and accept the chalice of pain and suffering, so that all persons might find forgiveness and all sin might be atoned for by His Sacrifice.

St. Luke tells us that after Jesus prayed in this way and accepted His sufferings, "there appeared an angel from heaven, strengthening him" (Luke 22:43). Now that the struggle was over and Christ had fulfilled the Father's will by His prayer of acceptance, the angels could gather around Him to comfort Him and to help Him go forward on the way of sorrow that would end in victory and glory. Once again, the humiliations and struggles that He endured as man were succeeded by the manifestation of the glories that are His as Son of God. That is why the angel came.

Yet, as the Passion of Our Lord proceeded, the angels were not mentioned again in the four Gospel accounts—not during the trials or the scourging, or on the Way of the Cross, or even at the Crucifixion. Mystics and visionaries describe them, in their own contemplations, as present and active at every moment, watchful, waiting, loving, and serving. But the Passion of Jesus was a human drama of inhuman acts. The angels could neither intervene nor interfere. They could only adore the Father's plan and watch its unfolding in the obedience of the Son. The Gospels speak instead of the crowds who jeered, of the holy women who wept, and of Jesus' Mother, St. John, and Mary Magdalene.

Around these holy souls we can perceive the influence of the angels at work. Their presence made room in the midst of the pressing, shouting, stifling crowds for these holy ones to stay strong and to do what they could for Christ. The pious women of Jerusalem received a grace to be brave enough to come forward, offering their tears and laments, to listen to His words and to remember them as long as they lived.

Perhaps the Veronica whom we know from the Stations of the Cross was one of those women, with an angel at her elbow, telling her to try, to offer the little comfort that she could, to go forward with her linen veil in hand. Thinking that she was offering a charity, a small gesture of comfort, she received a gift of divine grace. She saw the Innocent One who takes away the sins of the world; she wiped away blood and mud from Him who will wash us clean. Because of that courage, she became herself a true image of the One whose Face was impressed upon her veil. Veronica will always be for the Church the sign of a woman who is forever changed by the good she sought to offer another.

St. John, accompanying the Blessed Mother, saw Simon of Cyrene forced into carrying the Cross behind Jesus. The Beloved Disciple, who would have done anything to help Jesus, watched the stranger awkwardly take the weight of the wood from His shoulders for a few minutes. Simon did not know at the time that the wood was the least of Christ's burdens; he did not know that Jesus was carrying Simon's own sins on His back that day. But he came to understand this later; for he and his family became part of the early Jerusalem church.

Did St. John feel a pang of jealousy at this stranger's privilege, a moment of rebellion that he was not chosen to help carry the Cross? We might perhaps think so, for his was still a fiery nature. But perhaps the presence of Mary and the inspiration of his guardian angel was enough to "let it be done according to His will." It would be enough for John and the holy women to stand at the foot of the Cross, to remain with Him until the end, offering their silent presence in faithful love and accepting the mission that the dying Lord would grant to each of them. Perhaps it was this *Marian silence* and unflinching gaze upon Jesus that allowed John to see in the piercing of Christ's side so much more than what it seemed. Instead of proving that Jesus was finally dead, John realized that the blood and water that flowed out was the Sign, the evidence, the power of overwhelming, ever-flowing eternal life for us. When he bent down to look into the open Tomb on Easter Sunday, John had no questions to ask: "He saw and he believed" (John 20:8).

There are so many things that the angels can help us to contemplate as we meditate on the Passion, so many lessons and truths hidden from our busy minds and hearts that we easily overlook. When we become silent within, when looking becomes seeing, the angels will guide our contemplation in ways that will have immense spiritual value for us. The spirits of love will help us to contemplate the Passion in today's world too; for though Christ is seated at the right hand of the Father and suffers no more, is not His Passion continuing in the life and sufferings of every human person for whom He suffered? Is that not part of the mission entrusted to our angel guardians—that we come to see the Face of Jesus in every man and woman around us?

What Did Jesus Himself See?

As Jesus met His Mother on the way to Calvary, He saw in her the Immaculate Conception and the Church purified, made whole and beautiful. Not only is Mary His Mother, but she represents His Bride, the Church, for she is the first among believers. It was for this reason that St. Francis of Assisi, in one of his beautiful prayers, refers to her as "Virgin made Church." Mary is the pattern for all believers in our life of faith, trust, and obedient love. Though not washed in the sacramental waters of Baptism, she shares in the Redemption won by her Son uniquely and preeminently. She was "pre-redeemed," we might say, by the gift of her Immaculate Conception.

From this first grace that will encompass her entire existence, she will always stand before the Church, not only as Jesus' first disciple but also as Mother and Image of the Church. This is why, at Lourdes, Mary could call herself "the Immaculate Conception." And so, looking upon her as He carried His Cross, Christ was strengthened to accomplish His mission. Standing at the foot of the Cross, she was confirmed in her mission as Coredemptrix and Mediatrix of Grace. Whenever her Son's Sacrifice is renewed, she is there present by the side of the altar, lifting up her hands in prayer and calling down her Son's grace and mercy.

In John, the beloved disciple and faithful friend, Jesus saw the priesthood that will continue to perpetuate His atoning Sacrifice in the celebration of the Mass and the sacraments, the priesthood that will continue to offer the forgiveness of sins, even to the end of time. John accepted the care of the Blessed Mother, taking her into his home (John 19:27), even as he was entrusted to her loving care. She would share with Him her memories and contemplations and help to form him in his full maturity as beloved disciple, fearless apostle, priest, seer, and evangelist. He would become as an Eagle that soars to the heights of Heaven.

Fathers of the Church, as well as later saints and mystics, have seen in John the model of the soul completely transformed by Jesus and privileged to rest on His Heart. Saints from Gertrude the Great to Father Solanus Casey have spoken of their own "leaning on the Heart of Jesus" as an image of the spiritual life. The Eagle soars, but not alone; he draws us along with him.

St. Mary Magdalene is often depicted kneeling at the foot of the Cross, encircling it in her arms, her eyes wide with pain. Usually, she is shown unveiled, her long hair streaming down over her face in a gesture of sorrow, grief, and helplessness. Mary Magdalene represents all of us poor sinners who know that Christ is our only Savior, His Cross our final anchor of hope, the only rock to which we can cling. When one of the thieves cried out, "Save Yourself and us!" (Luke 23:39), she must have thought, "And save me, too!" She was sprinkled with His Precious Blood, even as she grasped the feet she had once anointed.

In her, the angels saw every repentant soul, every broken human heart, whose emptiness could only be filled up by the loving Christ. Until He would speak her name on Easter Sunday morning, not even their presence would succeed in consoling her. Then she could become "apostle to the apostles" and bearer of the best good news. The angels lead us to contemplate all the characters and figures of the Passion, even as they recede into the background, crying out with marvel, "Hosanna! Worthy is He, worthy of all praise!"

Three Days

Christian art often depicts angels surrounding the Cross. Sometimes they are portrayed in postures of mourning, but at other times we see them near the five wounds of Christ, catching the Precious Blood in chalices. These are spiritual and theological representations rather than historical ones, but they reveal to us a deep truth. Angels are always carrying the blood of Christ and His living Waters as they bear the graces of Christ to the world. They assist the Church as she brings forth the streams of life-giving blood and water in the sacraments of Baptism and the Holy Eucharist. They continue to assist in the worship of the Church by fulfilling their God-given roles. Angels do not share in the priesthood, but they do join themselves to the priests of the Church, strengthening their prayer and their praise and helping the whole community of the faithful so that we might receive more perfectly the gifts of salvation. We do not know from the Gospels what the angels experienced at Christ's death, though we may well imagine them darkening the sun in their sorrow, sundering rocks and tearing the veil of the Temple from top to bottom as signs of the mourning of Heaven and earth. We can picture them accompanying Him when He descended to the Limbo of the Just, bringing light to those who dwelt in death's shadows, awaiting the day of His preaching to the dead on Holy Saturday. This day is one of the most obscure of the mysteries of our Faith. We cannot fully know what the angels experienced as they waited, watching Mary in trustful faith as she anticipated the dawn of Easter Sunday and the rising of her Son.

But on that first Easter Sunday, the angels were present at the tomb, for we read:

And behold, there was a great earthquake; for an angel of the Lord descended from heaven and came and rolled back the stone, and sat upon it. His appearance was like lightning, and his raiment white as snow. And for fear of him the guards trembled and became like dead men. (Matt. 28:2–4)

This angel of the Resurrection was a messenger of power—of God's omnipotence. He came, too, as a messenger of purity, for the world is purified by the sufferings and the victorious Resurrection of Christ. And so the angel appeared clothed in white garments like lightning, revealing in his sublimity God's judgment on the world and the presence of the Risen One.

As we read the accounts of the holy women, those who had surrounded the Virgin Mother on Calvary and who had now come "to do what they could" on Easter morning, we see once again how the angels were present to reassure them. "Do not be afraid," the angels said—words full of tenderness and understanding as they pointed to the empty slab where the body of Jesus had been. According to St. Matthew there was one angel, and according to St. Luke and St. John there were two, but the details do not matter much. How could anyone expect to take it all in? What is important is the message: "Why do you seek the living among the dead?" (Luke 24:5).

This is the question of the angels to us, and it rings down through the ages. Even today they ask the same thing of us when we turn away from the Lord and settle for what is less. We can imagine the same angels imploring us today: Why do you seek God among false idols? Why do you look to things that are lesser than God to find happiness? Why do you seek truth, life, and love among the dead things of sin? Look to Heaven. Look to where Jesus is enthroned as Lord of the living and the dead. Look deep within your hearts and find there the grace of the triune God.

This is the message the angels give us to protect us from temptation, to ward off evil, to defend us from harm. "Why do you seek the living among the dead?" The angels continue to proclaim the Resurrection of Jesus and its meaning for our lives. They do so with joy, rapture, wonder, and awe as they encourage us to receive from the Lord the fullness of His gifts and to live His risen life abundantly.

Ascending Angels

In the forty days after Our Lord's Resurrection, Jesus continued to appear to His disciples. He spoke with them, ate with them, encouraged them, healed them of their obstacles to faith, and gave them teachings that have become part of the Sacred Tradition of the Church. There is no mention of the angels during those forty days, but we find them once again at the Ascension:

> As they were looking on, he was lifted up, and a cloud took him out of their sight. And while they were gazing into heaven as he went, behold, two men stood by them in white robes, and said, "Men of Galilee, why do you stand looking into heaven? This Jesus, who was taken up from you into heaven, will come in the same way as you saw him go into heaven." (Acts 1:9–11)

So, encouraged by the holy angels, the Apostles returned to Jerusalem to await the coming of the Holy Spirit — the anointing that allowed them to preach the gospel of salvation with courage and boldness.

Cardinal Jean Daniélou, in his wonderful little book *The Angels and Their Mission*, tells us that "the true mystery of the Ascension is the exaltation of human nature above all the worlds of the angels."[49] It is the conclusion of the cycle of Christ's glory and the defeat of Satan. This is the triumph of the victorious Christ, as the Incarnate Word returns to the Father in His glorious Risen Flesh. The Church historian Eusebius wrote of the angels, saying:

---

[49] Jean Daniélou, SJ, *The Angels and Their Mission: According to the Fathers of the Church*, trans. David Heimann (Westminster, MD: Christian Classics, 1976), p. 41.

The virtues of heaven, seeing Him begin to rise, surrounded Him to form His escort, proclaiming His Ascension as they cried, "Rise up, gates everlasting, and the King of Glory will enter."[50]

Psalm 23, which speaks these words about the Lord entering His Temple in Jerusalem, is here being applied to the Ascension of Jesus, the moment of His definitive entrance into the New and Eternal Jerusalem.

The angels in the life of Jesus appear always as ministering spirits caught up in the wonder and awe of reverent love. They inspire in us this same devotion, this same worship, this same fascination with the glory of God and the majesty of Christ, King of the Universe. When we come to adore Jesus in the Blessed Sacrament and to participate in Holy Mass, the angels surround us and inspire us to gaze upon the Lord with reverent love.

We see the elements under which He veils Himself, but they look directly upon His glory. We pray for the Church to continue Her mission, but they gaze on the Holy Spirit granting new Pentecosts to men and women at every moment of the day. That is why we call upon them and ask for their prayers:

Strengthen our faith! Focus our minds and hearts! Teach us how to adore as you do — from the depths of our being, with all that we are. Help us to embrace the Cross and never turn from Him. But strip away the selfishness, the pride, the laziness that prevent us from knowing Him as He wants us to know Him.

Jesus calls us to the life of grace here on earth, and He sends His angels to assist us so that we might appreciate more deeply

---

[50] Eusebius, *Comm. in Ps. 17*, cited in Daniélou, *The Angels*, p. 35.

and more joyously the great gifts that He gives us. Therefore, each day, give thanks to the Lord, who has called you to be part of His Church, who has shared with you His Gospel, who nourishes you with His Flesh. Praise Him in the sight of His angels and walk always in the ways of His truth.

Chapter 9

ANGELS IN THE NEW TESTAMENT: THE EPISTLES

✣

St. Paul the Apostle has been called "The Mystic of the Angels" because of his repeated references to the world of the angels throughout his epistles. Paul himself had been a Pharisee, a devout and learned Jew formed in the school of Gamaliel. Unlike the Sadducees, the Pharisees believed in the existence of angels and had developed an extensive angelology, which Paul brought with him at the time of his conversion. In his letters, Paul mentions angels frequently, and, though the references are usually brief, they are powerful. They reveal yet another dimension of how St. Paul's transforming encounter with Christ on the road to Damascus penetrated into all the parts of his theological formation and completed and perfected his cosmology.

Paul understood the angels as worshippers of the Lord and executors of divine missions. In the Old Covenant, they had been mediators, making known God's will and establishing the covenant with Moses; at times they spoke with or even in the voice of the Lord as His instruments. Now that time is over; God has spoken

His complete and supreme Word of truth and love in His Son, Jesus Christ, the Savior of the World.

In the Letter to the Hebrews, which is traditionally ascribed to St. Paul,[51] we read:

> In many and various ways God spoke of old to our fathers, by the prophets; but in these last days he has spoken to us by a Son, whom he appointed the heir of all things, through whom also he created the world. He reflects the glory of God and bears the very stamp of his nature, upholding the universe by his word and power. When he had made purification for sins, he sat down at the right hand of the Majesty on high, having become as much superior to angels as the name he has obtained is more excellent than theirs.
>
> For to what angel did God ever say, "Thou art my Son, today I have begotten thee"? or again, "I will be to him a father and he shall be to me a son"? And again, when he brings the first-born into the world, he says, "Let all God's angels worship him." Of the angels he says, "Who makes his angels winds, and his servants flames of fire." But of the Son he says, "Thy throne, O God, is for ever and ever, the

---

[51] The Catholic Church has traditionally accepted the Epistle to the Hebrews as St. Paul's fourteenth epistle, in keeping with the judgment of St. Jerome and St. Augustine. Recent scholarship has suggested that it is owed to another author, and even the Catholic Lectionary does not name Paul as author during the Mass readings. Even within the early Church, however, some recognized that while the *matter* of the epistle is Pauline, the *phrasing* seems to be different and more polished; Origen suggested that it might have been the work of St. Luke the Evangelist or St. Clement of Rome, faithfully recording St. Paul's teachings. These questions do not really belong to the present work, however. My desire is simply to survey the epistles of the New Testament and to comment on some elements of angelology as is useful for our spiritual purposes.

righteous scepter is the scepter of thy kingdom."... But to what angel has he ever said, "Sit at my hand, till I make thy enemies a stool for thy feet"? Are they not all ministering spirits sent forth to serve, for the sake of those who are to obtain salvation? (1:1–8; 13–14)

In his First Epistle to the Thessalonians, St. Paul uses the term "archangel" for the first time in a passage that describes Jesus' return in glory and the resurrection of the dead.

For the Lord himself will descend from heaven with a cry of command, with the archangel's call, and with the sound of the trumpet of God. And the dead in Christ will rise first; then we who are alive, who are left, shall be caught up together with them in the clouds to meet the Lord in the air; and so we shall always be with the Lord. Therefore comfort one another with these words. (4:16–18)

Paul does not give us the name of the archangel, though later Church tradition will ascribe the role of trumpeter of the resurrection of the dead to St. Gabriel.

In his Epistle to the Romans, which might be considered Paul's fundamental theological text, angels appear only once, when Paul lists ten cosmic realities in order to affirm that none of these have the power to separate us from the love of God present in Jesus Christ:

For I am sure that neither death, nor life, nor angels, nor principalities, nor things present, nor things to come, nor powers, nor height, nor depth, nor anything else in all creation, will be able to separate us from the love of God in Christ Jesus our Lord. (Rom. 8:38–39)

In the First Letter to the Corinthians, there are three mentions of angels (6:3; 11:10; 13:1). In the second, discussing the

145

traditional veiling of women in liturgical gatherings, Paul affirms that women should cover their heads because of the presence of the angels. This is a very early indication that the first Christians understood their celebration of the Eucharist, though it was not held in a beautiful cathedral or temple, to be a participation in heavenly worship. They understood that the angels mingled among them and joined their praise to the worship of the people. In the great hymn to charity in chapter 13, St. Paul speaks of the "tongues of angels," but reminds his readers that even such remarkable gifts are valueless without charity.

St. Paul's Warning

The Second Letter to the Corinthians refers to the Devil masquerading as an angel of light (11:14), a passage that has often been used to recall the need for discernment in matters of faith and the spiritual life. This discernment should be a frequent, even daily part of our prayers to our guardian angel. Lucifer seeks to bring shadow, division, and destruction into all the works of Christ, including our own souls.

In the Letter to the Galatians, Paul speaks of the immutability of the Gospel, responding to the dangers that his new believers were facing:

> I am astonished that you are so quickly deserting him who called you in the grace of Christ and turning to a different gospel—not that there is another gospel, but there are some who trouble you and want to pervert the gospel of Christ. But even if we, or an angel from heaven, should preach to you a gospel contrary to that which we preached to you, let him be accursed. (1:6–8)

These words are an important and perennial warning for all believers: The Gospel is unchanging and will never be improved upon.

The Church is indefectible; she can never fall away from the truth, nor will there ever be a need to exchange her or to supplement her with something else. Throughout the two-thousand year history of the Church, there have been many prophets and reformers who have appeared, claiming divine or angelic messages that led many out of the Church and into schism, heresy, and ultimately a rejection of many of Our Lord's essential teachings.[52] Peter's ongoing mission to confirm the brethren in the Faith is expressed in the guidance and authority of the pope and bishops in discerning the truth or falsehood of such claims of revelation.

In recent years, there have been a great many books and films about angels. Although the media has brought the angelic sphere before the eyes of many, we have to recognize that not all the angels portrayed in popular culture are in accordance with the truth of the Gospel or the teaching of the Church—in fact, very few

---

[52] Among other examples, we might consider the Church of Jesus Christ of Latter-Day Saints, which had its origin in American Protestantism. Its founder, the prophet Joseph Smith, claimed that an angel revealed a gospel that effectively denied the Trinity and the Virgin Birth, redefined the sacraments, restored various Old Testament laws and practices, and completely changed the Christian concept of the afterlife and union with God. The Jehovah's Witnesses, who also deny the Trinity, hold that Jesus was actually the archangel Michael, made visible in an "apparent" human form. Sects originating among Catholic believers have also claimed similar "divine mandates." The Army of Mary, a religious group founded in Quebec after Vatican II, has passed from a quite traditional form of Marian and Eucharistic spirituality to declaring its new identity as the "Church of [St.] John," supplanting and replacing the Church of Peter, worshipping a "Quinternity" of Persons, including the Blessed Virgin and its own recently deceased foundress, Marie-Paule Giguere. Once thought of as part of a "solution" to the problems of the Church in the modern world, it now celebrates a syncretistic version of the Mass, embodying pagan scriptures in its bizarre theology.

are. We must use the knowledge that the Church has given us to discern truth from falsehood — and always defer to the Church's judgment on such matters.

Often the angels we find in books on sale in supermarkets and airports are closer to the New Age movement, with its strange understandings of happiness and Heaven. Many volumes of "angelic messages" have also been published or appear on the Internet without Church approval or even any examination. Often, they mix traditional Catholic thought with secular sentimentality or unhealthy speculations. St. Paul warned the early Christians of Colossae and Ephesus against such beliefs. The angels, properly understood, always direct us to Christ. As St. Paul taught, if "angels" proclaim a gospel different from that of Jesus Himself, turn away from them. Do not walk. Run.

There are also many private revelations from centuries past that claim to reveal hidden truths about the angels, and again we must use the discernment of the Church in approaching these revelations. Even though a holy person has been beatified or canonized, it does not mean that the Church has recognized and validated every detail of his mystical experiences; oftentimes, these experiences of union with God and the unveiling of divine truths impressed themselves as images upon the mind and imagination of the holy person alone. Even the greatest and most articulate of saints and spiritual writers, such as Teresa of Avila and John of the Cross, found themselves at a loss to put what they "saw" into words. In some cases, as they themselves state, they struggled to find words to express what was given them as an inner illumination or conviction.

In one of her visions, St. Teresa saw the heavens opened and the throne of God revealed:

The throne seemed to me to be held up by some animals — I wondered if they were the Evangelists. But I could not see what the Throne was like, or who was on it—only a great multitude of angels, whom I thought of incomparably greater beauty than those I have seen in Heaven. I wondered if they were seraphim or cherubim, for they were very different in their glory and they seemed to be all on fire. There is a great deal of difference between angels, as I have said, and the glory which I felt within me at that time cannot be expressed in writing or even in speech, nor can it be imagined by anyone who has not experienced it.[53]

Such a passage helps us to understand that we cannot expect total accuracy regarding details that may have been secondary to the particular truth Our Lord wanted to impress on a mystic's soul. There are many mysteries about the angels that are disclosed to us in the pages of Scripture and in the Sacred Tradition of the Church, but there are other things that God doesn't need us to know. Those truths will be part of our joy and our glory when we come to Paradise—when we see the Face of God unveiled and live in the company of the holy angels and the saints for all eternity.

In the meantime, it is important for us to trust first in the teaching authority of the Church as we approach devotion to the angels and our practices of prayer. Doing so, we can never go wrong and we will never be deprived of any grace that we need for our holiness. The Lord's plan for the angels as cooperators in the work of our salvation is to be found within the Church and the practice of the Faith. As the Vatican's *Directory on Popular Piety and the Liturgy* explains:

---

[53] *Life of St. Teresa of Avila*, trans. Prof. Allison Peers (New York: Sheed and Ward, 1946), pp. 192–193; cited in D.D.C. Pochin Mould, *Angels of God* (New York: Devin Adair, 1963), p. 125.

Devotion to the Holy Angels gives rise to a certain form of the Christian life which is characterized by: devout gratitude to God for having placed these heavenly spirits of great sanctity and dignity at the service of man; an attitude of devotion deriving from the knowledge of living constantly in the presence of the Holy Angels of God; serenity and confidence in facing difficult situations, since the Lord guides and protects the faithful in the way of justice through the ministry of His Holy Angels. (215)

When we look at the lives of the saints, we see that the angels were sent to help to reveal the Word of God and to bear the joy of Christ into daily life. And that's what the angels still do for us. Their inspirations do not usually come in the form of long messages, but often simply as a word that echoes within the heart after a time of prayer or *lectio divina*. The message of an angel to you might be in the strength and joy that you feel as you approach the Blessed Sacrament. And then, as Jesus fills you with His love, ask the angel to praise the Lord with you—to adore Christ present within your soul.

Returning to St. Paul . . .

In his letters to St. Timothy, Paul reminds his disciple that as a bishop he must be a man of virtue, patience, and true Christian leadership, like Christ Himself. Paul invokes the angels twice in his first letter, quoting what seems to be a fragment of an early Christian hymn:

Great indeed, we confess, is the mystery of our religion: He was manifested in the flesh, vindicated in the Spirit, seen by angels, preached among the nations, believed on in the world, taken up in glory. (1 Tim. 3:16)

In the fifth chapter, Paul refers to the angels' seeing Timothy, when he writes:

> In the presence of God and of Christ Jesus and of the elect angels I charge you to keep these rules without favor, doing nothing from partiality. (5:21)

Though we have already spoken of some of the passages in the Letter to the Hebrews, there are two other points I want to make before passing on to the other epistles. As chapter 12 draws to a close, a contrast is drawn between the fear and trembling that accompanied Moses' revelations on Mount Zion and the gentleness and magnetic beauty of Christ's accomplished work of redemption:

> But you have come to Mount Zion and to the city of the living God, the heavenly Jerusalem, and *to innumerable angels in festal gathering*, and to the assembly of the first-born who are enrolled in heaven, and to a judge who is God of all, and to the spirits of just men made perfect, and to Jesus, the mediator of a new covenant, and to the sprinkled blood that speaks more graciously than the blood of Abel. (Heb. 12:22–24, emphasis added)

Whereas once the sight of angels filled the hearts of holy men and women with fear and trembling, now, since the coming of Christ as man, they are joyful signs of peace, blessing, and reassurance.

The final reference to angels in the Letter to the Hebrews is the mysterious and charming exhortation at the beginning of chapter 13:

> Let brotherly love continue. Do not neglect to show hospitality to strangers, for thereby some have entertained angels unawares. (13:1–2)

This passage is perhaps an allusion to the three mysterious visitors whom Abraham entertained under the oak tree at Mamre

(Gen. 18:1–33). These three men were addressed by Abraham by one name, "Lord," and were honored with the greatest signs of hospitality he could offer. They, in turn, predicted the birth of Isaac and the destruction of Sodom and Gomorrah. Abraham pleaded for the righteous who dwelled in those cities, and the Lord heard his plea. The words of the visitors were later fulfilled: Lot and his family were spared, and Isaac was born to Abraham and Sarah.

Both Orthodox and Roman Catholic traditions recognize the three mysterious visitors as angels who revealed a glimpse, or a *foreshadowing* or *image*, of the Holy Trinity, which would be fully manifest only with the coming of Christ. Mother Alexandra explains this image of the *One-in-Three*:

> That the three angelic figures were understood to be one is indicated thus: "So God finished speaking to Abraham and left him, and Abraham turned and went home" (Genesis 18:33)
>
> And, as such, the three angels must be seen rather as a self-revelation of God, than merely as an angelic apparition. The angels visually portrayed in their perfect unity and equal perfection the first fleeting glimpse of the great mystical doctrine of the Trinity, "admitting through the spiritual and unwavering eyes of the mind the original and super-original gift of Light of the Father who is the Source of Divinity, which shows to us images ... in figurative symbols towards its Primal Ray." [Dionysius the Areopagite][54]

It is this scene that inspired the famous icon, known simply as *The Holy Trinity*, by Andrei Rublev, which depicts the Three Angels seated around the table prepared by Abraham and Sarah.

---

[54] Mother Alexandra, *The Holy Angels*, pp. 12–13.

This icon has been the instrument of many graces for those who have contemplated it.

Moreover, the passage from the Letter to the Hebrews that evokes this visitation has inspired disciples of Christ to countless deeds of charity down through the centuries. There are many stories in the lives of the saints in which holy men and women have discovered that the poor whom they welcomed and aided were actually angels in disguise. Once St. Philip Neri was just about to place alms in a poor man's hand when suddenly the beggar was transformed before his eyes into a handsome and luminous angel. The angel refused the alms with a smile and disappeared with the words, "I was only testing you!" On another occasion, St. Charles Borromeo was kneeling to wash the wounded and dirty feet of a poor man when he looked up and saw Jesus Himself smiling back at him.

We do not expect such extraordinary signs, but I am sure that most people who have tried to live out this scriptural injunction have at one point or another received some divine inspiration that has confirmed the truth of these words and given them new courage in serving generously those who most certainly are not angels, but who have been committed to their care and ours!

Angels in the Catholic Epistles[55]

In his first letter, St. Peter alludes to the angels twice. The first reference is to the mysteries of the Faith that the believers have received, "things which have now been announced to you by those who preached good news to you through the Holy Spirit sent from

[55] "Catholic Epistles" is a collective term used for all the other New Testament letters that were addressed to various communities that the apostles visited on their journeys.

heaven, things into which angels long to look" (1 Pet. 1:12). The second, in reference to Baptism, speaks of Jesus Christ, "who has gone into heaven and is at the right hand of God, with angels, authorities and powers subject to Him." (1 Pet. 3:22).

St. Peter's second epistle also has two references to angels, with the first referencing the Lord's punishment for those angels who sinned:

> For ... God did not spare the angels when they sinned, but cast them into hell and committed them to pits of nether gloom to be kept until the judgment. (2 Pet. 2:4)

The second passage compares the curses uttered by the wicked and ungodly awaiting punishment with the angels who restrain their anger and keep silence, waiting on the Lord:

> Bold and willful, they are not afraid to revile the glorious ones, whereas angels, though greater in might and power, do not pronounce a reviling judgment upon them before the Lord. (2 Pet. 2:10–11)

The epistle of St. Jude was written at a time when heretical teachers were infiltrating the Christian churches with "gnostic" teachings, which claimed to reveal secret, mystical truths. Jude writes with authority and purpose, denouncing such teachings and demonstrating his own knowledge of extrabiblical Jewish texts that were often exploited by the false teachers. Some of his expressions are very similar to those used by St. Peter in his second epistle.

> And the angels that did not keep their own position but left their proper dwelling have been kept by him in eternal chains in the nether gloom until the judgment of the great day. (Jude 6)

In the next paragraph, St. Jude names St. Michael as an archangel—the second time that this category of angel is named in the New Testament and the first time that an archangel is identified by name— noting, like St. Peter, the angels' refusal to judge or to accuse:

> But when the archangel Michael, contending with the Devil, disputed about the body of Moses, he did not presume to pronounce a reviling judgment upon him but said, "The Lord rebuke you!" (Jude 9)

This verse references a Jewish tradition that Moses was buried in an unknown site in the land of Moab, evidently in order to prevent a cult of worship developing around him. This would have been the Devil's will to cause confusion among the Jews, and the archangel Michael was charged by God to prevent this happening.

When we read this passage as Catholics, St. Michael's refusal to rebuke Satan on his own authority, but rather to leave it to the Lord's will, is another demonstration of the power of humility to defeat the pride of the Devil. Michael's power is in service to the Lord; he rebukes as the Lord wills; he does battle when and how the Lord determines. His will is to do the will of God. And we must learn to do the same.

Chapter 10

ANGELS IN THE
BOOK OF REVELATION

✛

The book of Revelation, written by St. John in exile on the Isle
of Patmos, is a mysterious book filled with many strange and wondrous images — and also with angels. It is, in fact, a revelation *that
is mediated by the holy angels*, as was the case in the Old Covenant;
for the Risen Christ sends His angels to make it known to the
Church:

> The revelation of Jesus Christ, which God gave him to show
> to his servants what must soon take place; and he made it
> known by sending his angel to his servant John who bore
> witness to the word of God and to the testimony of Jesus
> Christ, even to all that he saw. (Rev. 1:1–2)

In recent years, there have been many wonderful works published on this remarkable book that have helped us to understand
its mysteries and its place in the canon of Scripture. Our purpose
here is much more limited: We seek to understand the role of the

angels for our spiritual good in this sacred text.[56] Here we find the angels as the messengers and executors of the divine plan for the triumph of goodness and the punishment of sin.[57] Their presence and example aid us to trust in God, to be faithful to the end, and to know that the promises of Christ will be fulfilled, for He has already won the victory. And if we stand by Him till the end, the reward will be ours.

The Carmelite nuns of Locarno suggest:

It seems that the simplest key to reading of the Apocalypse, the one most faithful to God's design is that He is offering each generation and each individual believer, a great sign (12:1) of hope and with it a pressing invitation to put into practice the words of this prophecy (1:3) in faith (13:10),

---

[56] In this chapter, I will draw heavily from the contemplative writings and insights of Mother Alexandra, the former Princess Ileana of Romania (1909–1991). Daughter of the king and queen of Romania, and granddaughter of Queen Victoria, Princess Ileana married a Habsburg prince, raised a family, fled from the Nazis and the Communists, and eventually found refuge in the United States. After many trials and adventures, she fulfilled her long-held dream of becoming an Orthodox nun. After some years in France, she returned to the United States and founded the first English-speaking Orthodox Monastery for women, located in Pennsylvania. A profound spiritual teacher, she had a lifelong devotion to the angels. Her classic book, *The Holy Angels*, first published in 1981, is at present, unfortunately, out of print. It is a masterful study of Orthodox and Roman Catholic angelology, composed by a scholarly mind and pure soul who lived in intimacy with God's mighty spirits. May her memory be eternal! My conferences that formed the basis of the *Angels of God* television series owed much to the chapter summaries to be found on pages 111–120 of her work. The present chapter incorporates a great deal of my later research.

[57] Monastero Carmelo S. Giuseppe, *In Comunione con gli angeli* (Conegliano: Editrice Ancilla, 2010), p. 272.

in fidelity (2:10), in endurance (13:10), in labors (14:13), and in constant watchfulness (16:15). Only in this way, on this foundation of virtuous commitment, will the final victory, achieved by Christ the Lord through his blood (12:11), have its accomplishment in the people of God and in each Christian believer.[58]

Introduction to Revelation

As the great Orthodox monastic foundress Mother Alexandra reflects,

> The Book of Revelation is composed in the traditional style of the Apocalypses of the Old Testament, and is full of allusions to other books of the Bible, thus in a remarkable way linking them together and writing "Amen" to what has now become "One Book."[59]

As we read through the book of Revelation, we see how God's plan unfolds over time. John has a clear message that he communicates throughout the book—that those who remain constant in their witness to Christ shall stand before the throne and behold the Face of God. On the other hand, those who have turned away and entered of their own will into the misery of sin will experience inexpressible suffering and loss.

The great Benedictine liturgist Dom Cyprian Vagaggini sees throughout Revelation "the profound union between the human world and the angelic world." In his classic work, *Theological Dimensions of the Liturgy*, he writes:

[58] Ibid., p. 273.
[59] Mother Alexandra, *The Holy Angels*, p. 109.

The general plan of this final book of the Scriptures is clear enough: the just both here below and in the heavenly Jerusalem comprise but a single city and a single kingdom, at the head of which is God and the Lamb. This single city, however is in two distinct phases of development which are converging to a unification in a single reality. There is the heavenly phase where, together with God and the Lamb, the faithful angels and just men who have already arrived at their goal are in peace and glory. And there is the earthly phase, made of the faithful who are still engaged in the struggle against the hostile city of Satan and the beast.[60]

The book of Revelation, then, is a series of images alternating between the calamities that befall the world of men and women and the blessedness of Heaven that awaits the faithful. These scenes are often shown juxtaposed, for all through the book we are made aware of the truth that God is triumphant even now. Good has already vanquished evil through the Cross of Christ.

We must not think that the book of Revelation is only or even primarily a book regarding the end times. It is this but more: a global vision of whole history of salvation from the beginning (Genesis) to the final triumph of the Lamb and the Church. And it is set against a framework of liturgical worship of God in Heaven.

The Angels' Roles and Functions

As we look at the angels in Revelation, we can be easily overwhelmed by images and language that are foreign to us. What is constantly underscored is the truth that the angels are concerned

---

[60] Dom Cyprian Vagaggini, OSB, *Theological Dimensions of the Liturgy* (Collegeville, MN: Liturgical Press, 1976), pp. 347–348.

with our struggles here on earth and assist us in every way possible, as Dom Cyprian affirms.

> The angels in particular serve as intermediaries between God and the faithful here below; they reveal to them the designs of God; they intervene in the battle as His ministers in order to punish the enemy, those who are attached to the beast, especially by means of the material elements, over which they have power. Under the leadership of their chief, Michael, they even engage directly in the struggle against Satan and his satellites.[61]

Mother Alexandra too provides us with a helpful understanding of the angels' appearances and responsibilities.

> In these pictures, the divine seer depicts the angels superbly as the executors of the will of God. They are God's messengers, sent to illumine our faulty and limited understanding. They hold back or let loose, as the case may be, the elements in their charge, and they herald great tidings, while they interpret, punish, and reward.[62]

Mother Alexandra then provides a helpful list of twenty functions[63] that angels undertake in the book of Revelation, which may be helpful for our prayerful contemplation:

[61] Ibid., p. 348.
[62] Mother Alexandra, *The Holy Angels*, p. 111.
[63] I say *functions*, because it is clear that certain of these tasks are accomplished by the *same angel*; for example, in numbers 9 and 10, the Angel of the Great Oath is also the one who carries the Little Book (or scroll), and perhaps also the Seven Angels of numbers 15 and 16 are the same group of seven. One of them also will serve as the Interpreter in chapter 17. Mother Alexandra omitted the Angel with the Millstone, bringing the number of roles we are considering to twenty.

1. The Interpreting Angel, who speaks the words of Jesus to John and is his mentor and guide for all that follows
2. The Seven Angels of the Seven Churches of Asia (1:20–3:4)
3. The Heralding Angel (5:2)
4. The Four Angels of the Four Winds (7:1)
5. The Angel of the Seal of the Living God (7:2)
6. The Seven Angels of the Seven Trumpets (8:2–10)
7. The Angel of the Incense (8:3)
8. The Seven Angels of the Seven thunders (10:1–4)
9. The Angel of the Great Oath (10:5–7)
10. The Angel of the Little Book of Life (10:8–11)
11. The Angel of the Good Tidings (14:6)
12. The Angel of Judgment (14:7)
13. The Angel of Fire (14:8)
14. The Angel of the Sharp Sickle (14:17–20)
15. The Seven Angels of the Last Seven Plagues (15:1)
16. The Seven Angels of the Seven Bowls of Judgment (15:5–8)
17. The Angel of the Waters (16:5)
18. The Angel of Prophetic Doom (18:1–3)
19. The Angel with the Millstone (18:21–24)
20. The Angel Having the Key of the Bottomless Pit (20:1)[64]

Chapter 1 serves as an introduction to all that will follow, placing us in the presence of the Living God and revealing the mission given to St. John. The next two chapters, then, include the messages sent to the particular angels of the Seven Churches of Asia. These messages communicate heavenly judgment: The churches are both commended for the good that they do and rebuked for what is lacking in their work. Note that each Christian community

---

[64] Mother Alexandra, *The Holy Angels*, p. 112.

has its own angel assigned to it; the local bishop is in some sense the earthly counterpart of the angel, though the bishop's mission is a share in the high-priestly mission of Christ, which the angels do not possess.

In chapter 4, St. John suddenly brings us back into the presence of God, who is Maker and Ruler of the whole universe. The focal point in this vision is the throne of God, an unchanging symbol of God's eternal stability and steadfastness that recurs throughout the book. Here we see the four angels upon whom the throne of God rests. And from this throne flows forth authority and justice and unchanging beauty.

In the next chapter, John introduces the book of the reign of God. In the hands of the Maker, it is sealed with seven seals that none can open, save the One Who has already redeemed what lies bound within it. The One is, of course, Christ Himself. And then, in chapter 6, we see the opening of the first six seals and the appearance of the four riders of the Apocalypse. These riders are charged with carrying out judgment, using mankind's sins to forge the means for executing God's Justice and Judgment. The first rider is bent upon conquest, while the second signifies war, the third famine, and the fourth death. One leads to another.

When the sixth seal is broken, it lets loose a terrible cataclysm over the face of the earth, but the angels of the four winds bring quiet. The servants of the Lord are reassured, and the seal of the living God is set upon their foreheads, once again to assure us that victory is ours with the Lamb. This scene should encourage us as we face the day-to-day tribulations that are part of our cross here on earth. The Lord has set His seal on us—first in Baptism, when we were signed with the Cross of Christ, and later in Confirmation, when we were sealed with the anointing of the Holy Spirit. He has given us grace for our state in life. These graces sustain us in every age of the Church's life.

The Seventh Seal

Just before the seventh seal is opened, there is a pause—a silence in Heaven that lasts about a half hour. This is a mysterious interlude, and it is important for us to reflect upon it: Quietness and reflection have their place in Heaven as well as on earth, as Cardinal Sarah has reminded us. Both rest and action are part of God's Kingdom. This short time of silence seems to indicate a time of trial and suffering, when the prayers of the faithful apparently go unheard.

But then we read:

> And another angel came and stood at the altar with a golden censer; and he was given much incense to mingle with the prayers of all the saints upon the golden altar before the throne; and the smoke of the incense rose with the prayers of the saints from the hand of the angel before God. (8:3–4)

As Eric Peterson has shown, the Heavenly Liturgy in which the angels participate unites and unifies our prayers and joins them to their own. The incense is joined to the prayers of God's faithful and holy ones so that they may receive His grace and withstand the time of judgment and punishment. We use incense at Mass to designate something as holy and to inspire prayer. As the incense rises to God, it leaves behind a pleasing fragrance that purifies all those present, both interiorly and exteriorly, awakening even deeper prayer, adoration, and trust in the goodness and justice of God.

> The angels who do not share man's fallen, but redeemable nature, still join them in the grand worship of the Lamb. Thus it is in Vespers that we sing: "Let my prayer be set forth before as incense (Ps. 140:2)."[65]

---

[65] Ibid., p. 114.

John passes from the image of the incense and its mercy to the unfolding of judgment. The angel hurls the burning coals from the altar upon the earth, triggering thunder and lightning and earthquakes. And in this cataclysm, following abruptly upon that moment of silence, the first of the angels sounds his trumpet.

If the seven seals represented divine decision and decree, the seven trumpets signify divine action and accomplishment. The Lord's actions echo throughout creation: The earth, the sea, the sun, the moon, and the stars are under the guidance and dominion of the angels, so they must be part of this final drama of judgment. In every age, the light of the book of Revelation will guide us and direct us to trust in the Lord's triumph.

Mother Alexandra sums up this aspect of the angelic mission and of God's everlasting love in this way:

> Above all, the Book of Revelation has the angels appearing as the executors of God's holy will, the personification of his detailed power, by which ultimately, even the forces of evil are placed under the divine control. Therefore, the tormenting afflictions which befall those who choose a way that is not God's, can do no permanent harm to the faithful who are under God's own guardianship, and who need fear no evil, for their guardian angel is powerful to protect them.
>
> Evil is self-destructive; the sounding of the seven great trumpets heralds deathly, fearful retribution both through the agency of so-called natural forces, as that of the malignant spiritual powers. But none of these disastrous events is senseless, for their determinative goal is to induce repentance.[66]

That evil is self-destructive is a truth that is not always evident to us, since our minds are limited and often clouded by sin and

---

[66] Ibid., p. 115.

falsehoods—which may be themselves the residue of sin. That is why prayerful reading of the Sacred Scriptures (*lectio divina*) is so important for us; it purifies our minds of such confusion and strengthens us to take up the path of conversion, which leads to peace.

The Angels and the Woman

In chapter 10, John sees another mighty angel clothed in beauty and majesty: "wrapped in a cloud, with a rainbow over his head, and his face was like the sun, and his legs like pillars of fire" (v. 1). The angel calls out like a roaring lion, and the Seven Thunders respond (v. 3); he speaks an oath that calls forth the fulfillment of all prophecies of old into an eternal moment. Mother Alexandra reflects on this scene with profound insight: "Time has no more reality than transient things; now is really only a part of eternity, for without eternity the present would be in an instant nothing but the past."[67]

John enters into this scene personally when he is told to take the scroll from the angel and to eat it; the angel warns him that it will be sweet to the taste but bitter to the digestion. He experiences the truth of this, but is nonetheless enjoined to preach and prophesy without fear (vv. 8–11). This scene is often used as an image of the spiritual life and of the trials that await us as we draw closer to the realities of the mystery of the Cross.

> In the little book that the angel holds the past and future meet. It is sweet to taste, but bitter to digest, because although the glad tidings of companionship with God are like honey to the tongue, to do the business of God demands austere discipline and many a bitter abnegation. To digest

[67] Ibid.

the little book of knowledge calls for a deeper understanding in our judgment of events. We must study history with Christian discernment, having the mental penetration of the anointed and the sealed. We must acquire the insight which will permit us to single out the clues that will bring all knowledge and the history of recorded incidents into correlation and under the authority of the Word. The great angel of Christian understanding stands astride land and sea, mastering every element, physical and abstract. This same great angel stands astride our lives, claiming our attention, bidding us call all men to God before it is too late, for the seventh trumpet is about to sound![68]

Chapter 11 speaks of the olive trees and the lampstands, the unfolding of the persecutions wrought by the Beast, and the punishments meted out to evildoers (vv. 1–14). Then the seventh angel blows his trumpet, and John hears the voices of the elders and the blessed in Heaven crying out in praise and thanksgiving, "The kingdom of the world has become the kingdom of our Lord and of His Christ, and He shall reign for ever and ever" (v. 15).

As the chapter comes to an end, St. John sees the temple of God in Heaven revealed, and "the ark of His covenant was seen within His temple" and there were lightning, earthquakes, thunder, and hail (v. 19). This may seem to some readers to be the dramatic conclusion of the prostration and prayer of the twenty-four elders, summarized simply and briefly in one verse before St. John relates his distinct vision of the Woman clothed with the sun and the moon in chapter 12.

I would invite you not to rush into chapter 12, however, without pausing to consider this final image. Remember that the assignment

---

[68] Ibid.

of chapter headings is not a matter of divine revelation, but simply a useful contribution of later scribes. What is the Ark of the Covenant that John sees? He may have seen the image of the gold-covered chest in the Holy of Holies, but that Ark was itself only an image, a type, of something else, or rather of *someone* else: The Ark of the New Covenant is Mary, the Mother of Jesus, who *tabernacled* Him within her body for the nine months of her pregnancy. He is the New and Everlasting Covenant, which is effected in the Sacrifice of His Body and Blood.

John's vision of the Ark within the Temple is the preface to his seeing *Mary* as the Woman persecuted by the Dragon. He who had stood beneath the Cross by her side and taken her into his own home and care now sees her clothed with a greatness and a power that must have been overwhelming for him. She who had loved him and confided in him her private memories and singular understanding of Jesus is now revealed as the magnificent and powerful Woman who will crush the head of the serpent under her feet (Gen. 3:14–15).

> And a great portent appeared in heaven, a woman clothed with the sun, with the moon under her feet, and on her head a crown of twelve stars; she was with child.... And the dragon stood before the woman who was about to bear a child, that he might devour her child when she brought it forth; she brought forth a male child, one who is to rule all the nations with a rod of iron, but her child was caught up to God and to his throne, and the woman fled into the wilderness, where she has a place prepared by God, in which to be nourished for one thousand two hundred and sixty days. (Rev. 12:1–6)

This passage, so mysterious and so fascinating, so frightening and yet so reassuring, contains many levels of meaning: John himself could not have comprehended them all in a single instant. Now, perhaps, he understood for the first time why Jesus called His Mother "Woman." Now the words of the Lord God in Genesis had found their fullness: "I will put enmity between you and the woman, and your seed and her seed; she shall crush your head and you shall lie in wait for her heel" (3:15).[69]

Mary is the Mother of Jesus, but also the Image and Mother of the Church, giving birth to Christ-in-us. The Dragon sees her as his enemy and attacks those who are her children.

> Then the dragon was angry with the woman, and went off to make war on the rest of her offspring, on those who keep the commandments of God and bear testimony to Jesus. (Rev. 12:17)

Angelic Warfare

[69] Though I have used the Revised Standard Version (Catholic Edition) of the Scriptures throughout this book, for this passage I must rely on my rendering of the traditional Catholic translations, based on the Vulgate. Modern versions claim that the pronouns refer to the "seed," not the Woman. In that case, it is Jesus who crushes the Serpent's head—something with which all Catholics would agree. However, since Jesus came into this world through Mary and, moreover, since the Vulgate and many of the early Fathers of the Church understand the passage as referring to *the Woman's foot*, let us not exclude Mary from her role in this truth of the Faith. As Father Randall Payne points out in *His Time Is Short: The Devil and His Agenda*, to do otherwise would entail a great loss to the Catholic *sensus fidelium* and require a massive redesign of Catholic statues and medals of the Blessed Mother. See Father Randall Paine, *His Time Is Short* (St. Paul, MN: Leaflet Missal Company, 1989), p. 75.

But between the beginning and the end of this chapter, we find St. John's vision of the warfare in Heaven, which is the source of our understanding, limited though it is, of the enmity that exists between the Devil and his dark angels on one side and St. Michael and his armies on the other. This is the battle that began before time and will be completed only when all things are consummated in Christ.

> Now war arose in heaven, Michael and his angels fighting against the dragon; and the dragon and his angels fought, but they were defeated and there was no longer any place for them in heaven. And the great dragon was thrown down, that ancient serpent, who is called the Devil and Satan, the deceiver of the whole world—he was thrown down to the earth and his angels were thrown down with him (12:7–9).

This scene, which we considered in our chapter on the fall of the rebel angels, reveals itself as a *cosmic battle* that begins in the Heavens but continues here on earth. St. Michael, whose very name expresses the humility of his service to the Lord, "Who is like unto God?," does battle through love. Lucifer is no longer the "light bearer," as his name would have it; he has become dark, for he no longer reflects the Light. He has become the adversary (Satan) of God, the liar (the Greek *diabolos* means "slanderer")—first the deceiver of his fellow angels, later the deceiver of the world of men and women—and our *accuser*.

But John's vision is not over until he is reassured of God's final victory—and the Church's part in it:

> And I heard a loud voice in heaven, saying, "Now the salvation and power and the kingdom of our God and the authority of his Christ have come, for the accuser of our brethren has been thrown down, who accuses them

day and night before our God. And they have conquered him by the blood of the Lamb, and by the word of their testimony, for they loved not their lives even unto death. Rejoice then, O heaven, and you that dwell therein. But woe to you, O earth and sea, for the devil has come down to you in great wrath, because he knows that his time is short!" (12:10–12)

Michael and his angels are victorious because their weapons are humility and faith in God; the saints of earth are joined to them, so that, by the power of Christ's blood, all victory and all glory might be God's. We may possess neither the intellect nor the will of the angels but Satan is nonetheless undone when we "love not our own lives" even to the point of laying them down for Christ. Martyrdom is the fullest expression of witness. It is the seal of love and of humility, just as death on the Cross was the seal and the final and fullest expression of Christ's love, obedience, and humility. All the sufferings of Jesus' Passion express His *kenosis* — His self-emptying of divine glory and even human dignity in order to die for us a death of perfect atonement and infinite significance.

In chapter 13, St. John goes on to describe the reign of the beast, who seeks to place his evil mark upon all. Yet even then, the Lord is faithful and calls his holy ones to bear witness by their faith and endurance (v. 10).

Chapter 14 opens with the radiant vision of the Lamb surrounded by the "hundred and forty-four thousand" who surround the Lamb and follow Him wherever He goes. Those who were sealed by the angels with the sign of the Lamb are filled with strength and grace to persevere to the end. This, of course, is the mark of the baptized and the confirmed. The angels also continue their mission of revelation, counsel, and the execution of judgment, symbolized by the sharp sickles (vv. 16ff.). The angels not only share in the destruction of the city of the beast, an image that unites Babel, Babylon, and pagan Rome as cities of sin and death; they also build up the New and Heavenly Jerusalem, together with the believers and the faithful ones.

The next chapter reveals the seven angels of the last plagues, whose mission is a priestly one: Robed in pure, bright linen and girded with golden bands, they receive the Lord's judgment in golden bowls, which they pour out as He commands. Even as John recounts the enormity of these punishments, God's justice is revealed in the sobriety and order of His providence. After the angel of the third plague has poured out his bowl into the rivers and water sources, the angel who stands as guardian of the waters of the earth calls out:

> Just thou art in these thy judgments, thou who art and wast, O Holy One. For men have shed the blood of saints and prophets, and thou hast given them blood to drink. It is their due!" And I heard the altar cry, "Yea, Lord God the Almighty, true and just are thy judgments!" (16:5–7)

In chapter 17, one of the plague angels serves as interpreter and guide as John again sees the awful unfolding of wickedness revealed in symbolic form. And then in the succeeding chapter, an angel of even greater authority and splendor proclaims the end of evil and the machinations of evildoers. A second great angel casts a millstone into the sea as a sign of judgment and the finality of God's decree.

The End

Chapter 19 introduces us to the culmination of the divine plan in the "marriage supper of the Lamb." Just as God had revealed Himself to Israel using bridal language and bridal imagery to prepare them for the coming of His Son, who wed Himself to human nature by the Incarnation and weds us to Himself in His faithful love for the Church, so now in the final chapters of the book of Revelation, we see how the Father's eternal plan is made perfect in the triumph of Christ the Redeemer, the unity of the angelic world and the human world, and the completion of the Church's mission. Faith is replaced by sight, hope by possession, and charity (divine love) reigns in the hearts of all creation.

John hears the triumphant acclamations of a great multitude, "like the sound of many waters and like the sound of mighty thunderpeals" (19:6), crying out their hallelujahs: "Salvation and glory and power belong to our God, for his judgments are true and great" (19:1–2). He is overwhelmed by the immensity of it all; when an angel commands him to write down the words, "Blessed are those who are invited to the marriage supper of the Lamb," he falls down at his feet, ready to worship him. But the angel quickly draws him up again, though with apparent kindness and understanding, "You must not do that! I am a fellow servant with you and your brethren who hold the testimony of Jesus. Worship God!" (19:9–10). These words tell us much about who the angels truly are and how they have come to see us through the unfolding of God's plan.

But before the Heavenly Jerusalem begins its celebration, John is shown the stark realities of evil's final defeat and the glories of the Captain of Heaven's armies: He sees Jesus as a warrior, Faithful and True, mounted on a white horse, His robe dipped in blood (19:11). He is crowned with many crowns, identified as King of Kings and Lord of Lords, but His name ultimately remains a mystery, though He is known by all as "Word of God" (19:13). He goes forth with His white-robed armies and defeats His enemies in every age, casting them into the lake of brimstone and slaughtering their minions.

John then sees an angel coming down from Heaven, key in hand, whose mission is to bind Satan for a thousand years. In an overwhelming series of images, the seer glimpses the battles yet to unfold, the final victory of Christ and His saints, and the beauty of the Bride—Christ's Church, the New and Eternal Jerusalem:

> And I saw the holy city, new Jerusalem, coming down out of heaven from God, prepared as a bride adorned for her husband; and I heard a great voice from the throne saying, "Behold, the dwelling of God is with men. He will dwell with them, and they shall be his people, and God himself will be with them; and he will wipe away every tear from their eyes, and death shall be no more, neither shall there be mourning nor crying nor pain any more, for the former things have passed away. And He who sat upon the throne said, "Behold, I make all things new." (21:2–5)

One of the angels who had borne the plague bowls now comes to John to show him more closely the beauties and the glory of this new Jerusalem as she descends from the Heavens. He sees the twelve mighty angels who stand sentry above her twelve gates, named for the original twelve tribes of Israel—but her twelvefold foundations, made of precious stones and jewels, bear the names of the twelve apostles (21:12–14). The holy people of God, from the age of the first covenant to the New Covenant made in the Blood of the Lamb, are forever united in this city whose Temple is the Lord God Almighty and the Lamb (21:22).

As we ponder John's description, we begin to realize that we can understand his words and imagery only through the Church, Christ's Mystical Body and inseparable Bride, which we experience even now and in which we dwell here on earth. As we increase in divine life, through an ongoing process of conversion and sanctification, of consecration and sacramental grace, and as we are slowly transformed and renewed by Mary's loving presence and constant cooperation with her Son's plan, we read the book of Revelation ever more gratefully and confidently. It is not a "sealed book," but a gift to increase our hope, trust, and humility.

Jesus has sent His angel to John and to us with this book's message (22:16). It prepares us to do battle each day against the world, the flesh, and the Devil. It reminds us that we must conquer our pride, arrogance, lust, and selfishness and rediscover our first fervor. We must be faithful and true to Him. All wickedness and all evil will be overcome. The Lamb who was slain is risen and victorious. His birth was announced by angels; in His time, His justice will be accomplished by their faithfulness too. And we shall be united with them around His throne in Heaven. The angels assist us and bid us come to Christ, Who says:

> I am the Alpha and the Omega, the first and the last, the beginning and the end.... I Jesus have sent my angel to you with this testimony for the churches. I am the root and the offspring of David, the bright morning star. (Rev. 22:13, 16)

Part 3

THE ANGELS IN THE CHURCH

Chapter 11

ANGELS IN THE EARLY CHURCH

There are many scenes in the Acts of the Apostles that describe the angels' presence in the life of the young Church. The book of Acts was written by St. Luke, the conscientious historian whose Gospel describes with great beauty the appearances of the angels from the first pages to the last. Indeed, Luke seems to have a particular delight in relating angelic encounters.

When the Lord ascended into Heaven, two angels were in the midst of the apostles to remind them of their duty: "Men of Galilee, why do you stand looking into heaven? This Jesus, who was taken up from you into heaven, will come in the same way as you saw Him go into heaven" (Acts 1:11). After hearing these words, the apostles went back to Jerusalem, and there in the Upper Room with Our Lady and the holy women, they awaited the coming of the Holy Spirit at Pentecost. Then the apostles, with bravery and conviction, began to preach Christ in all His glory and truth. In this way, and with the grace of God, they converted many to Christ.

The angels must have looked on with great joy as they witnessed the beginnings of the Church. Their prayer and their presence continued to strengthen and to animate the apostles as they went about their first works and undertook their first missionary journeys.[70] In fact, in St. Luke's account we see the angels coming and going with an ordinariness that shows us how the natural and the supernatural are woven together in the life of the Church.

For instance, in the fifth chapter of Acts we read about how the apostles were arrested by the Sadducees. "But at night an angel of the Lord opened the prison doors and brought them out and said, 'Go and stand in the temple and speak to the people all the words of this Life'" (Acts 5:19–20). This direction of the angel for the apostles to return to their duty—preaching the gospel—is stated clearly and with great boldness.

The angel freed them from prison, but not from danger. On the contrary, he sent them out to face danger by preaching openly. This reminds us that part of the angels' mission is to strengthen our commitment to God as well as our heart and mind so that we might undertake arduous tasks for the glory of God in keeping with our vocation. The apostles accepted the message of the angel and unhesitatingly obeyed, rejoicing that they were counted worthy to suffer shame for Christ's sake. And so they overcame the terrors that were all around them as they began their work of salvation.

There are many deep lessons for us in the Acts of the Apostles, not the least of which is the intimacy and active cooperation between the angels and the early Christians. It should be a model for us as we undertake our own missions for Christ and His Church: Docility to the guidance of the angels helps us to bear spiritual fruit.

---

[70] In *The Holy Angels*, Mother Alexandra writes with true spiritual insight about the role of the angels in the life of what she lovingly calls "The Young Church." See pp. 96–102.

St. Peter

St. Peter, the first pope, had a particularly powerful experience with the ministry of the angels:

> About that time Herod the king laid violent hands upon some who belonged to the church. He killed James the brother of John with the sword; and when he saw that it pleased the Jews, he proceeded to arrest Peter also. This was during the days of Unleavened Bread. And when he had seized him, he put him in prison, and delivered him to four squads of soldiers to guard him, intending after the Passover to bring him out to the people. So Peter was kept in prison; but earnest prayer for him was made to God by the church. (12:1–5)

In this brief passage we see the early Church strengthening the Vicar of Christ with their prayers on his behalf—and the prayers of the Church were heard.

> The very night when Herod was about to bring him out, Peter was sleeping between two soldiers, bound with two chains, and sentries before the door were guarding the prison; and behold, an angel of the Lord appeared, and a light shone in the cell; and he struck Peter on the side and woke him, saying, "Get up quickly." And the chains fell off his hands. (12:6–7)

We need to picture for a moment what this scene describes. St. Peter has been arrested by Herod, who also played a very important role in the condemnation of Jesus. He is now chained, seated on the floor, his back against a wall, his arms outstretched. At his right and his left there are two guards. In Peter's half-sleeping, half-wakeful state of anxiety, he must have been thinking about the Crucifixion of Jesus. We know that before the Ascension, Jesus had spoken to

Peter about his coming death. After giving him the charge "Feed my lambs.... Feed my sheep," Jesus told the Rock of His Church that in his old age there would be those who would fasten a belt around his waist and take him where he would not want to go (John 21:15, 17–18).

Despite Jesus' reference to martyrdom in his "old age," Peter must have been frightened in that cell. As he slept in a posture that physically conformed him to the Crucified Lord, with soldiers who would have reminded him of the two thieves as well as the soldiers at Calvary, he must have been wrestling with his own fears, even as he made interior acts of submission, trust, and hope for his deliverance.

And then suddenly the angel awakened him by striking him in the side, perhaps with his foot. In his fitful state of sleep, it may very well have been to him like the blow of the lance that Christ had received. Why else would the angel have roused the sleepy Vicar of Christ in that fashion? The angel took command of the situation immediately and directed him step by step: "'Dress yourself and put on your sandals.' And Peter did so. And he said to him, 'Wrap your mantle around you and follow me.' And he went out and followed him." And Luke very clearly tells us, "He did not know that what was done by the angel was real, but thought he was seeing a vision" (12:8–9). Peter thought that he was still asleep and that the angel was revealing to him a pathway through death.

But instead, he was about to be restored to the Church. "When they had passed the first and the second guard, they came to the iron gate leading into the city. It opened to them of its own accord, and they went out and passed on through one street; and immediately the angel left him." And Peter only then fully woke up, saying, "Now I am sure that the Lord has sent his angel and rescued me from the hand of Herod and from all that the Jewish people were expecting" (12:10–11). Just as once the Lord had sent

His angel to protect Daniel from the lions in the den and just as once the Lord had sent His angel to protect the three young men in the fiery furnace, so now the Lord sent His angel once more to the first pope, the Vicar of Christ, to protect him and to ensure that the nascent Church might continue to grow and to be strengthened.

St. Stephen

God's holy angels also appear in the story of another one of the great saints of the book of Acts. This time the intervention of the angels was not to save someone from martyrdom but rather to fortify the first martyr of the Church, St. Stephen.

Stephen was a man of outstanding courage and insight. He not only looked after the material needs of the Church with the other deacons, including caring for those who were in need, but he also dedicated himself to preaching and to the study of Scripture. Standing before his accusers, Stephen spoke to them of Moses and the angels of the Lord:

> Now when forty years had passed, an angel appeared to him in the wilderness of Mount Sinai, in a flame of fire in a bush.... This Moses whom [the Israelites] refused, God sent as both ruler and deliverer by the hand of the angel that appeared to him in the bush.... This is he who was in the congregation in the wilderness with the angel who spoke to him at Mount Sinai, and with our fathers; and he received living oracles to give to us.... You stiff-necked people, uncircumcised in heart and ears, you always resist the Holy Spirit. As your fathers did, so do you. Which of the prophets did not your fathers persecute? And they killed those who announced beforehand the coming of the Righteous One, whom you have now betrayed and murdered,

HIS ANGELS AT OUR SIDE

you who received the law as delivered by angels and did not keep it. (7:30, 35, 38, 51–53)

Stephen's testimony is remarkable because it shows how, as a devout and believing Jew, he understood the importance of the angels, especially their involvement in giving the Law.

We know that among those who were present and gave silent consent to Stephen's murder was a young man named Saul. Many years later, under the name of Paul, he would use the same words as he approached his own martyrdom: "[The law] was ordained by angels through an intermediary" (Gal. 3:19).

St. Stephen's deep faith so transfigured him that those at his trial "saw that his face was like the face of an angel" (Acts 6:15). His faith had purified him, and so he bore on his face the reflection of the guardian to whose care he was entrusted. His faith even allowed him, while yet on earth, to see the heavens open before his eyes with Jesus standing on the threshold to receive him (7:55–56).

There is another dimension of St. Stephen's martyrdom that we should not overlook here. In the very moments of his final witness, Stephen teaches us to pray as Christians.

And as they were stoning Stephen, he prayed, "Lord Jesus, receive my spirit." And he knelt down and cried with a loud voice, "Lord, do not hold this sin against them." And when he had said this, he fell asleep. (7:59–60)

Stephen addresses these two prayers directly to Jesus, using the words that Jesus had spoken from the Cross to the Father: "Father, into thy hands, I commit my spirit!" (Luke 23:46), and earlier, "Father, forgive them for they know not what they do" (Luke 23:34). This is an important moment in the history of Christian prayer: It is proof that the very earliest Jewish converts addressed their prayers to Jesus in the same way that He (and they) had prayed to the Father previously. In other words, Jesus was praised and adored in the same manner as the Father from the very beginning of the Church's life. This was not a later development; it was part of the Church's understanding of the Risen Lord since Pentecost.

Cornelius

As the book of Acts continues, we see another wonderful episode in which the angels intervened in the life of the Church. While Peter was staying in Joppa, he heard the Lord Jesus' voice commanding him to eat non-kosher food. This was a preparation for the next chapter in Peter's mission. Shortly thereafter Peter was informed that a group of Gentiles was outside, calling him to go to the house of a certain Cornelius, a Roman centurion in Caesarea.

> He said to them, "You yourselves know how unlawful it is for a Jew to associate with or to visit any one of another nation; but God has shown me that I should not call any man common or unclean. So when I was sent for, I came without objection. I ask then why you sent for me."
> And Cornelius said, "Four days ago, about this hour, I was keeping the ninth hour of prayer in my house; and behold, a man stood before me in bright apparel, saying, 'Cornelius, your prayer has been heard and your alms have been remembered before God.'" (10:28–31)

These words are almost exactly the words that the angel Raphael speaks in the book of Tobit. We do not know whether the angel who appeared to Cornelius was Raphael himself or another of the "seven who stand before the throne of God," but the language is reminiscent of that promise of assistance that was made in the Old Testament. The angel went on to tell Cornelius:

"Send therefore to Joppa and ask for Simon who is called Peter; he is lodging in the house of Simon, a tanner, by the seaside." So I sent to you at once, and you have been kind enough to come. Now therefore we are all here present in the sight of God, to hear all that you have been commanded by the Lord. (10:32–33)

And St. Peter, impressed by this angelic message that confirmed the revelation made to him in Joppa, replied:

Truly I perceive that God shows no partiality, but in every nation anyone who fears him and does what is right is acceptable to him. You know the word which he sent to Israel, preaching good news of peace by Jesus Christ (he is Lord of all), the word which was proclaimed throughout all Judea, beginning from Galilee after the baptism which John preached: how God anointed Jesus of Nazareth with the Holy Spirit and with power; how he went about doing good and healing all that were oppressed by the devil, for God was with him. (10:34–38)

Our Lord uses His angels as messengers in this critical moment when the first Gentile convert to Christianity, together with his family, was received and baptized by Peter. A centurion was a proud and feared soldier, a leader whose men obeyed him unquestioningly, and he was formed by the violence and discipline of an often brutal military culture. The conversion of such a man required nothing less than an overwhelming transformation. Grace had already invaded his soul, since he told Peter that he was keeping a time of prayer when the angel appeared to him.

This beautiful sign shows us how the angels participate in the work of conquering the world for the love of God with the weapons of faith, hope, and love — and through the grace of the living Christ that God has entrusted to His Church. This love is so powerful and transcendent that it unites men and women of every nation in a common work that the world might be lifted up and the redemption of Christ might bear fruit in the hearts of all men and women.

St. Philip the Deacon

In the story of St. Philip the deacon, we see another instance in which an angel arranged all things for God's plan and purpose. Philip was one of the seven original deacons, together with St. Stephen, and he preached in Samaria among the people the Jews considered to be heretics. His preaching was marked by many miracles, especially by the casting out of demons. But as he completed his work there, an angel appeared and said to him, "Rise and go toward the south to the road that goes down from Jerusalem to Gaza" (Acts 8:26).

Philip followed the angel's message immediately. Along the road, he came upon an important servant of the queen of Ethiopia. This man was a eunuch who had come to know the Jewish faith. He was seated in his carriage reading aloud (as was the custom of the time) from the scroll of Isaiah, but he was confused about the meaning of the passage. Philip immediately realized that the reason he had been brought to that place at that moment by the angel was to speak to this man—to answer his need and to preach to him the Gospel of Christ. The man immediately responded to this grace and asked for baptism, which Philip conferred.

This passage is especially important because, in enlightening and baptizing the eunuch, Philip did something extraordinary for the building up of the Church. Eunuchs were outside the community of Israel (Deut. 23:1), and so this baptism initiated the extension of the preaching of the gospel to all peoples of the world.

St. Philip's acceptance of the angel's message should remind us that when we receive in our prayer an inspiration to do an act of charity or to speak a word of comfort, we should always respond with trust. In this way we become the instruments of His love — sometimes with an impact that goes well beyond anything we could imagine. Even a single inspired word might be the first step in bringing about a conversion.

After people have been away from the Church for a long time, their return to the Church often begins with a simple invitation, from a friend or a family member, to Mass or to a special church event. Fallen-away Catholics and non-Catholics who attend the funeral Mass of a Catholic friend frequently find great grace in that moment. They look within themselves and begin to realize what God is offering in the Catholic Church — the life of joyful faith, love, peace, and forgiveness of sins. The Liturgy in which the angels participate and for which they serve as models — and from which flows the grace of God — is one of our greatest resources for evangelization. This is another reason for us to pray for our priests and deacons at every Mass we attend, particularly funerals, so that they may have the grace of touching souls and healing them.

Over and over again, we realize in the course of our lives that when we're more concerned about our Father's business than the trifling things that too often fill the hours of our day, God makes of us instruments of His love to touch the hearts of others and draw them closer and closer to Him. I will always remember a man I met at my first parish. He had been married to a Catholic for thirty years and regularly attended Mass with his wife. One Sunday I said to him, "When are you going to come into the Church?" And he stopped, looking confused, and said, "No one's ever asked me before. I'd love to come into the Church." Within a week he began his instructions, and since he had attended Sunday Mass for so long and had participated in raising Catholic children, his time of catechesis was very short indeed. And a very little while later, I experienced the joy of receiving him into the Faith and giving him his first Holy Communion.

His wife was amazed; she thought that she had done everything in her power to bring her husband into the Church—and she had! His conversion was the result of her long years of faithful and patient witness, her loving prayers, and the wonderful family relationship they had formed. But it took only one question—one invitation at the right time—to complete the process.

When the angels suggest to you to say a word of love, of comfort, of truth, or of invitation, speak that word, and you will find that the Lord will work through you, just as He worked through Philip and all the great saints, known and unknown, who have gone before us. You, too, with the angels by your side, will help to build up His Kingdom and to bring His joy to many others.

Holy guardian angel, my friend and companion, my elder brother and teacher, keep my mind and heart always open to your words and guidance. You see better than I how much good there is to be done. Open my eyes to the needs of those around me. Open my ears to their unspoken prayers and soundless cries. Open my heart so that I may be brave and unashamed in loving my neighbor with the very love of Jesus. Do not let me hold back in doing even a little good for others. Like the widow in the Temple who gave all she possessed, though it was only a penny, inspire me to do even the very smallest things with great love, for anyone whom I can help. Amen.

Chapter 12

ANGELS IN THE LITURGY

✛

As we have seen in many passages from Sacred Scripture, the holy angels bear our prayers to God and unite them to the Heavenly Liturgy — the worship that the saints and the blessed offer to God in Heaven. The *Catechism of the Catholic Church* declares:

> In her liturgy, the Church joins with the angels to adore the thrice-holy God. She invokes their assistance. (CCC 335)

But how do we *engage* their assistance more deeply? How do we inform our prayer and participation in daily and Sunday Masses according to the spirit of the angels? What dispositions of mind and heart should we cultivate?

In the book of Revelation, St. John describes his vision in these words:

> After this I looked, and behold, a great multitude which no man could number, from every nation, from all tribes and peoples and tongues, standing before the throne and before the Lamb, clothed in white robes, with palm branches in their hands, and crying out with a loud voice, "Salvation

belongs to our God who sits upon the throne, and to the Lamb!" And all the angels stood round the throne and round the elders and the four living creatures, and they fell on their faces before the throne and worshiped God, saying, "Amen! Blessing and glory and wisdom and thanksgiving and honor and power and might be to our God for ever and ever! Amen." (7:9–12)

This is the worship of Heaven. It is sublime and perfect in its joyous praise. But our worship of the Lord here on earth, when the Church gathers to celebrate the saving mystery of Christ's Body and Blood, is not something separate from that heavenly worship. The angels and saints contemplate the Father ever-loving; His Son the Word, Who continues to be our Mediator; and the Holy Spirit, Who is their love breathed forth upon all creation.

Every Mass offered on earth, whether in a soaring cathedral or in a simple mission outpost, whether in the presence of thousands or by a single priest all alone, is in essence a perfect and true fore-taste of that heavenly worship. They participate in one another. Just as our participation in the Eucharist is a pledge of eternal life, so, in the East and in the West and in the writings of the Fathers of the Church and in the great founders of religious orders, we find this emphasis on the richness of the interaction between the heavenly and earthly liturgies. If the angels rejoice at the conversion of a sinner, so do they also rejoice when we participate in the Mass, the Divine Office, or any other liturgical service.

Some Practical Counsels for Holy Mass

When we come to Mass, we must truly be aware of raising our eyes, our minds, and our hearts — and, in turn, of being lifted up on high to the Lord's presence. Remembering that the Lord had spoken to Moses on Sinai and that the prophets often encountered Him in "high places," devout Jews always spoke of "going *up* to Jerusalem," even if they were traveling south. When we attend Mass, we too are ascending the mountain of the Lord; we are going up *mystically* to Calvary, the meeting place of earth and Heaven. As we prepare for the Mass, we should be mindful of this cosmic, universal dimension of worship. In this way we can be open, in the most catholic (which simply means "universal") sense of the term, to the glory of God and to the wonder and awe the blessed experience in Heaven before the throne of the Lamb, Who was slain for us. Whether we are able to look forward in faith to that eternal day, or whether we are just seeking the strength to go on for one more day, we are entering into the presence of Divine Mercy.

In the past, it was commonly believed among Catholics that each parish church had its own angel who watched over it, adored the Eucharistic Jesus, and welcomed the faithful who entered to pray, affirming and influencing the individuals' guardian angels. Teaching Sisters would tell children to greet these angels whenever they passed a church. This pious belief is corroborated by St. Faustina Kowalska, who wrote in her *Diary*:

> When I was riding on the train, I saw an Angel standing on every church we passed, but surrounded by a light which was paler than that of the spirit who was accompanying me on the journey, and each of these spirits who were guarding the churches bowed his head to the spirit who was near me (630).[71]

[71] See the wonderful study by Father Titus Kieninger, ORC: *The Angels in the Diary of Saint Faustina Kowalska* (Carrolton, OH: Order of the Holy Cross, 2014), p. 58. I recommend this little book to all who are devoted to the Divine Mercy.

St. Faustina wrote of seeing angels whose very appearance increased her yearning for God (see *Diary* 471); their luminosity, their demeanor, and even their vesture revealed to her the glories and infinite beauty of the Triune God. Perhaps if we were to greet the angel of our parish when we arrive for Mass, we could ask him to assist us with the same grace, so that our yearning for Christ might be strengthened. Instead of "killing time" or reading the parish bulletin, we could engage in real prayer with this parish guardian. If we do this, we will also grow in charity toward those around us, each of whom is carrying his own cross, each of whom is seeking the same living water and divine life that we seek. We will begin to understand better that the One Bread truly makes us One Body with those around us.

In the Tradition of the Church, many liturgical norms have been tied to our understanding of the angels. In the early Church, for instance, it was thought by some that the Gloria ("Glory to God in the Highest ..."), which was prayed while catechumens—those who were preparing to be brought into full communion with the Church—were present, was made in union with the *lower choirs* of angels. After the catechumens left and only the baptized remained, the Preface to the Eucharistic Prayer, which is said to invoke the *higher choirs*, especially in the Sanctus ("Holy, holy, holy ..."), brought the baptized together with these angels to the worship of the Trinity, as God comes down to earth in the Consecration.

In preceding chapters, we have mentioned the angels lifting up the prayers of the just to God like bowls of incense (Rev. 5:8; 8:3–5). Dom Cyprian Vagaggini, OSB, writes of this "angel of sacrifice":

> When the Apocalypse speaks of the angel who, in paradise, on the symbolic golden altar which stands in the presence of God's throne, offers to the Most High the prayers of the

saints (Apoc 8:3–5), it must be inferred that this is, in a broad way, what happens with the greatest prayer of the faithful, the Mass. The implication, therefore is that the sacrifice which the faithful offer here below is presented in heaven before the throne of God through angelic mediation. This concept is common to the various liturgies [of the Apostolic Churches].[72]

This had been recalled in the Extraordinary Form of the liturgy with an invocation of the archangel St. Michael in the blessing of incense. And as the priest would incense the altar, he would pray, "Let my prayer be directed to You as incense." In the present Roman Canon (the First Eucharistic Prayer), the celebrant invokes the ministry of the angels after the Consecration, asking that the gifts may be carried by the Angel to God's altar in heaven, and that those who will receive the Holy Eucharist may be filled with all graces and blessings.

This leads us to another very important consideration about Holy Mass. We are never just a small community. Even if we are only two or three gathered in His Name (Matt. 18:20), our celebration of the Liturgy is a cosmic event; we are worshipping the one Lord, Who holds all creation in His Heart. We are united not only to Heaven's worship, but to every other offering of the Mass that is occurring around the world in this hour or on this day. We are not and must never become a community *turned inward toward itself*.

In part, this is why there has been a renewed discussion in recent years of *ad orientem* celebrations of the Mass, in which priest and people face a common direction, usually focused on a large crucifix, as a sign of being inwardly and communally turned toward the Lord and awaiting His return in glory. Many people

---

[72] Vagaggini, *Theological Dimensions of the Liturgy*, p. 349.

find this a difficult concept to grasp, let alone adopt. Some priests and bishops have returned to the practice of using a prominent crucifix on the altar to assist their focus and ours on this fundamental reality.

Our purpose here is not to enter into polemics about liturgical matters, but to remember what the angels can teach us about Almighty God and the divine life He shares within us. All the choirs of angels in Heaven participate and share in the worship of the Triune God, Who saves us through the Cross. Their attention, their gaze, is directed to Him. Our worship is in a certain sense completed and perfected by theirs, as the One Sacrifice is re-presented before our eyes and they inspire and enlighten us to see the invisible Reality behind the visible signs and gestures. Reverence, awe, and fascinated wonder must characterize our communion in love with Christ. That is what the angels want for us.

At Mass, as St. John Chrysostom wrote in his treatise *On the Priesthood*, the whole of the sanctuary is filled with angels. And he describes in that same work how he had heard from an old and reliable man — and perhaps St. John is talking about himself — that once at the Consecration of the Mass he had seen a whole host of angels encircling the altar and bowing their heads to the ground like "soldiers in the presence of their King."[73]

Dom Cyprian Vagaggini provides us with another image, this time from the sixth-century Egyptian Liturgy. At the kiss of peace, the deacon announces:

Have your hearts in heaven. If anyone has had any dispute with his neighbor, let him be reconciled.... For the Father of men, His only Son and the Holy Spirit are present, watching

[73] St. John Chrysostom, *On the Priesthood*, bk. VI, no. 4.

our actions and examining our thoughts; *and the angels are moving among us and mingling with us.*[74]

These words are very different from the casual heartiness with which the Sign of Peace is so often exchanged in our parishes today. Perhaps this is because we have lost our awareness in faith of the angels' presence, their exultation, their endless praise. We must rediscover the fullness of worship in order to participate in it, whether here on earth or in Heaven. The Sign of Peace is meant to be a real expression of fraternity, Christlike peace, and mutual forgiveness.

"May the *peace of Christ* be with you!" These words may seem uncomfortably formal on our lips, whether spoken to family members or to strangers around us, but they need to be said. They are an important part of our preparation for Holy Communion, whether sacramental or spiritual. They do not disturb our prayers before Communion. Rather, they are meant to symbolize the laying down of all enmities before approaching the altar with the gift of our hearts. Flashing peace signs, waves, and other greetings may indeed be distractions; but looking someone in the eye with Christian love and murmuring this *"Pax Christi"* — whether or not accompanied by a handshake — is a gesture of which the angels surely approve.

Active Participation Is More Than You Think It Is

An Leabhar Breac is a medieval Irish manuscript containing a treasury of prayers, histories, and catecheses from the early years of the Church in Ireland. In one of these documents, the *Instructions on the Sacraments*, we read this beautiful description of the Mass:

[74] See Anton Baumstark, in *Oriens Christianus* (1901), pp. 1ff., as cited in Vagaggini, *Theological Dimensions of the Liturgy*, p. 351, emphasis added.

For Christ is both Priest and Oblation there, for there are three things at the oblation of Christ's Body and Blood to wit the priests, visibly ministering in the presence of all in general, and the angels and archangels witnessing it and as witnesses for Him as minister of Christ and Christ Himself changing and blessing and consecrating the bread and wine so that He makes His Body and Blood of them.

When we think of the angels present at Mass, we must also realize — as the Fathers of the Second Vatican Council pointed out so beautifully — that all baptized men and women have a particular role in the Mass. That is, all are called to an "active participation" in the celebration of the Liturgy. But, we must ask, what does that active participation mean?

Active participation is something much greater than simply reciting the responses or joining in the hymns or even adopting a common posture; these are the external manifestations of interior attitudes of worship, thanksgiving, expiation, and petition. Our role as baptized men and women is to unite ourselves to God the Son in His obedience to and trust in His Heavenly Father — expressed especially by listening attentively to the readings and the homily, and professing our Faith in the Creed and our dependence on His loving care in the Prayers of the Faithful. Then we are to offer up, to the same Father, the Lamb who was slain, the now glorious and ascended God the Son, whose Body and Blood, Soul and Divinity are sacramentally present in the consecrated elements on the altar. After the words of institution, you and I *join ourselves* to the offering of Christ. We lift up Christ to the Father, and we say to Him:

Eternal Father, I accept the sacrifice of Your Son on my behalf. I lift Him up to You, for He is the only acceptable gift. He is the only Treasure that I possess that I can offer to You in atonement for my sins and for the sins of the whole world.

He has made Himself mine by His coming as man. I have made myself His by the grace of divine life and redemption shared with me and the free-will gift of my heart, my mind, my body, my all. Through Him I can offer You worthy praise, for He alone adores You perfectly. With Him, I offer You everything that I am; I give You my body and soul so that I may be changed into Him and You may see Him in me. In the sight of the angels, O Lord, in the company of the blessed, Your Church in Heaven and on earth, with Mary my Mother, I praise and magnify Your Holy Name.

This is a prayer that the angels cannot offer as we do, since they do not share our human nature, nor do they have physical bodies. Their participation in the plan of redemption is different from ours. The angels worship in awe and glorify God while *we offer back to the Father the once-Bread and once-Wine*, the elements the priest has consecrated to become our daily and Divine Food. This is the special privilege that is ours and this is how, as we deepen our love for the Liturgy, we come to understand more deeply our call to become who we really are—the Body of Christ, members of His Church.

When we receive the Eucharist, we do not change or assimilate His Body into ours, as happens with ordinary food, but instead we are changed into Him; we become ever more truly members of His Mystical Body. And then we can renew our offering again, as the transforming Christ changes us into His own self, day by day, moment by moment, Communion by Communion.

As we go forward to receive Jesus, we can prepare for His coming with four simple steps:

  † An act of faith: Jesus, I believe that You are really here before me.

  † An act of love: Jesus, I love You because You are all good and deserving of all my love.

† An act of desire: I want to receive You in Holy Communion, the Gift You have chosen.

† An invitation: Please come into my heart, my life, and everything I am and everything I do.

As you become accustomed to using these four steps, you will find yourself growing in the particular graces that Jesus wants to use to guide you to receiving Him in the best possible way. You may feel drawn to ask Our Lady to accompany you, to share her faith, her love, and her desire with you as you approach her Son. Or you may find yourself asking your holy angel to prompt your words and thoughts. Sometimes, particular inspirations come to us, depending on what is going on in our lives at present. For instance, we may ask for St. Mary Magdalene's tears of gratitude or St. John's courageous resolution to supplement our faith, trust, and love.

When we return to our place, our angel accompanies us "as if at a respectful distance," to use one holy old priest's expression. The angels are amazed, fascinated by what has happened for us, to us, and in us. St. Faustina was given a particular grace to understand and write about this in her *Diary*:

> Hidden Jesus, Eternal Love, our Source of Life,... before creating heaven and earth, You carried us in the depths of Your Heart.... I do not envy the Seraphim their fire, for I have a greater gift deposited in my heart. They admire You in rapture, but Your Blood mingles with mine. Love is heaven given us already here on earth. Oh, why do You hide in faith? Love tears away the veil (1049).[75]

When we receive the Eucharistic Lord, our first thought should be one of joyful gratitude. Christ has come to me! He dwells in me now so that I may always dwell in Him!

[75] See Kieninger, *Angels in the Diary*, pp. 89–90.

Jesus, You have left altar and tabernacle, ciborium and chalice, to come into my body, my heart, my soul. Those vessels are works of art, beautiful and shining, but they cannot love You as I can, for, despite their beauty, they are only things of cold metal. You have given me a heart that can be filled only by Your infinite love and a mind that can be satisfied only by Your absolute truth. You have now come to me once again in the greatest union that Your divine mind and human heart could offer. You are inviting me to a friendship that will transform me entirely and continue for all eternity. I adore You as my God; I love You as my Friend and Hero. I give You all that I am, with all my strengths and my weaknesses, my best desires and my most recurring faults. Lord, receive all of me. Give me only Your love and Your grace so that I may never sin again or offend You in any way. Show me how to do good this day and to assist my neighbors, whoever they may be, to come closer to You.

You do not need to say exactly these words as your thanksgiving after Communion, but they may be helpful to you in formulating your own prayers and renewing your baptismal consecration to the Lord. Our words will vary in accordance with our personality, state of life, and other circumstances. Men and women will phrase things differently; the ordained and the religious will use language that is different from married or single people; the young will look forward with eager zeal and dreams, while older people will look back, perhaps, with improved self-knowledge and understanding of God's ways in their lives.

What is most important is that we speak and listen to the Lord with sincerity, simplicity, and self-awareness, using the best words and sentiments that we can *today*. If we do so, and do not fall into serious sin, our next reception of Holy Communion will be even more beneficial. And onward we will go, carrying out the mission that Christ Jesus entrusts to each of us personally.

When we have finished speaking to Our Lord in this fashion, we may kneel or sit quietly for a time and then make use of some vocal prayers, such as the Anima Christi or others that are proposed in our missals or prayer books. We should ask Our Lady to help us to remain with her Son throughout all the demands of our daily lives. We can also make intercession for loved ones and friends, for the needs of the Church, and for other special intentions in our hearts.

We can certainly involve the angels in our thanksgiving. We can invite our guardian angel to join us in our grateful adoration; we may pray the Sanctus one or more times in union with all the angels in our church. We can also offer prayers of gratitude to Jesus for having entrusted us to the care of our angels and for their faithfulness.

One of the marvelous women saints of the Middle Ages, Gertrude the Great (1256–1302), has left us a marvelous testimony of her gratitude to the angels and how she sought to show her thanks:

> As the Feast of St. Michael approached, St. Gertrude prepared herself for Holy Communion by meditating on the care which the Angels had of her, by the Divine command, notwithstanding her unworthiness; and as she desired to render some return to them, she offered in their honor the life-giving Body and Blood of Jesus in the Most Holy Sacrament, saying: "I offer Thee this most august Sacrament, O most loving Lord, for Thy eternal glory, in honor of the princes of the kingdom, and for the increase of their felicity and beatitude." Then Our Lord drew this oblation to Himself in an ineffable manner, thereby causing the greatest joy to these angel spirits, who appeared even as if they had never before experienced such blessedness and superabounded in delights.

Then each of the choirs of Angels, according to their rank, inclined respectfully before St. Gertrude, saying: "Thou has indeed honored us by this oblation, and we will therefore guard thee with special care," the Guardian Angels adding, "We will guard thee night and day with ineffable joy, and will prepare thee for thy Spouse with the utmost vigilance."[76]

By this prayer, St. Gertrude was not giving away the sanctifying effects or merits of her Communion; those belong to the recipient and cannot be given over to someone else. Instead, she was receiving Jesus in a spirit of gratitude for the ministry of the angels and asking Him to increase their happiness and union with Him in virtue of the sacramental Communion she was receiving. Her prayer was not only an act of worship of Jesus but also an act of loving union with the angels; and her prayer was pleasing to Our Lord.

Can we do the same? We cannot ask that the angels receive Communion, for that is not God's plan for them, but we can ask Our Lord to give them an increase in love and glory because of the Communion that they are helping us to receive worthily. We can ask that as we grow in union with Our Lord through the sacraments, so they may rejoice ever more as they accomplish their mission on our behalf. And at the same time, we can promise them to be always docile (which means "teachable"), listening to their inspirations, heeding their warnings, and learning from their example.

The Divine Office and the Other Sacraments

St. Benedict, the father of Western monastic life, wrote in his rule for religious life about the Divine Office — that is, the daily prayers said at regular hours especially by priests and religious, and which

---

[76] *The Life and Revelations of Saint Gertrude the Great* (Charlotte, NC: TAN Books, 2002), pp. 441–442.

are now often prayed communally in our parishes or by individual members of the faithful:

> We believe that the Divine Presence is everywhere and that the Eyes of the Lord behold the good and the evil in every place. Especially should we believe this without any doubt when we are assisting at the work of God. Let us ever remember what the prophet says, "Serve the Lord in fear." And again, "Sing ye wisely." And again, "In the sight of the angels, I will sing praises unto Thee." Therefore, let us consider how we ought to behave ourselves in the presence of God and of His angels and so assist at the Divine Office that our minds and our voices may accord to gather. (chap. 19)

So, in order to pray the Office well—in order to sing the psalms and to praise the Lord—our voices must be united not only with the community around us, but with the voices of the angels. That is why the Church in Her Liturgy makes abundant use of Psalm 103: "Bless the LORD, O you his angels, you mighty ones who do his word, hearkening to the voice of his word! Bless the LORD, all his hosts, his ministers that do his will!" (vv. 20–21).

Our prayer is also nourished by what we can learn from the traditions of the Church and the treasures left us by the early Fathers. Father Vagaggini tells us that there is a clear tradition in the early liturgies of the Church and in the writings of the Fathers that there is "an angel of baptism, who takes special care of the catechumen, intervenes in the sanctification of the baptismal water, is present at the solemn moment when the sacrament is conferred, and afterwards takes the baptized under his special protection for the rest of the lifetime of the baptized person."[77]

---

[77] Vagaggini, *Theological Dimensions of the Liturgy*, p. 354.

Both St. Cyril of Jerusalem and St. Ambrose of Milan speak of the angels' admiration and delight in the newly baptized. St. Cyril explained to them:

> The angels dance around you in chorus, saying, "Who is this who comes up in white garments and leaning on her beloved?"[78]

Though the idea of dancing angels might seem excessive or even inappropriate to our way of seeing things, Father Vagaggini reminds us:

> If there is joy among the angels of God over one sinner who does penance, who can deny their joy at the birth of a sinner into divine life?[79]

Angels at the Side of Deacons and Priests

The role of the angels in the Liturgy is commonly compared to that of deacons. Sacred art often depicts the angels in the vestments of deacons, signs of their service and assistance at heavenly worship, whether here on earth or before the throne of God above. Perhaps this understanding also drew on the Acts of the Apostles, which tells us that the face of St. Stephen the deacon looked like that of an angel to the onlookers at his martyrdom (Acts 6:15).

These ancient understandings about the angels have continuing relevance for participation in and celebration of the Holy Mass. The great sixth-century priest Narsai, though a Nestorian,[80] wrote these beautiful words about the Liturgy:

[78] Ibid., p. 355.
[79] Ibid., p. 356.
[80] Nestorians were an ancient heretical sect that held that the divine and human natures of Christ were separate.

An angel is great and we should say he is greater than you, oh priest. Yet when he's compared with your ministry, he is lesser than you are. Holy is the seraph and beautiful the cherubim and swift the watcher, yet they cannot run with the fleetness of the word of your mouth. Glorious is Gabriel and mighty is Michael, as their name testifies. Yet every moment, they are bowed down under the mystery which is delivered into your hand. On you they are intent, when you draw near to minister and for you they wait that you would open the door for their Holy of Holies. With voices fraught with praise, they stand at your right hand. And when you have celebrated the mysteries of the redemption, they cry out with praise. With love they bow beneath the will that is concealed in these mysteries and they give honor to you for the office that is administered by you.[81]

This beautiful passage calls to mind the life of St. Francis of Assisi. Many do not know that he was an ordained deacon, but not a priest. Although he is known throughout the Franciscan family as "Father Francis," he refused to be ordained to the priesthood because of his humility. He loved his role as a deacon and participated in it gladly. At Greccio, Francis was a deacon for the Midnight Christmas Mass when he established the first Nativity scene.

St. Francis famously said that if he met a priest coming down the road and saw his guardian angel at the same time, he would kiss the priest's hand first—out of respect for the hand that consecrates the Host—and then greet his angel afterward. Francis also demanded that his friars pay great attention to the dignity of churches and the manner in which they celebrated the Eucharist. They were to make sure that everything was spotlessly clean and

[81] Mar Narsai, Homily XXI.

that the most beautiful vessels, linens, and vestments were used in divine service. As the Friars spread throughout Europe, they brought this tradition of attention and devotion to the Eucharist everywhere. They were among the first promoters of the "new custom" of elevating the Host after the Consecration, which began in France in the early thirteenth century.[82] We should certainly give thanks to whatever angel was responsible for inspiring this beautiful gesture from which we all benefit!

Among the remarkable priestly saints whose lives have illumined the Church in modern times is the much-loved Père Lamy, who died in 1931. Fr. Jean-Edouard Lamy was a humble parish priest in the village of La Courneuve. His parishioners were for the most part poor people; one of his first biographies is called *The Priest of the Rag Pickers*. In many ways Fr. Lamy was like his patron, St. John Vianney, the Curé (parish priest) of Ars — a man of great simplicity who was rich in his understanding and experience of God's love, and who had a very special relationship with Our Lady and the holy angels.

St. Francis of Assisi would also recognize Père Lamy as a kindred spirit: He exhausted himself in the service of the poor and shared the simplicity of their lives. He became a profound spiritual teacher, appreciated by many, ignored or overlooked by still more. The great philosopher Jacques Maritain often sought his counsel and spiritual direction, and was happy to sit at his feet — quite literally.

On several occasions, Father Lamy saw Christ physically present before him as he celebrated Mass. Jesus appeared to be rising

---

[82] The elevation of the chalice seems to have evolved from this practice shortly thereafter. The elevations have become such an integral part of our experience of the liturgy that it seems strange to think they are less than eight hundred years old!

from the altar, embracing the old priest, with the chalice and host in between the two. As Father Lamy experienced these visions, he saw around the altar the angels filled with wonder, their eyes continually passing from Christ's to his own. He realized that they were marveling at the gift he possessed: the gift of priesthood, in which vessels of clay—ourselves—are joined to the Lord's work. Father Lamy also had a special relationship with St. Gabriel, whom he saw often and called the "shining friend" and champion of Our Blessed Lady.

Another such mystic was Father John Baptist Reus, a German Jesuit missionary who spent his priesthood in Brazil and died in 1947. Unknown to his fellow Jesuits, Father Reus led a life of intense mystical intimacy with Christ. Outwardly, he was a quiet, ordinary seminary professor, but inwardly he was a soul on fire with love, consumed by adoration and zeal for souls. Often, when saying Mass, he saw Jesus on the altar, surrounded by the angels, who lifted up the petitions and prayers of the faithful to the throne of the Most High. Father Reus's journals and diaries contain many descriptions of his raptures accompanied by very simple drawings of these visions—and in these sketches the angels abound. Hundreds of people visit his grave every week, and his cause for beatification continues.

I have recounted the story of these simple priests for a reason: As we grow in our appreciation of the Liturgy of the Church and the role of the angels, we must not think that the angels can praise God so much better than we that our worship and praise mean little or nothing in comparison. Undoubtedly, they sing better than we do; after all they are "choirs of angels"! They see Him face to face, but we do not yet. They love Him with angelic (even seraphic) love.

But always remember this: You have a human heart, and so you can respond to the Lord's love by giving Him your heart completely. You can love Him with all your strength, with all the powers of your mind and your will and your body. You can love Him with all your own brokenness, which He longs to heal, and with all your own littleness, which He longs to complete. You can offer yourself together with Jesus Christ to God the Father, uniting your human sufferings to His Holy Passion and Cross. The angels cannot do that.

Both St. Thérèse the Little Flower and St. Faustina understood how important this is in God's eyes.[83] You can offer the prayers and sufferings of everyone around you, asking that they take on a new beauty and a new power in virtue of your union as members of Christ's Mystical Body, the Church. This is beautiful and profound worship. And it will in turn be united to the worship offered by the angels, whose praise complements and supplements our own.

Angels in the East

In the Eastern Liturgy there are marvelous hymns and chants that amplify and extend the great song of the angels heard by the prophet Isaiah: "Holy, holy, holy is the LORD of hosts; the whole earth is full of his glory" (Isa. 6:3). One of these is the Trisagion, which in the West we sing on Good Friday: "Holy God, Holy Strong One, Holy Immortal One, have mercy on us." This beautiful hymn has now re-entered Western devotion through the Chaplet of Divine Mercy and is prayed by millions of people each day. And so, even in that

---

[83] St. Thérèse said to her sisters in one of her last conversations, "The Angels can't suffer; therefore, they are not as fortunate as I am. How astonished they would be if they suffered and felt what I feel! Yes, they'd be very surprised because so am I myself." St. Thérèse of Lisieux, *Her Last Conversations* (Washington, DC: Institute of Carmelite Studies, 1977), p. 150; cited in Kieninger, *Angels in the Diary*, p. 91.

prayer that calls down the mercy of God through the Passion of Christ, we unite ourselves to the holy angels and borrow their words.

In the Byzantine Rite, this resplendent hymn is part of every Mass, and it is believed that the angels join the faithful in song. While the choir sings the Trisagion, the priest sings:

> O God Who art Holy and rests in the Holy, O God Who art hymned by the seraphim with the cry of the Trisagion, Who art glorified by the cherubim and adored by all the Hosts of Heaven, Thou Who didst bring all things from nothing into being, do Thou, O Lord, receive from the mouth of us sinners the hymn of the Trisagion and look down upon us in Your goodness.

After the catechumens are dismissed and the Mass of the Faithful begins, there is also the great "Hymn of the Cherubim," which was introduced into the Byzantine Liturgy during the reign of Emperor Justinian II. In this hymn, the Church calls upon the glorious angels known as "the many-eyed ones":

> We who mystically represent the cherubim, who sing the life-giving Trinity, the Trisagion hymn, let us now lay by all earthly cares that we may receive the King of the world Who comes escorted by unseen armies of angels, Alleluia.

What a joy for angels and men to see the Church at prayer! Prayer becomes our delight over time, a delight that fills our hearts and reminds us that we must focus our lives, above all else, on the worship and the glory of God.

Every Sunday morning and in Her great feasts throughout the year, the Western Church joins together in the Office of Readings to proclaim the glory of God in the ancient hymn known as the Te Deum. There, all of Heaven and earth unite in the praise of the Father with these words.

We praise Thee, O God. We acknowledge Thee to be the Lord. All the earth doth worship Thee, the Father Everlasting. To Thee all angels cry aloud, the Heavens and all the powers therein. To Thee, cherubim and seraphim continually do cry, "Holy, Holy, Holy, Lord God of Hosts. Heaven and Earth are full of the majesty of Thy glory."

As we pray this prayer and unite ourselves to the whole Church on earth, let us with living faith look forward to the day when we will praise the Lord in the sight of the angels and look upon the Face of God unveiled. But in the meantime, here on earth, as we kneel before Jesus in the Eucharist, let us remember that the angels surround us with wonder and praise.

Chapter 13

SAINTS AND THEIR ANGELS: OUTSTANDING EXAMPLES OF ANGELIC FRIENDSHIPS

—————— ✤ ——————

When we read the lives of the saints, we can be sure that the angels played a large part in their spiritual formation and the development of their interior lives, but we do not always find detailed evidence of this in their biographies, beyond perhaps a brief mention of their devotions or prayers. When we do find evidence of a real collaboration — a covenanted friendship between the angels and one of God's servants — it is a very special gift indeed. Here too, however, it is helpful to make a distinction between what is admirable and what is imitable — between the exceptional mystical gifts that many saints experienced and the heroic though often unnoticed responses to angelic influence given by others.

The writings of great mystics such as Teresa of Avila, Veronica Giuliani, or Anne Catherine Emmerich reveal many wonderful insights into the angelic world, but each of those holy women — as well as their guardian angels — would tell you that the most important aspect of the angels' role in their lives was found in their understanding of the Cross, their growth in divine charity toward their neighbor, and, ultimately, their transformation in Christ. The angels are messengers of these truths, guides to these mysteries, and spiritual teachers of this way of life.

Angelic Saints

St. Bernard of Clairvaux (1090–1153) was a monastic founder, reformer, preacher, adviser to popes and crusaders, and one of the greatest intellectual figures of any age in Church history. He is often called "the last of the [Church] Fathers," and his writings continue to inspire, delight, and challenge. Bernard was above all else and before all else a man of deep prayer, even a mystic. His love for Christ and the Virgin Mary penetrated his personality and all his actions.

He was also a great friend of the angels: They delighted, charmed, and challenged him in his "return to God," the great journey of the spiritual life that was the goal for Bernard and his followers. Bernard wrote of the angels in two great series of sermons, as well as in many of his other written works. As Steven Chase notes in his introduction to Bernard in *Angelic Spirituality*:

> The angels serve to reveal God as all in all (cf. 1 Corinthians 15:28). God loves in the Seraphim as charity, knows in the Cherubim as truth, is seated in the Thrones as equity, reigns in the Dominations as majesty, rules in the Principalities as principle, guards in the Powers as salvation, acts in the Virtues as strength, reveals in the Archangels as light, assists in the Angels as piety.[84]

---

[84] See Bernard of Clairvaux, *On Consideration* V.5.12, quoted in Chase, *Angelic Spirituality*, p. 107.

Perhaps the most angelic of all the saints is Francis of Assisi. He has become known far and wide as the "Seraphic Saint," and within the Franciscan family he is called the "Seraphic Father." In other words, his love for Jesus was so great, so intense, so fiery that he could be compared only to that highest choir of angels. Just as the seraphim do not simply burn with the love of God but also inflame others with that love, so too St. Francis gathered followers who caught fire with the love of God.

The likeness to God that came from this great love reached its perfection when the Lord sent His seraphim to seal St. Francis with the five wounds of the stigmata, impressing in his flesh the marks of the Cross. Every age needs to rediscover Francis, because that rediscovery represents a new finding of Christ Jesus. To Christians of every stripe and to many outside the Church, St. Francis's "seraphic love" is a mysteriously attractive and fascinating proof of God's presence among us.

Though the little church of San Damiano will always be remembered as the place where Francis began his mission, it was the church of Our Lady of the Angels that St. Francis loved most in his final years, and it was there that he died. This small chapel, now enclosed in a beautiful basilica, is the heart of the Franciscan family, and the title has become the distinctly Franciscan name for Mary. Countless Franciscan churches and chapels—and even the entire City of Los Angeles—have been named in her honor.

When Mother Angelica came to Irondale, Alabama, she too could think of no more fitting name for her Poor Clare foundation than that of Our Lady of the Angels. This name not only evokes the Immaculata's special relationship with the Lord's messenger-servants, but also calls to mind her protective care—so often expressed by angelic means—over us, her children.

Among the Seraphic Saint's many gifts to the Church, one that is not widely known outside the Franciscan family is the beautiful

"Salutation to Our Lady," which he composed. Rich in fervor and theological poetry, the prayer reveals Francis's sublime understanding of heavenly works:

> Hail holy Lady, most holy Queen,
> Mary, Mother of God, Virgin Made Church,
> Chosen by the most holy Father in heaven,
> Whom He consecrated with his most holy beloved Son
>   and the Paraclete Spirit!
> You in whom was and is all plenitude of grace and all
>   good!

The great Franciscan theologian and cardinal St. Bonaventure (1221–1274) continued Francis's devotion to the angels in his own mystical and theological writings. He pondered the angelic gifts and their ways of knowing and compiled a devotional list of their activities on behalf of souls, drawn from the Scriptures. His theological studies and writings often led him to experience mystical contemplation and to conclude his written works in loving praise of God—a truly *seraphic expression* of Franciscan theology.

Another saint from the Middle Ages who is known for his relationship with the angels is St. Thomas Aquinas—known as the "Angelic Doctor" due to his marvelous intelligence and his ability to view truth from every single aspect, comprehensively, almost like the angels themselves. Early in his religious life, Thomas experienced a remarkable grace of confirmation in chastity when two angels appeared by his side and wrapped a cincture (a rope-like belt) around his waist as a symbol of that divine gift. The Dominican Order has translated this mystical experience into a religious movement called "The Angelic Warfare" for people young and old to maintain purity of body and spirit. Members wear a special medal or cord and participate in prayers for this gift of integrity of body and soul.

Thomas Aquinas is venerated throughout the Church as the patron of all theologians and the chief teacher of all who are in preparation for the priesthood. The collection of prayers he composed for the Feast of Corpus Christi is the source of the hymns used at Benediction throughout the Catholic world. In these hymns and his other prayers, we see Thomas's soul ascending to God, his mind and heart seeking Him and Him alone, even as he dedicated all his physical and mental labors to leading his fellow men and women to the Beauty he had contemplated. The purity of his thought has never been surpassed, and the passionate love of his heart has never been forgotten.

The great Benedictine St. Hildegard of Bingen (1098–1179) provides us with an outstanding example of monastic-angelic life. She understood her vocation to be an imitation of the angels' life of praise and glory offered to the Lord, which she expressed in her writings, the illustrations of her manuscripts, and, especially, her music. St. Hildegard is an extraordinary example of a woman who used all her human talents, skills, and creativity to translate her unique mental and mystical enlightenments so that others could benefit from them.

She made great truths perceptible to the senses. In the exquisite miniatures that translate her visions into pictures, we see the fall of the angels in the form of dark stars that have lost all their light and have been cast down to earth. She saw the nine choirs arranged in nine concentric circles around Almighty God, each choir and sphere displaying its own characteristics, in a marvelous synthesis of her own visions and the theology of Dionysius. Though the subject of many controversies during her life, her mission in the life of the Church took on a new impetus and luster when Pope Benedict XVI declared her to be a Doctor of the Church in 2012.

St. Frances of Rome, who lived in the fifteenth century, enjoyed ongoing intimacy with her guardian angel. She was a noblewoman married to a man from a noble family, and the mother of many children. And yet, in the midst of all of her activities, occupations, and obligations, she lived a life of intense prayer and union with God. To help her on her way of faith, the Lord gave her the visible presence of her guardian angel. For more than twenty-four years, she saw the angel constantly at her side; he became her teacher and her guide in the ways of prayer and charity; and in her last years, a second angel was given to her, to perfect and complete the teachings of the first.

In addition to providing St. Frances with wonderful insights into the ways of God and the mysteries of His love, the angel also helped her to get along with difficult in-laws and demanding neighbors. Her crosses became more bearable, day by day, as her angel inspired her with practical advice and support. (You see, the troubles and sufferings of the saints are not so different from ours.) Before she died, St. Frances founded a religious house of Benedictine Oblates and later retired to the convent, where her sisters still pray for the Church and promote devotion to the holy angels.

Angels at Their Side

In the lives of the saints we also find many simple men and women for whom the angels were companions and helpers in their daily life and work. St. Isidore the Farmer, who is venerated throughout Spain and the Hispanic world, received assistance from the angels with his work in the fields. It is said he would become wrapped in prayer and the angels would carry on his plowing and other labors for him.

The angels came repeatedly to Blessed Anna Maria Taigi (1769–1837), the poor Roman housewife and mother of seven children who was graced by God with extraordinary gifts of prophecy and prayer. Though illiterate, she was able to see events of the past, present, and future — all for the purpose of bringing comfort and strength to Christ's Church and to souls who were burdened with heavy crosses. But these gifts were not the source of her holiness; Anna Maria was first and foremost a wife and mother. Her husband was a good but uneducated man who sometimes had a difficult temper. Her children were her constant concern, even after they had married and left home.

Anna Maria Taigi did everything in the presence of her guardian angel, sending him to bring comfort to the sick and protection to those who were tempted. We can do the same thing: Every day we can speak to the angels of the poor, of the sick, and of the strangers whom we see in the streets. If you find yourself distracted by someone in church, speak to that person's guardian angel, apologize for your distraction, and tell him that you pray that his work will be successful this day and that he will bring his charge ever closer to Christ.

Not all the saints saw their guardian angels; most of the saints, in fact, went through their lives as we do, without extraordinary visions or phenomena of this kind. But they were conscious of the ministry of the angels in their daily lives, and they knew that the angels were conscious of them. They knew that the Lord had placed an angel at their side, just as He has for us, and that made a great difference in their lives. We want to realize this same truth and benefit from this same blessing. We must be aware of these great helpers in our needs, and we must ask them for what is most important: that we might grow deeper in faith, in hope, and in love of God. By their presence and protection, the Lord gives to us tangible signs of His awareness of all our needs; every little thing that we do and every cross that we bear, however small, is known to Him.

There are many riches to be found in the world of the angels as we grow in our understanding of how the Lord unites angel and man in His service and for His glory. Every day when we open the Sacred Scriptures, we ask the Lord to reveal Himself to us, to open our mind and our heart: "Holy angel, help me. Take away from me all lukewarmness and narrowness of mind. Let me see the wonders of the Lord in all their fullness and glory. Let me grow in discipleship. Let me realize the vocation that God has given me."

The Lord calls each one of us by name to love Him. Every morning when we wake, our first thought should be: "Today I can give glory to God. Today I am loved by God. Today the angel is at my side. My Heavenly Mother watches over me. The Lord Jesus calls me." When we begin our day in this way, we begin with the joy and vitality of the grace of the Gospel and the life of the Church. Each morning, let us ask the Lord to give us the clear-sightedness to see His will so that we might become His instruments and so that we might be guardians for others, stewarding the gifts of God within them and cooperating with His grace so that with our elder brothers, the angels and the saints, we might praise Him always.

Modern Saints

One of the great gifts given to the Church over the past four decades has been the extraordinary number of beatifications and canonizations of saints. During the reign of St. John Paul II, the Church recognized 482 saints and 1,327 blesseds (beatified persons, one step before sainthood); while Pope Benedict XVI sat on the Chair of Peter, there were 45 new saints and 843 new blesseds; through the end of 2017, during Pope Francis's pontificate, 885 saints and 1,121 blesseds have been named.

There are many reasons for these extraordinary numbers. The first is the number of large groups of martyrs from times of revolution and persecution in France, Spain, Poland, China, Vietnam, Korea, and elsewhere. The remarkable improvements in communications, research, travel, and methodology have also had a revolutionary effect on speeding up the canonization process. But more important than any of these factors is one great theological truth: God wants it so. Only the Lord *makes* saints; the Church just *recognizes* them.

Almighty God wants to let His glory be seen in His holy ones, men and women of times long past and time more recent, whose lives are recognizable to us and who became friends of God, neighbor, and stranger alike, loyal and faithful servants of Jesus Christ, and courageous witnesses to His truth and love. They are among the most powerful evidence for the truth of the Catholic Faith. Reading their lives inspires, challenges, and fascinates—encouraging us to hear our own invitation from the Lord, "Come, follow me.... Be perfect as Your heavenly Father is perfect.... I no longer call you servants, but friends" (see Matt. 19:21; 5:48; John 15:15).

Women Religious and Their Angelic Benefactors

Many of these newly beatified and canonized holy people have left testimony of their devotion to the holy angels and the depth of their intimacy with them. Some lived in centuries past, in ages of faith and often in monastic lives of prayer and labor *in conspectu angelorum* (in the sight of the angels). St. Crescentia Hoess (1682–1744) was a German Franciscan mystic whose spiritual gifts were joined to the kind and practical heart of a wise religious superior. A poor girl without a dowry, she was able to enter the convent only because the local Franciscans owed the town's Protestant mayor a favor. (At the Sisters' request, he had purchased a tavern that was too close to the convent walls and shut down the business.)

Among the mystical graces that characterized her religious life was a great intimacy with her guardian angel, as well as the angels of souls in Purgatory who were the object of her prayers, penances, and charity. The angels also gave her good advice for dealing with the other sisters and for encouraging them to a deeper spiritual life. In chronic poor health because of her childhood poverty, Crescentia suffered from migraines and toothache. Arthritis later crippled her hands and feet and caused her to assume a permanently crouched posture before her death. With true Franciscan verve—and, no doubt, to the admiration of the angels—she would cry out, "Oh, you bodily members, praise God that He has given you the capacity to suffer!" She passed from this life into Heaven on Easter Sunday, 1744.

One of Pope Francis's canonizations was St. Marie of the Incarnation Guyart (1599–1672), a widow from Tours in France who became an Ursuline nun and later one the founders of the Church in Canada. Marie of the Incarnation was both a mystic and a missionary, translating the mysteries that she contemplated experientially into the spoken language and heartfelt aspirations of the pioneer settlers of "Ville-Marie" and the New Canadian frontier. She was granted special insight into the life of the Holy Trinity in her mystical experiences through a series of intellectual visions and illuminations; but her divine enlightenments always included the choirs of angels, in whom she saw the Perfections of the Trinity reflected and praised.

Among the recent beatifications and canonizations have been a number of women mystics who have borne the wounds of the stigmata and whose spiritual path has been a gospel of suffering and an evangelization of pain. The lessons taught by these modern mystics are well-suited to the needs and experiences of people today. St. Anna Schaeffer (1882–1925) was horribly burned in a work accident she suffered just before her nineteenth birthday. Working as a laundress in order to help her family and to save up for a convent dowry, she lost her footing and slipped into a large washing vat of boiling lye soap and water. Burned from her heels to her hips, she underwent more than thirty surgeries and skin grafts to no avail. She found herself confined to bed, in constant pain and unable to fulfill her hopes of a vocation.

Through the ministry of a kind, wise parish priest, Anna learned to offer her sufferings to Christ and to make of her injuries a "straight path for the Lord." She spent her days doing needlework for poor persons and churches, writing letters of comfort to other shut-ins, and giving advice and consolation to all who sought her out. She responded to every act of kindness with affectionate gratitude, but she also knew rejection, poverty, and the loneliness of chronic pain.

Our Lord consoled her with visions and visitations from her guardian angel and the saints; Anna received these gifts simply and gratefully, but referred to them simply as her "dreams." While receiving Holy Communion one morning, she saw five rays of light come from the Host and mark her with the wounds of the stigmata. She quickly asked that these wounds remain invisible, so as not to attract attention. In 1925, she developed colon cancer, which developed into paralysis; later, a stroke made it very difficult for her to speak. Yet she never lost her peace of heart or her hope in Christ Jesus and His victorious Cross.

Her life might be summed up simply as: What God took from her, she gave; what God gave her, she accepted. Shortly before her death, one of her visitors complained that she would be left without anyone to listen to her. Anna replied, "Just go to my grave. I will understand you." This beautiful soul, a worthy companion to the angels, died on October 5, 1925, at the age of forty-three. She is considered the patron of all hospice patients and of those who care for bedridden loved ones.

Other mystics who have left behind testimonies of their relationship with their guardian angels and other angelic guides include the charming St. Mary (Mariam) of Jesus Crucified, OCD (1846–1878), the first saint born in the Holy Land in modern times. The life of this remarkable Carmelite nun reads like a Bible story. The child of a devout family, Mariam lost both her parents as a child and was raised by a loving uncle and his family. Moved by an inner calling from Christ, she rejected the marriage arranged by her family and thus experienced their rejection.

A servant then made an attempt to woo her and force her conversion to Islam. Rejecting his advances, the young man attacked her with a knife, slashing her throat. Miraculously healed and protected by the Virgin Mary and an angel who appeared in human form, she eventually made her way to France, where she entered a convent at Marseille. Because of the miraculous phenomena that surrounded her, the sisters did not permit her profession of vows. However, she was welcomed into a Carmelite cloister that soon sent her to India as one of the foundresses of an Indian Carmel.

There followed an increase in mystical phenomena around Sister Mariam, including her joining in the songs of angel choirs during her ecstasies. Levitation, the stigmata, and other gifts became an ordinary part of her life. Yet she continued to live humbly as a lay Sister, dedicating herself to hard labors and constant duties. Eventually she returned to France, but then she became part of a second foundation in Bethlehem in her native Palestine. Returning to her home, she alleviated many problems for the foundation through her gifts of language and cultural identity. Acting under mystical inspiration, she designed a round, Davidic monastery and was the instrument in the rediscovery of the Crusader shrine of Emmaus. She died at the age of thirty-three, in the presence of the angels, whose songs she delighted to share.

The late nineteenth century also saw the foundation of two religious communities dedicated to the angels: First, in Bilbao, Spain, Rafaela Ybarra de Vilallonga (1843–1900), a married woman and mother of a family, founded the Sisters of the Guardian Angels in order to work with young children, assuring them of religious education, maternal love, and protection from exploitation and child labor. She began this work when she realized the care needed by her nephews after the death of her sister. Upon the death of her husband, she fully devoted herself to the congregation. She was beatified in 1984.

A second community is the Sisters of the Angels, founded by the Blessed Seraphina (Clotilde) Micheli (1849–1911). Clotilde Micheli saw her guardian angel throughout her childhood, and when she was eighteen, the Blessed Virgin appeared to her, telling her to found a community to be known as Sisters of the Angels. Despite this apparent divine approbation, her road was a long and difficult one. The Blessed Virgin's words told her that she was to be a true "sister to the angels" by adoring the Most Blessed Trinity with them and serving the needs of her brothers and sisters.

But when the young woman was told by Monsignor Agostini, the future cardinal archbishop of Venice, that she should begin to write a rule of life for the future institute, she became frightened and left her family, seeking work in another city. It was only after some fourteen years had passed that she sought entrance into another community in Rome. After four years with those sisters, she was finally ready to begin her own work.

In 1891, at the age of forty-two, she was clothed in her new habit and became Mother Seraphina of the Sacred Heart, foundress of the Sisters of the Angels, Adorers of the Most Holy Trinity. The Sisters dedicated themselves to the poor, orphans, and all children at risk. Later, her community would become known for the "interpenetration" of adoration and assistance, like the angels who never cease gazing upon the Face of God, even as they serve as guardians and messengers from God to us. Her life continued to be marked by supernatural interventions, and she often began instructions to her nuns with the words, "My angel showed me ..." or "My angel told me ..." She had a clear understanding of what her Sisters needed in order to grow in the spirit of her charism, as her prayers demonstrate:

> O Holy Angels I would like to pray like you. Help me today and always in the life that I want to undertake, joined to your own. Yes, I would like to be your imitator, your companion. You contemplate the Lord in heaven, face to face. If only I, here below, could see God in everything, love Him as you do, and always cry out: Holy, Holy, Holy! I must be an Angel for those who surround me. Like you, I must lead souls to heaven, pray for them and build them up with good example, assist them with wise counsels and supply for them whatever is lacking![85]

Angels at the Turn of the Twentieth Century

The late nineteenth century was also an extraordinary time for bold pastoral works throughout Italy. In Pompei, near Naples, the Blessed Bartolo Longo (1841–1926), a lawyer who had dabbled in Satanism while in university, converted to the True Church because of the grace of the Rosary and began a life of truly astonishing social and spiritual works, motivated by profound faith and a compelling urge to do whatever charity demanded of him. Bartolo sought to focus the devotion of the poor folk whom he was serving by obtaining a painting of Our Lady of the Rosary, which showed the Blessed Mother and the Christ Child giving the Rosary to Sts. Dominic and Catherine of Siena. When the painting arrived, atop a donkey cart hauling manure, it was damaged and of very poor quality, but even so it had a magnetic effect.

---

[85] Suor Giuseppina Romano, "Gli angeli di Suor Serafina Micheli" in Marcello Stanzione, ed., *Gli Angeli dei Mistici* (Tavangnacco, Udine, Italy: Edizioni Segno, 2007), pp. 256–257.

Eventually repaired and restored, the beloved image, crowned and jeweled, is enshrined in a magnificent basilica shrine, which in turn is surrounded by the many centers of charity founded by Bartolo Longo and his benefactress—and later wife—the Countess de Fusco: orphanages, schools for the poor, rehabilitation centers, trade schools, shelters for women and children at risk, and halfway houses for prisoners returning to society. All are united by the prayer of the Rosary and the ceaseless repetition of the angel Gabriel's words, "Hail, Full of Grace."

Bartolo Longo was deeply devoted to the archangel Michael and to the choir of archangels whom he venerated as the "Seven Assisting Spirits before the Throne of Mary." Bartolo had taken this term from Raphael's words in the book of Tobit and *adapted them* to the Blessed Mother, reasoning, no doubt, that she who carries the Christ Child on her lap has become the throne of the Most High, the new Seat of Wisdom and Mercy. He had a beautiful altar to Michael and the other archangels constructed in the main church and commissioned for it a special painting, *The Moment after the Angelic Victory*, depicting the Seven after the fall of Lucifer. St. Michael was named guardian and patron of the basilica, and supplications to him were composed for frequent use, both public and private.

Bartolo wrote and published many booklets of prayer and Church teaching, including several on the angels. He inspired many other prominent holy persons in their devotion to the seven archangels, notably St. Hannibal di Francia (1851–1927), founder of the Rogationist Fathers and the Daughters of Divine Zeal, and St. John Calabria (1873–1954), founder of the Poor Servants of Divine Providence. Bartolo's gifts were particularly evident in the many prayers he composed, combining both fervor and poetry in his words. These are excerpts from his Prayer to the Seven Assistant Spirits before the Throne of God for Peace:

O Most Noble and Powerful Spirits of the Eternal Kingdom of God, O sublime Intelligences, who, like flames of purest love, burn in the abyss of inaccessible light that forms the throne of the Most High, I greet you. You are those Highest of Princes, Sovereign Ambassadors of the King of Kings, who more than any others remain at the Seat of the Eternal One, charged to range over the earth, bearing the Grace of God and Peace to the faithful. O Holy Archangels, you announced peace to men of goodwill at Bethlehem and always and everywhere, you are bearers of heavenly grace and peace of heart to mortal men and women. Call down upon us, from Jesus, the Prince of Peace, and from Mary, Queen of Mercy, who has placed her Throne in the Valley of Pompei, this precious gift of Grace and Peace, which the world cannot give!

Peace we ask of you, O Angels of Peace: peace in our souls, peace in our families, peace among the nations; peace in the Church of Jesus Christ; and peace especially for all those who have come together to build the Sanctuary of Pompei. O chosen and most pure Spirits who surround the Throne of Mary, your Queen: may the light of her Immaculate Conception be reflected in the most pure ocean of Your intellectual light, and make you ever more beautiful and lovable in our eyes. Oh, for the love that you bear for Mary your Queen, care for us and our homes always and watch over the Pontifical Basilica of the Rosary of Pompei. Flee from us, Satan and all you our enemies, both visible and invisible! Strengthen us in faith, holy Angels; make fervent our prayers; enflame our soul with the pure love of God! Obtain for us a forgetfulness of ourselves, the spirit of oblation and abandonment in God, in which is all Peace! Aid us in our needs, heal us in our infirmities, protect us with your powerful arm! Assist us, console us, and bless us, now and always, in life and in death. Amen.[86]

Blessed Bartolo Longo was not a visionary, but he walked with eyes of faith; his mystical experience was a profound union with Christ experienced through daily Mass and Holy Communion, holy hours of adoration, and especially the constant prayer and meditation of the Holy Rosary. He saw Christ in the Eucharist; He saw Christ in His Blessed Mother; he saw Christ in the poor and the needy. And he never turned away.

Bartolo Longo was beatified in 1981 and is entombed in the basilica that he gave to Mary; in his casket, he wears the mantle and insignia of the Equestrian Order of the Holy Sepulchre of Jerusalem, in which he was invested by the Holy See. The Church celebrates his feast day on October 5. He is particularly well-known among priest exorcists, who find him a powerful advocate against Lucifer and his forces of darkness.

Blessed Bartolo Longo's devotion to the Seven Archangels was shared by the Blessed Father Justin (Giustino) Russolillo (1891–1955), a Neapolitan priest and the founder of the Vocationist Priests and Sisters, as well as of the consecrated laity known as Apostles of Universal Sanctification. At a time when "vocations directors" did not yet exist, Father Justin dedicated himself entirely to the promotion of vocations to the priesthood and religious life, the inspiration of young people, and the establishment of religious houses called "vocationaries," in which young men and boys could nourish the first signs of a priestly vocation in themselves and develop the human and spiritual maturity necessary to foster and to discern a true

---

[86] Marcello Stanzione and Carmine Alvino, *I Sette Arcangeli: Storia di un culto cattolico contestato e dimenticato* (Milano: Sugarco Edizioni, 2014), pp. 155–156.

229

calling from Christ. Reading his biography and his own writings, one cannot help but be struck by the purity and joy of his priestly enthusiasm: He never lost the spirit of gratitude and wonder that marked his vocation.

Father Justin's understanding of creation is rooted in God's desire to establish us in a relationship of personal love with the Blessed Trinity. This is a universal call, not one reserved for the privileged; it is achieved through constant, gradual ascent; and it is lived out through imitation of the Holy Family in their relationships with the Trinity, which he compares to spousal love. He counseled that all community prayers end with these words:

O my God and my All! Father, Son and Holy Spirit, may your will be done, your love reign, your glory shine always more in me and in everyone, as in yourself, O My God and my All.[87]

In his book *Spiritus Orationis*, a true spiritual masterpiece revealing his own "itinerary to God," Blessed Justin provides remarkable guided meditations and prayers for the formation of young men's hearts and their transforming union with the Holy Trinity. This is his "plea" to the angels:

O Sovereign Creatures, O Celestial Princes, O First-Born of the Created World, O Masterpieces of the Sanctifying Spirit, my soul longs for and soars toward you, my soul bows before you and applauds you, my entire soul is open and united to you!

O my Angels, O my Archangels, O my Principalities, O my Powers, O my Virtues, O my Dominations, O my Thrones,

---

[87] "Vocationist Spirituality," website of the Vocationist Fathers and Brothers, http://www.vocationist.org.

O my Cherubim, O my Seraphim, O my seven Spirits Assisting at the Throne of God, O my own Angel!

For the love I have for you, allow me to call you mine, as every soul calls its own, The Guardian Angel! As your Prince, St. Michael and Mary, your Queen, call you their own! As Jesus, your ruler and the Blessed Trinity call you their own!

All of you together, each Choir and each Angel, call me yours and possess me as yours; in a very special way, I want to be a servant of the Angels, brother of the Angels, priest of the Angels: Grant that I may be such, O Prince of the Angels!

With the mind and the heart of the Church, with the mind and the heart of Mary, with the mind and heart of Jesus, I rejoice for all the good you do; with you, in you, and through you, I glorify the Lord!

In the spirit of the Liturgy of the earthly and heavenly Church, every day I intend to celebrate a group of the Angels, along with a group of Saints of the day. In communion with you, in your Heaven, at your banquet, I intend to court the Lord with the glory of love!

O my Angels, every moment I expect from each one of you a gift of humility, purity, and love. Flood my soul with all the graces that flow among you, sweep away my soul with the currents of glory that circulate among you!

May my spirit reflect all the images and likenesses of the Blessed Trinity that shine in each and every one of you! May my heart offer to the Blessed Trinity that glorious, loving feast which It receives from each and every one of you!

O Holy Trinity, grant that I may live totally in communion with the Angels, so that I may be like a little angelic world! I unite myself to all the pleasures with which You are glorified in Your Angels; and to all the pleasures that the Angels enjoy in You, O Blessed Trinity![88]

The symbol that Father Justin designed as the seal or coat-of-arms for his community is an intricate pattern involving a triangle for the Holy Trinity and three interlocked circles representing the Holy Family. Framing this design are seven pairs of wings for the holy archangels, the Seven Spirits before the Throne of God.[89]

A contemporary of Blessed Justin and certainly a symbol of evangelization in the modern age is the Blessed James Alberione (1884–1971), founder of the Society of Saint Paul, the Daughters of St. Paul, three other communities of sisters, four secular institutes, and a lay third order. He is revered as the apostle of social communications and mass media; in his long life, he guided his community in the use of penny newspapers, traveling book-selling nuns, bookstore centers of evangelization, and film production and radio and television apostolates. Since his death, his religious communities have taken up the challenges of the Internet and

---

[88] Website of the Vocationist Fathers and Brothers, http://www.vocationist.org/files/Spirit-of-Prayer.pdf.

[89] St. Faustina also received the special assistance of one of seven assisting angels: "One day, when I was at adoration, and my spirit seemed to be dying for Him, and I could no longer hold back my tears, I saw a spirit of great beauty who spoke these words to me: 'Don't cry—says the Lord.' After a moment I asked, 'Who are you?' He answered me, 'I am one of the seven spirits who stand before the throne of God day and night and give Him ceaseless praise.' Yet this spirit did not soothe my yearning, but roused me to even greater longing for God. This spirit is very beautiful, and his beauty comes from close union with God. This spirit does not leave me for a single moment, but accompanies me everywhere" (*Diary* 471).

social media; they are on the cutting edge of evangelization in the public square.

Father Alberione's admiration for the apostle St. Paul and his devotion to Jesus the Master (Teacher) and Mary, Queen of Apostles, places him in the classic tradition of Italian piety and traditional devotion. But his ability to translate the strengths and gifts of his own piety into a multicultural and international family of religious congregations makes him a unique apostle in any age. Father Alberione, who was lovingly called *Primo Maestro*, or "First Teacher," among his spiritual children, had a deep and constant devotion to St. Gabriel and to his own guardian angel. He devoted one of his secular institutes for consecrated laymen to the archangel and dedicated the first Thursday of the month in community to honoring the guardian angels. He felt strongly that to honor the angels is to honor God Himself, for they are His representatives. Throughout his conferences, letters, and sermons we find continuing exhortations for his evangelizing sons and daughters to remain in close contact with the first messengers of the good news.

St. Padre Pio, the great Franciscan mystic who died in 1968 and who bore the stigmata for some fifty years, had such a wonderful relationship with his guardian angel that several books have been written about their friendship and the friar's contact with other angels. In his early letters and in later private conversations, Padre Pio called his angel the "shining man," and it is clear from his descriptions that he saw him as his true and inseparable friend. The angel not only served as protector and guide but, at times, even preached to him. According to Padre Pio's early letters, his angel would correct him when he was not acting as he should have.

The angel helped Padre Pio to adapt himself to the mission that Jesus entrusted to the friar-priest: He would carry the Cross of Jesus in a visible and unending Via Crucis for a full fifty years, exposed to the eyes and demands of friends and enemies alike. As the Lord had once received the ministrations and comfort of the angels in the Garden of Gethsemane, so He sent these same spirits to the friar of San Giovanni Rotondo.

The words and example of these recently canonized and beatified men and women should be a special confirmation to us that Almighty God always keeps His promises. The means of holiness are still the same; the wounds we bear are not new, and His remedies are always powerful. He calls us to do great things for Him because He does great things in us. If He asks us for more than we think we have, He will provide what we do not possess. The Lord is near, and He hears every prayer that we make. Just as St. Raphael gathered up the prayers and good works of Tobit, so our guardian angels join their prayers to ours in all our "contemporary" needs and concerns, our sufferings and labors. They bring us closer to Jesus so that we in turn may bring Him to others.

Chapter 14

MICHAEL, RAPHAEL, AND
THE ANGEL OF FATIMA

———— ✛ ————

A few specific angels have left their distinctive mark on the history
of the Church. We have already discussed St. Gabriel at length,
and so here we will consider the other two archangels whose
names have been recorded in the Scriptures: Michael and Raphael. Both of these extraordinary figures have appeared elsewhere
in this book — their importance is so great that it is impossible
to talk about the angels without mentioning them — but here we
will focus briefly on the Church's devotion to them.

Finally, there is one unnamed angel who has made a particularly important mark on Church history in our time: the Angel of
Fatima. We have just passed the centenary of the Blessed Mother's
appearance to the three Portuguese children Lucia, Jacinta, and
Francisco, and yet Her message — and the message of the Angel
who preceded Her — is as urgent as ever.

St. Michael the Archangel

Saint Michael is the great defender of the holiness and omnipotence, the rights and dignity of Almighty God. From the earliest times of the Church's life, he has been regarded as the leader of Heaven's armies in the battle against Lucifer and the protector of the Church, the New Israel, and all God's people.

Various titles and responsibilities have been attributed to the holy archangel over the centuries: He is sometimes called the "thurifer" (see Rev. 8:3ff.), and he has often been seen as the guide of the souls of the dead to their particular judgment, or even "the weigher of souls (Job 31:6; Dan. 5:27ff.). For this reason, he is frequently shown holding a balance or scales as a symbol of judgment and reckoning. The holy archangel is also invoked by those whose vocations are defense and protection: soldiers, police officers, and first responders of all kinds. Many police officers, particularly in the United States, wear or carry medals of St. Michael in the form of a badge or shield.

Sanctuaries and shrine churches have been erected in Michael's honor over the centuries and have become popular places of pilgrimage, healing, and protection. Usually they are found on high mountains or isolated high places, such as Skellig Michael in Ireland or Mont-Saint-Michel in France. It is an extraordinary fact that seven major sanctuaries of the archangel lie on a straight line that extends from Skellig Michael, off the coast of Ireland, through Cornwall, France, Italy, Greece, and Israel. The most important of these is the Cave or Grotto of Saint Michael of the Gargano in the south of Italy. Hundreds of thousands of people have made pilgrimages there to the underground church that is believed to have been consecrated by the archangel himself.

St. John Paul II, during his visit to the fifteen-hundred-year-old Gargano shrine in 1987, spoke at length of the archangel's role as protector of the Church:

To this place, as so many of my predecessors on the Chair of Peter have done in the past, I too have come ... to venerate and invoke the Archangel Michael, that he might protect and defend the Holy Church in a moment in which it is difficult to render an authentic Christian testimony without compromises and without accommodations....

However fragmentary they may be, the references in Revelation to the personality and role of Michael are very eloquent. He is the Archangel (Jude 1:9) who upholds the inalienable rights of God. He is one of the princes of heaven (Daniel 12:1), the protector of Israel from whom will come forth the Saviour.

Now the new people of God is the Church. This is the reason for which she considers him as her own protector and sustainer in all her battles for the defense and the diffusion of the Kingdom of God upon earth. It is true that "the gates of hell shall not prevail" according to the Lord's promise (Matthew 16:18), but this does not mean that we are exempt from trial and from battles against the attacks of the Evil One.

In this battle, the Archangel Michael is at the Church's side to defend her from all the evils of the age, to help believers to resist the demon who is "like a roaring lion going about seeking whom to devour" (1 Peter 5:8). To this battle, the figure of the Archangel Michael recalls us once again, to whom the Church in the East as well as the West, has never ceased to pay special devotion.[90]

St. Michael appeared to Pope St. Gregory the Great in the year 590 while the pope was making a penitential procession through the

---

[90] John Paul II, Discourse to the people of Monte Sant'Angelo, May 24, 1987, in *In Comunione con gli angeli*, pp. 72–73, translated by the author.

streets of Rome, asking for the end of a plague that was devastating the city. Looking up, he saw the figure of the archangel standing atop the emperor Hadrian's tomb, sheathing a bloody sword in its scabbard—a sign that the plague was over. The tomb became known as Castel Sant'Angelo (the Castle of the Holy Angel) from that time forward, and a large bronze statue of Michael crowns the edifice.

St. Francis of Assisi also had a great veneration for St. Michael; he kept a forty-day fast in preparation for his feast day in September. He taught his friars to venerate the archangel particularly as the angel who presents the souls of the dead to God. St. Joan of Arc saw him surrounded by a company of angels when he appeared to her and told her to take up arms to defend France. He also admonished her to behave well and to go to church often.

St. Francis de Paolo said that Michael appeared to him in a vision and gave him the motto *caritas* ("charity") for his order. The great missionary Francis Xavier invoked him as his protector on all his missionary journeys. Founders such as Alphonsus Liguori and Paul of the Cross made him patron and protector of their religious communities, and mystics such as Blessed Anne Catherine Emmerich, Blessed Rosa Gattorno, and St. Faustina found in him a special friend and guide.

In 1884, Pope Leo XIII had a vision of the battle between Satan and St. Michael, which moved him to compose a prayer to be said after Low Mass throughout the Catholic world. It became known to Catholics everywhere and was prayed after Mass until the reforms of the Second Vatican Council. It has experienced a rebirth of popularity among many Catholics today.

> St. Michael the Archangel, defend us in battle. Be our protection against the wickedness and snares of the Devil. May God rebuke him, we humbly pray, and do thou, O Prince

of the Heavenly Hosts, by the power of God, cast into Hell Satan and all the evil spirits who prowl about the world seeking the ruin of souls. Amen.

Saint Raphael the Archangel

St. Raphael, whom we know from the book of Tobit, is venerated as the "angel of healing." He is the only angel who completely conceals his identity until the fulfillment of his mission, appearing as a human friend and companion to the young Tobias, son of the virtuous and devout Tobit. Because of this, Raphael is often considered to be the model and pattern of our understanding of the guardian angels' role in our lives.

In the Scriptures, Raphael appears as the providential guide and companion of Tobias, who must travel from Nineveh to Medea to collect money loaned to his father's kinsman. He identifies himself as Azarias ("the Lord's help"), son of Ananias ("the Lord's goodness"), names that reveal his true mission, but not his identity. On the way, he saves the youth from an attack by a vicious fish (6:2), teaches him the spiritual and therapeutic use of the animal's organs (6:5–8), and advises the marriage of Tobias to Sarah (6:9–12), whose seven attempted marriages resulted in the deaths of each bridegroom at the hands of the demon Asmodeus.

While Tobias arranges the marriage with Sarah's father, "Azarias" completes the journey to Medea to retrieve the money loaned. But before he sets off, he instructs Tobias and Sarah in prayer, and bids the bridegroom to burn the fish's heart and liver, which drives the demon away (see 8:5–7). On his return to Tobias's home, Raphael heals his father, Tobit, of cataracts, by having Tobias use the gall of the fish as a balm (11:10–14).

It is only when he has completed all these tasks and deeds of defense and healing that he reveals his true identity:

Then the angel called [Tobias and Tobit] privately and said to them: "Praise God and give thanks to him; exalt him and give thanks to him in the presence of all the living for what he has done for you. It is good to praise God and to exalt his name, worthily declaring the works of God. Do not be slow to give him thanks. It is good to guard the secret of a king, but gloriously to reveal the works of God. Do good, and evil will not overtake you. Prayer is good when accompanied by fasting, almsgiving, and righteousness. A little with righteousness is better than much with wrongdoing. It is better to give alms than to treasure up gold. For almsgiving delivers from death, and it will purge away every sin. Those who perform deeds of charity and of righteousness will have fullness of life; but those who commit sin are the enemies of their own lives.

I will not conceal anything from you. I have said, "It is good to guard the secret of a king, but gloriously to reveal the works of God." And so, when you and your daughter-in-law Sarah prayed, I brought a reminder of your prayer before the Holy One; and when you buried the dead, I was likewise present with you. When you did not hesitate to rise and leave your dinner in order to go and lay out the dead, your good deed was not hidden from me, but I was with you. So now God sent me to heal you and your daughter-in-law Sarah. I am Raphael, one of the seven holy angels who present the prayers of the saints and enter into the presence of the glory of the Holy One. (12:6–15)

Before the angel leaves their home, he imparts these final words, which explain the nature of an angel's mission and the manner in which he appeared to their eyes:

But he said to them, "Do not be afraid; you will be safe. But praise God for ever. For I did not come as a favor on my part, but by the will of our God. Therefore praise him for ever. All these days I merely appeared to you and did not eat or drink, but you were seeing a vision. And now give thanks to God, for I am ascending to him who sent me. Write in a book everything that has happened." Then they stood up; but they saw him no more. So they confessed the great and wonderful works of God, and acknowledged that the angel of the Lord had appeared to them. (12:17–22)

Throughout the book, Raphael reveals himself as a wise and ever-helpful servant and friend by aiding, protecting, and advising Tobias. His advice is both practical and spiritual; his support immediate and also long-ranging.

Revealing himself as "one of seven," he establishes the existence of a special group among the angels. These words, along with those of St. Gabriel to Zechariah (Luke 1:19) and the designation in St. Jude's epistle of St. Michael as an *archangel* (Jude 9), are the basis for the traditional notion that the seven who stand in the presence of the Lord are the *seven archangels*.

In the life of the Church, St. Raphael is held as the principal patron of the city of Cordova in Spain, where he is believed to have appeared to end a plague in 1278. His feast is kept there on May 7. St. Frances of Rome mystically visited Hell and Purgatory in his company, and St. John of God invoked him as a special patron for his nursing congregation and its hospitals. The eighteenth-century Neapolitan lay Franciscan St. Mary Frances of the Five Wounds (1715–1791) was very devoted to the archangel, who also appeared to her frequently and even administered Holy Communion to her.

In 1842, Alphonse Ratisbonne, a young Alsatian Jewish banker, converted to Catholicism after he experienced a vision of Our Lady of the Miraculous Medal over the altar of St. Michael in the Church of Sant'Andrea delle Fratte in Rome. Ratisbonne was baptized less than two weeks later and would become a priest, dedicating himself to the foundation of the Priests and Sisters of Our Lady of Sion. Reflecting later on his conversion, Alphonse noted that his middle name was Tobias and that, like his biblical namesake, he had been guided and directed by an angel of the Lord to the right place at the right time.

St. Raphael is traditionally considered the special patron of travelers, the blind, happy meetings, nurses, physicians, pharmacists, medical workers, matchmakers, Christian marriage, and those seeking spouses. Since the Middle Ages, parents have entrusted their children who are traveling great distances for the first time to his care. We could well do so for students going off to college or those moving away from home for the first time.

The Angel of Fatima

The apparitions of the Blessed Virgin, Our Lady of the Holy Rosary, at Fatima in 1917 are not only one of the most important events in the Church in the twentieth century, but also one of the greatest *Mariophanies* in the life of the Church. Because of the spiritual movements that arose from these appearances, a tremendous wave of prayer, devotion, writings, and spiritual works of all kinds spread across the globe. Pope St. John Paul II was unquestionably "the Pope of Fatima," who believed that the personal and historic events of his reign—from his shooting to the fall of Communism in the Soviet Union and beyond—were inextricably linked to the messages of the Mother of God and the secrets she entrusted to the children she appeared to.

One of the secrets they kept, however, regards not the Virgin's words, but the appearances of the "Angel of Peace," who came to the children three times in the years before the Virgin's first appearance and who made a profound impression upon their minds and hearts. These apparitions offered a catechesis of grace and sacrifice that disposed Lucia, Jacinta, and Francisco to receive the coming of the Holy Virgin and her message with a depth of commitment and maturity that far exceeded their years or education.

Lucia did not speak about these appearances at all until 1924, and Sts. Jacinta and Francisco never did so at all before their deaths. Though Lucia confided in a priest about the angel's visits, she was advised not to speak about them, lest they confuse the importance of Our Lady's words. It was only in her 1937 memoir that she revealed their story in full.[91]

The first appearances took place in 1915, when Lucia and two other girls saw a white transparent figure appear in the sky at the *Cabeço* — a secluded hillside — not far from their homes. The figure was of natural height, but seemed like a brilliant snow-white statue made of cloud. Though they saw this figure on three occasions, they did not reveal the experience to anyone.

In the spring of 1916, Lucia and her two cousins, Jacinta and Francisco, were tending their sheep at the *Loca do Cabeço* and had just finished their shortened version of the Rosary. A figure approached them through the sky coming from the east — a transparent, luminous figure of a youth of perhaps fourteen or fifteen years. The children were amazed and overwhelmed by what Lucia would describe as the "supernatural atmosphere" that penetrated and surrounded them. As she recounts in her memoir, the angel spoke to them words of reassurance and authority:

"Do not be afraid! I am the Angel of Peace. Pray with me."

[91] All the references from Sister Lucia's memoirs are taken from *Fatima in Lucia's Own Words*, 16th ed. (Fatima, Portugal: Postulation Centre, 2007).

Kneeling on the ground, he bowed down until his fore-head reached the ground. Led by a supernatural impulse, we did the same, and repeated the words which we heard him say:

"My God, I believe, I adore, I hope and I love Thee! I ask pardon of Thee for those who do not believe, do not adore, do not hope and do not love Thee!"

Having repeated these words three times, he rose and said:

"Pray thus. The Hearts of Jesus and Mary are attentive to the voice of your supplications."

Then he disappeared.

The children remained with their heads bowed to the ground for some time, filled with this supernatural splendor. The prayer that they heard, now commonly called the Angel's Prayer, remained fixed in their minds; Lucia said they often knelt with their heads on the ground, repeating this prayer for long periods of time.

This first message has many rich graces for us to consider: The angel reveals himself as the "Angel of Peace" in the midst of the First World War, but the peace that he comes to bring is based in union with God and intercession for others. His words call us back to the greatest commandments of the Old Law: total and complete love of God and neighbor. The prayer he entrusts to them is brief, but it expresses both adoration and intercession in a posture of total reverence: kneeling and with forehead touching the ground. It is a gesture that the children understood and that they imitated constantly.

The second apparition took place in the summer, after the children had pastured their sheep in the morning. Then, in the heat of the afternoon while they were playing quietly in the shade by the well near Lucia's house, the angel appeared suddenly and said:

"What are you doing? Pray, pray very much! The Holy Hearts of Jesus and Mary have designs of mercy on you. Offer prayers and sacrifices constantly to the Most High."

Lucy asked: "How are we to make sacrifices?"

"Make of everything you can a sacrifice, and offer it to God as an act of reparation for the sins by which He is so offended, and in supplication for the conversion of sinners. You will thus draw down peace upon your country. I am its Angel Guardian, the Angel of Portugal. Above all, accept and bear with submission the suffering which the Lord will send you."

The angel's first words are abrupt and echo the Lord's voice to Elijah on Mount Horeb: "What are you doing, Elijah?" (see 1 Kings 19:9–13). Yet they are immediately followed by reassurance and strength. Once again, the angel speaks of the Hearts of Jesus and Mary, but this time he does not call them "attentive" to the children, but rather he says that Christ and His Mother have "plans of mercy" for them — a suggestion of an upcoming mission.

Then the angel speaks of sacrifices, both those voluntarily undertaken and those the Lord will send to the children. The sacrifices that they generously take upon themselves will serve as reparation for sins, contribute to the conversion of sinners, and bring about peace for the nation. These are weighty responsibilities to give to the three children. And the angel points out too that the greatest sacrifice of all is the sacrifice of our own will, through acceptance and willing submission to God's plan. These are words on which we must meditate, just as the children did. They cannot simply be *heard*; rather, we must *listen to them* with open and trusting hearts. Let us pray: "Jesus, I want what You want for me."

The angel also identifies himself specifically as the guardian angel of Portugal, hearkening back to St. Michael's role as prince and guardian of Israel in the book of Daniel. In premodern times, many nations, kingdoms, and cities celebrated their own "guardian angels." The Portuguese nation had celebrated a feast in honor of its guardian angel since 1514, though by the eighteenth century, it had fallen into disuse and the feast was suppressed under St. Pius X a few years before the apparitions took place. Some have suggested that the angel who appeared to the children was actually St. Michael, to whom Portugal had at one time been consecrated; others note in contrast that St. Michael has always announced himself by name in other apparitions, as he did to St. Joan of Arc. The question of the angel's identity has not been answered, nor will it ever be, it seems, this side of Heaven.

The third and final apparition of the angel is the most extraordinary of all, since it is focused on the mystery of the Holy Eucharist. While other saints and blesseds have received Holy Communion from the hands of an angel (St. Bonaventure, St. Stanislaus Kostka, St. Paschal Baylon, St. Mary Frances of the Five Wounds, Blessed Marguerite Bays, and others), the Communion of the children of Fatima would seem to have an added *ecclesial significance* in keeping with the importance of their whole mission:

> The third apparition must have taken place in October, or towards the end of September, as we were no longer returning for siesta.
>
> After our lunch, we decided to go and pray in the hollow among the rocks on the opposite side of the hill. To get there, we went around the slope, and had to climb over some rocks above the Pregueira (south of the Loca do Cabeço). The sheep could only scramble over these rocks with great difficulty. As soon as we arrived there, we knelt down with our foreheads touching the ground, and began to repeat the prayer of the Angel:

"My God, I believe, I adore, I hope and I love Thee ..."

I don't know how many times we repeated this prayer, when an extraordinary light shone upon us. We sprang up to see what was happening, and beheld the Angel. He was holding a chalice in his left hand, with the Host suspended above it, from which some drops of Blood fell into the chalice. Leaving the chalice suspended in the air, the Angel knelt down beside us and made us repeat three times:

"Most Holy Trinity, Father, Son and Holy Spirit, I offer Thee the most precious Body, Blood, Soul and Divinity of Jesus Christ, present in all the tabernacles of the world, in reparation for the sacrileges, outrages and indifferences by which He Himself is offended. And through the infinite merits of His Most Sacred Heart, and the Immaculate Heart of Mary, I beg of Thee the conversion of poor sinners."

Then, rising, he took the chalice and the Host in his hands. He gave the Sacred Host to me, and shared the Blood from the chalice between Jacinta and Francisco, saying as he did so:

"Take and drink the Body and Blood of Jesus Christ, horribly outraged by ungrateful men! Make reparation for their crimes and console your God."

Once again, he prostrated on the ground and repeated with us, three times more, the same prayer: "Most Holy Trinity ..." and then disappeared.

Moved by a supernatural force which enveloped us, we had imitated the Angel in everything; that is, we prostrated as he did and repeated the prayers that he said.... We remained a long time in this position, repeating the same words over and over again. It was Francisco who realized that it was getting dark, and drew our attention to the fact, and thought we should take our flocks back home. I felt that God was in me.

The Eucharistic prayer that the angel teaches the children is a magnificent summary of the Catholic Faith: It speaks to us first of the Trinity; then it summarizes, almost like a catechism, the definition of the Real Presence of Jesus in the Eucharist; then it moves us to offer Christ to the Father, accepting His Passion for our sake and uniting our will to His will as an act of expiation and reparation; and finally it turns us to the very core of His redeeming love, his Sacred Heart, always united to His Mother's pierced Heart for the salvation of sinners.[92]

The angel offers this prayer in preparation for the children's Communion and as the most fitting thanksgiving thereafter. We too can benefit greatly from this prayer, receiving it as a gift from Heaven and incorporating it into our own Eucharistic Communions.

The children see the Host bleeding into the chalice, a visual image that unites the two Species and links this extraordinary reception of the Eucharist to the Sacrifice of the Cross and its renewal upon the altar. Lucia has already received her First Holy Communion in the parish church of Fatima, so she is accustomed to the reception of Holy Communion. Francisco and Jacinta have not yet received their First Communion, but are communicated with the Precious Blood from the chalice. This first mystical union with Christ affected the children profoundly, leaving them in a state of joy, silence, and exhaustion.

In the third apparition, the presence of the Angel was still more intense. For several days, even Francisco did not dare to talk. He said later on: "I love to see the Angel, but the

---

[92] I recommend the marvelous study of Father William Wagner, ORC, *The Angel of Portugal at Fatima* (Carrolton, OH: Order of Canons Regular of the Holy Cross, 2016), for a fuller spiritual and theological analysis of the apparitions and their effects on the children's spiritual development.

trouble is that later on, we are incapable of doing anything. I could not even walk any more. I didn't know what was the matter!"

It was a grace so sublime, and so intimate, that Francisco, all absorbed in God, did not have a clear consciousness of the mystical grace that he had received and felt in a confused way. Once the first few days were over, and we had returned to normal, Francisco asked: "The Angel gave you Holy Communion, but what was it that he gave to Jacinta and me?" "It was Holy Communion, too," replied Jacinta, with inexpressible joy. "Didn't you see that it was the Blood that fell from the Host?" Francisco replied: "I felt that God was within me, but I did not know how!"

Though Francisco could not articulate his experience as clearly as the others, his words reflect the truth and beauty of what he felt, with all the candor and simplicity of a child. We know that he never heard the words of the angel—nor, later, the words of Our Lady—but rather he depended on Lucia and Jacinta to repeat them to him. But he did see the angel with the Host and the chalice, and he shared in the others' adoration and prayer; this was enough to prepare him for this moment of union with Christ the Savior.

Why did the two younger children receive their mystical First Communion from the chalice rather than with the Host? Perhaps this was because the chalice is a biblical image of suffering, both in the Old Testament and the New. Sharing in the Blood of Christ—drinking of His chalice—is a sign of willingness to undergo martyrdom for the sake of His Name. Jacinta and Francisco were both destined to die at a very early age, and both offered their sufferings consciously and courageously to the Lord, as the angel had taught them. Jacinta was drawn to reparation for sinners, while Francisco spent many hours of the day in their parish church, "consoling God."

Now, from their place in Heaven they have become evangeliz-ers, teaching us to do good with all our sufferings — and to do good toward those who suffer. The prayers they learned from the angel can be taught to the great and the small, the young and the old. In them we find a message from Heaven to each of us. Through such prayers and the generous offering of our own sacrifices, may we come to share in this life in the wonder, reverence, and joy that the children of Fatima experienced. And may we one day be their companions in Heaven!

Part 4

THE ANGELS AND YOU

Chapter 15

SPIRITUAL FORMATION
WITH THE ANGELS

✦

Christ is Lord of the angels. They are His servants, ministers of His truth and of His grace. They accompanied Him throughout His life on earth, adore Him in the unceasing Liturgy of Heaven, and remain enraptured by the mystery of His Eucharistic life that He shares with us. And so, if we want to have an authentic reverence and devotion to the angels, and if we want to collaborate with them in their work, we must always remember that Christ is at the center of our prayer and love—and the love and service of the angels.

With this in mind, we can look at five roles that the angels take on in their love and service for the Lord: messengers, stewards, warriors, guardians, and adorers.[93]

---

[93] The Church's tradition of these five roles can be found at the Opus Sanctorum Angelorum website.

Messengers

As we said earlier in this book, the word "angel" means "messenger." These pure spirits are sent from God to communicate to us His grace, His goodness, and His truth. They do this ordinarily through illuminations, inspirations, and intuitions that come to us in the course of our prayer and our daily lives. The angels bring messages from God because, first and foremost, they remain ever in His presence, contemplating His perfections. If we want to hear what the Lord is saying to us, we must practice the same contemplation by focusing our mind and our will on Him.

The Fathers of the Church wrote about the angels encircling God, contemplating and adoring Him. What do the angels see as they gaze on the Face of God? With their remarkable minds, so much superior to ours, they see with a special clarity the existence, the stability, the order, the truth, the beauty, and the love of God. They contemplate the Holy Trinity—Father, Son, and Holy Spirit—in His infinite perfections. In God the Father, they see the greatness of God Himself and His plan for creation and growth. In God the Son, the Word Made Flesh, they find the pattern for all creation, for through Him and by Him all things were created. In His Incarnation, they see the Truth of God come down to earth—the sign of hope for all mankind. In God the Holy Spirit, Who is the Love of the Father and Son personified, they find manifest the transforming power of perfect love. Stop and consider what each of these words mean, and remember that our human concepts pale before the perfections of Almighty God.

The angels receive graces from their contemplation and then communicate them to us according to God's plan. As they enlighten us in prayer, they receive our responses of praise and petition to God. And as they lift our prayers to God, they enhance and enrich them by joining their supplications to ours.

We know this from the pages of Scripture. Remember the words of Raphael from the book of Tobit:

> And so, when you and your daughter-in-law Sarah prayed, I brought a reminder of your prayer before the Holy One; and when you buried the dead, I was likewise present with you. When you did not hesitate to rise and leave your dinner in order to go and lay out the dead, your good deed was not hidden from me, but I was with you.... I am Raphael, one of the seven holy angels who present the prayers of the saints and enter into the presence of the glory of the Holy One. (12:12–13, 15)

In the book of Revelation, too, John sees angels holding bowls of incense, the smoke of which represents the prayers of the holy ones that rise to God (Rev. 8:3). Not only is the smoke of the incense a sign of worship, but it leaves behind a pleasing fragrance that signifies the transformation worked in the one who is praying. As the charcoal and the incense burn, they are consumed—consumed in divine service, just as our lives are lived out in the love and service of the Lord. The hotter the fire burns, the more fragrance is released; in the same way, the more ardently our love for Christ burns, the purer will be our acts of loving worship and spiritual service. That is why we pray at Vespers, "Let my prayer be counted as incense before Thee, and the lifting up of my hands as an evening sacrifice" (Ps. 141:2).

The sense of smell is also linked to the memory center of the brain; pleasing fragrances can help trigger memories and aid us, with the assistance of the angels, to link ideas and thoughts that help us to understand the ways of God in our lives. This is another reason why incense is used in the worship of so many different peoples. Thus, we are purified by our prayers, just as a pleasing fragrance drives away an unpleasant one. And we bear into the world the fragrance of Christ, in virtue of our Baptism, Confirmation, and, for the clergy, Ordination.[94]

In the Roman Canon, or First Eucharistic Prayer of the Mass, the priest prays that the Lord's angel may carry the sacrifice of the Church here on earth to His altar on high, so that as we in turn receive the Eucharistic Christ, we may be filled with every grace and blessing.

So the angels both deliver our prayers to the Lord and relay His messages to us. Stories of angels as deliverers of special messages from God are to be found throughout the lives of the saints. St. Michael spoke to Joan of Arc. The Angel of Peace appeared to the three children at Fatima. Padre Pio developed a special relationship with his guardian angel and with many other of God's ministering spirits. The angels joined their praise to that of St. Gertrude as she and her fellow nuns prayed the Divine Office. St. Margaret Mary Alacoque, the great mystic of the Sacred Heart, once saw a vision of the seraphim in the garden of the convent; she was going about her daily duties when she saw before her the trees filled with the angels, and the seraphim cried out to her and invited her to praise the Sacred Heart of Jesus with them. St. Gemma Galgani benefited from the teachings of her guardian angel, who revealed his presence to her frequently and helped her communicate with her spiritual directors.

Often when we are at prayer the angels inspire in us a deeper understanding of God's love and presence. When we enter a church and place ourselves before the Blessed Sacrament, the angels call us to inner silence and a fascinated and deep reverence for the Lord present in the Holy Eucharist. As we grow in our life of faith, they

---

[94] Chrism, consecrated oil infused with the perfume of balsam sap, is the material sacramental indication of this sealing and change. Its fragrance indicates the hidden beauty of Christ within our souls.

will also call us to a new reverence for those around us. The angels help us see the poor, the marginalized, and the outsider with the eyes of Jesus. We begin to see that the strangers around us are not as strange as we had first thought—or judged. They too are our sisters and brothers, children of the one Father, redeemed by the same Precious Blood.

We are part of the universal family of the Church. Christ is at work in every soul we meet or pass on the street. The angels help us to be aware of this truth and to be ready to cooperate in the salvation of others. At first this may seem daunting. Yet, throughout our day, when we speak to friends and strangers and colleagues and coworkers, we can call upon the holy angels so that they might enlighten us to say the right word—a word that will bring truth, a word that will bring comfort, a word that will express pardon.

Pope Pius XI and St. John XXIII recommended that we speak to the guardian angels of the people we meet in the course of a day. This was a practice that they developed in their early years in the Vatican diplomatic corps! What a marvelous idea! We priests can speak to the angels of the people who attend Mass and listen to our sermons so that these men and women might be open to the words of the Liturgy and take in what Christ wants them to receive. When priests are going to hear confessions, too, it is good for us to speak to the angels of all those who will come to our confessional— that they may experience an increase in contrition and that we may receive inspiration to say the right words in our roles as the instruments of God in the sacrament. Penitents can address their confessor's angel so that he might have clarity in understanding, compassion in speaking, and wisdom in guiding.

There are many ways in which we can imitate the angels as messengers. The Fathers of the Church believed that the higher angels had a role in enlightening those lower in the angelic hierarchies. In the life of the Church, the Holy Father has this role as he

confirms the college of bishops in their responsibilities as succes-
sors of the apostles. The bishops in turn act as messengers of God's
love and truth, particularly in their relationship with the priests
of their diocese. And priests in turn bring that enlightenment by
teaching authentic Christian doctrine and encouraging prayer and
right living among parishioners.[95] Parents, too, have the responsibility to be messengers of God's truth and love to their children.
Indeed, if we have influence over others as part of our vocation or
our profession, we cooperate with the angels whenever we inspire
goodness and truth and encourage others in the ways of holiness.

These angelic responsibilities remind us that the angels are not
just objects of our devotion. They are winds and flames, spiritual
messengers and warriors; but they are also elder brothers, fellow
servants of the Lord, companions, and teachers on our journey.
We may even call them friends, for if their Lord has given us that
intimate privilege with Himself, they too will joyfully enter into
that relationship with us. In addition, the angels help us in the
practical aspects of daily Christian life as we carry our cross and
help others to carry their crosses.

Stewards

The second responsibility of the angels is stewardship. The angels stand over all of creation. There is not one atom or particle
that is not somehow under their care. We use the word "stewardship," rather than "guardianship," because here we are not speaking about individual human beings who have guardian angels but

---

[95] This is not meant to be a full vision of ecclesiology, of course, but
only an image of the principle of subsidiarity that may help us to
understand how we can receive spiritual gifts from those who are
more advanced in the ways of God.

rather about the principles and forms of all creation. The holy angels carry the laws of God into creation. They bear these truths of His order, beauty, and creative love into the material world so that the material world might reflect these divine perfections. We tend to forget these dimensions of the angelic life, and consider these spirits primarily in their relations with us. But this reduces the wonderful scope of their missions, which are not only personal but cosmic.

Blessed John Henry Newman, in his *Apologia pro Vita Sua*, recalled the deep and reverent awareness that he had of the angels, even during his Anglican years. In a sermon written for St. Michael's Day (Michaelmas) in the early 1830s, he said:

> I say of the Angels, "Every breath of air and ray of light and heat, every beautiful prospect, is, as it were, the skirts of their garments, the waving of the robes of those whose faces see God." Again, I ask what would be the thoughts of a man who, "when examining a flower, or a herb, or a pebble, or a ray of light, which he treats as something so beneath him in the scale of existence, suddenly discovered that he was in the presence of some powerful being who was hidden behind the visible things he was inspecting, who, though concealing his wise hand, was giving them their beauty, grace, and perfection, as being God's instrument for the purpose, nay, whose robe and ornaments those objects were, which he was so eager to analyze?" and I therefore remark that "we may say with grateful and simple hearts with the Three Holy Children, 'O all ye works of the Lord, &c., &c., bless ye the Lord, praise Him, and magnify Him for ever.'"[96]

---

[96] John Henry Newman, Sermon on St. Michael's Day, 1831, quoted by him in *Apologia Pro Vita Sua* (London: Penguin, 2004), p. 45.

Part of this task of stewardship has long been seen as defending the material universe — that is, preserving the laws that govern science and reality. The angels do battle against the evil spirits who cannot attend God directly but who vent their anger and frustration at His creative plan by exploiting the weaknesses of creation and attacking human persons, for our material world bears in itself what theologians call the *vestigia Dei*, usually translated as "the footprints of God." At the summit of this creation stands man — men and women, material and spiritual, created in His image and likeness and called to transformation and divinization (*theosis*) by the grace of Christ Jesus our Savior. The holy angels will maintain their stewardship over all creation until the time when the new Heavens and the new earth will come among us. As we read in the book of Revelation, this, too, is part of God's plan. We imitate the stewardship of the holy angels by preserving the gifts of God to ourselves and others. First, these are the spiritual gifts of sanctifying grace. We must guard and cultivate our spiritual life through diligent prayer, the reverent reception of the sacraments, and the practice of charity and all the other virtues. We especially need to pray for all those around us who have a mission from God on our behalf. We need to pray for our Holy Father that he may have strength and health and joy in preaching the Gospel and in being the sign of unity for the whole Church. We need to pray for our pastors in their mission; we need to pray for parents; we need to pray for teachers; we need to pray for all those who have spiritual responsibilities so that they might practice virtue and use the gifts of God as He intends — for the good of those in their charge.

We should also pray for our friends, who have a very powerful influence upon us (and we upon them), so that the goodness that first attracted us to friendship may always grow and increase. This is a sign of gratitude for these human relationships and an expression of our desire for our friends' holiness and salvation. In fact, it is also very good spiritual practice to pray for past friends and others whom God has placed upon our path even for a short time. We can thank God for having created them and for sending them into our lives, praying a Glory Be for each of them. If they are still living, our prayer may avail them to greater grace; if deceased, our prayer contributes to their final purification. In either case, we are spiritually catching up in the net of our memory the souls whom Jesus wants to bring to everlasting life. And we may well be cooperating with the angels, who often bring such unexpected memories into our minds and hearts.

Gratitude for such blessings and persons not only makes us more aware of Our Lord's providence in our lives, but acts as a great defense and remedy against sadness, depression, and many kinds of temptation.

There are temporal gifts, too, of which we must be stewards if we are to be faithful to God. We have to be stewards of our physical and mental health, and we need to share our material blessings with others, especially the needy, which is our duty in justice. Generosity to those in need, called "almsgiving" in times past, has always been an expression of spiritual conversion and union with Christ. To see with His eyes means to see the needs of those around us. To love with His Heart means that we are compelled interiorly to do what we can and to share what we have. Certainly the angels desire such Christlike love from us. Care of the material world and of the environment itself is an important aspect of how we practice the stewardship of the angels in our daily life. Pope Francis has certainly taught this wisely in his encyclical letter *Laudato Si.*

Warriors

Throughout Scripture we find the angels defending us against evil and supporting the plans and purposes of God. They are the protectors of

Israel, both ancient Israel and the New Israel of the Church, formed through Christ's saving action.

Angelic warfare is not carried out with weapons. The tradition of the Church is that the warfare of the angels—both the warfare at the trial of the angels at the beginning of time and their day-to-day warfare on our behalf—is carried out with virtue—that is, their power of spirit. The archangel Michael, who is venerated as the head of all of Heaven's armies, derives his name from the Hebraic phrase he cries out, "Who is like unto God?" Those words, shouted at Satan and his supporters, are a cry of humility, the humility of one who places all his trust and his allegiance in God and Him alone. It is by his humility and his trust in God that he vanquishes Lucifer, who has been cast down from Heaven.

In the same way today, the angels by their holiness seek to defend us against the attacks of the Evil One. Why does the Evil One tempt us? Why is Satan interested in us? It is because Almighty God has created us with such an important place in His plan and because the Lord of Heaven and earth has come down to us as man. Jesus shared the flesh of Mary so that we might be transformed—raised to Heaven and divinized to share the vision of the Father, Son, and Holy Spirit that will fill us with joy for everlasting life.

The jealousy of the fallen angels causes them to attack the image and likeness of God in us, in order to show God that He made a mistake in creating us. But the love of God strengthens us. His Son has united Himself to us, sharing our human nature and life. The words of Christ reveal truth to us. The Cross of Christ heals us. The victory of Christ at Easter assures us that victory will also be ours if we remain faithful to God, a fidelity that expresses itself in humility of heart and in charity—love of God and love of neighbor.

When we respond to the Lord and practice our love in obedience, we experience the help and the defense of the holy angels.

Our angels impress upon us God's graces and stir up our memories of His blessings, His protection, and the example of His saints. They give light to our intellect, which clarifies our thinking and shows us the way to fulfill God's holy will. To our wills, the angels bring strength and determination so that we might accomplish what God asks of us in our daily life. We learn to accept and to love the Cross of Jesus in the crosses of daily life. And to our souls, the holy angels bring encouragement and refreshment, consolation so that we might persevere in doing what is good and right and just. We begin to see with the eyes of faith and to experience even here on earth the wisdom and beauty of God's plan.

The evil spirits, on the other hand, bring to us very different "gifts." To the intellect, they bring darkness and confusion. In fact, theologians say that the first punishment of sin is spiritual darkness, even spiritual blindness. We lose the ability to see what is good and true, and to discern good from evil. We can see this in the lives of many who have turned away from the Church because the Devil insinuated in them darkness and confusion that compounded their own weakness. They become bitter and cynical about all things spiritual.

We have hope and trust that by God's grace the fallen-away can come back. And so we make atonement and reparation for the sins of those who have turned away so that they might find that enlightenment once more — so that weakness and hesitancy in their wills might be replaced by strength and tenacity in doing God's will. We remain strong and persevering in our prayer because we are convinced that Our Lord loves them even more than we do. We pray, too, that Satan's sadness — the despair that fills the hearts of those who wander in darkness and sin — might once again be replaced by the peace of Heavenly grace. The witness of our own inner peace and trust in Our Lord has a powerful role in this.

HIS ANGELS AT OUR SIDE

The angels had only one battle in which they had to overcome selfishness. What they accomplished for their eternal beatitude in one moment takes us a lifetime of seemingly countless struggles. But our struggles bring victory when we realize that in God's plan of love we can turn back to Him when we falter. He goes in search of us, like the Good Shepherd seeking the lost and wandering sheep. The Lord calls us home; through the sacrament of Reconciliation we can once more find the grace of God and that new life of Christ.

We will understand the wonders of God's mercy only when we enter into Heaven and become part of the Communion of the Saints. I am sure that when we get there, we will be very surprised by many of the souls whom we see, battle-scarred by the healed wounds of their sins, and glorious in their victory. But, as I often remind my parishioners, the wonderful thing about Heaven is that everyone is so well-mannered and polite that they won't show that they're surprised to see us!

The power of the holy angels to enter into the fray of our struggles on our behalf is very great indeed. But we need *to call upon them* so that we might have this assistance, so that we might grow strong with their aid.

In order to imitate the warrior nature of the angels, we first need to maintain spiritual good health. First, of course, we have to turn away from mortal sin. But we also have to learn to overcome habits of venial sin that weaken us, slowing down our advance in grace and cooling the fire of charity within us. When we grow in grace in this way, we also advance in discipline of the mind and body. This training happens as we grow in the knowledge of God and in the teachings of the Faith, acquiring virtues through obedience to God's commands and identification with the mind of the Church. As part of this process, the angels lead us to a deeper sense of the spiritual life through spiritual reading and meditation, the practice of prayer, and pondering the teachings of the Holy Fathers and the saints.

The sacrament of Reconciliation has a very powerful role to play in our lives, one that many Catholics seem to have forgotten. In Confession, we go to the foot of the Cross, drawing near to the wounded body of Christ. In gazing up at Him, we realize how much He truly loves us, and that we are suffering ourselves from the wounds of our own sins and the fever of our own disordered desires. The practice of frequent Confession has been replaced by a twice-a-year habit for many "good Catholics." But a Catholic who is receiving Communion every Sunday — let alone a daily Massgoer — should try to receive absolution much more regularly. A good habit of monthly Confession will soon lead to an even better habit of Confession — every two weeks, or even weekly. The less often we go to Confession, the less we have to say, because we become desensitized to our sins and temptations, and blind to our concessions and compromises in thought, intention, and deed. The first punishment of sin is spiritual blindness, and the darkness increases when we stay away from Jesus' forgiving grace.

In confessing our sins, it is good to declare any frequent or particular temptations that we are wrestling with, even if we have not given in to them; temptations frequently bind us with shame and embarrassment. Declaring them briefly to a priest shatters their "hold" over us; that is why experienced confessors will sometimes tell us, "A temptation confessed is already half-conquered."

When we confess our sins simply, trustingly, and sincerely, we not only experience Christ's forgiveness, but we also receive special grace against the particular sins that attract us and cause our falls. Our contrition joined to a strong desire for amendment may also bring us to a deeper level of love for God than we had before we fell. Asking the angels, particularly our guardian angels, to help us with our examination of conscience can be very useful.

They assist us to see ourselves honestly and objectively, but at the same time they help us to see ourselves *in the Heart of Jesus, as His beloved, for whom He has given everything.* In this way, we are not overwhelmed or discouraged by our sins, but rather are drawn to His mercy.

Oftentimes, we end up repeating the same sins over and over again to our confessors, which is not at all surprising. We incline toward certain sins and patterns of selfishness, each according to our own particular disposition and history. Certain sins and temptations will probably be part of our struggle right up to the final confession we make. We need to remember the advice St. Teresa of Avila gave to one of her young nuns: "Don't let those sins of yours turn into bad habits!" In other words, do not let them become routine or ordinary. Never use the excuse "That's just me" or "I have a weak temperament."

Struggle. Pray. If you fall, do penance and confess. Reboot and repeat as needed. Be serious about every confession you make, and be sincere in your purpose of amendment. Ask your confessor for advice and follow through with it. When you have found a good confessor, keep seeing him—even if you have to drive an hour to get to him. (Consider that a part of your penance!) Bad habits can be broken; dependencies can be overcome; and "crutches" can be thrown away. Great sinners make great saints. *Your misery can never outweigh Christ's mercy.* That sentence is the most important thing you can read on this page.

And your guardian angel loves a challenge.

When we leave the confessional and as we begin to pray the prayers of our penance, our first thoughts should be of gratitude and joy. Our penances are not punishment, but rather thanksgiving. Our restitutions are acts of justice and expiation that purify. After Confession, we should look up at the tabernacle and the Crucified Lord, and smile. We are at peace with Him. We can address God again as "Our Father"; we can speak to Our Lady with a pure heart; we have made the angels rejoice. And the demons are literally as mad as Hell.

When you leave the church, I suggest that you immediately do something kind, charitable, and selfless, or make an act of atonement that is above and beyond your penance, even if your confession had nothing particularly intense about it. Make such an act of your own free will as a generous and spontaneous expression of your purpose of amendment—your desire to live a more Christlike life. It does not have to be a heroic act—you will know when such a thing is required—but it should be motivated by love of God and love of neighbor, to "seal" the grace of your confession and to let the priest's absolution bear fruit. Make another such act the next day and the next.

Thinking and acting like this, advancing step by step on the way, we receive help and grace from the most important weapons that God gives to us—the sacraments, especially Confession and Holy Communion. This is how we overcome selfishness, sin, and pride. This is how we stand by the side of the prince of the angelic armies and call out in our own voice, "God is God. Who is like unto God?"

Each time we receive Our Lord in Holy Communion, we have within us the Divine Trinity. The one true God sanctifies us, transforms us, and changes us. Little by little, His Heart becomes our heart; the fire of His love enkindles our own, burning away whatever is impure and singeing us with the fire of repentance and new life. Theologians and spiritual authors remind us that if we do not put up impediments to God's grace, we really do advance and progress in the spiritual life from one Mass and Communion to the next. St. Anthony Mary Claret, archbishop of Havana and founder of the Missionaries of the Immaculate Heart of Mary (the Claretian Fathers), experienced a mystical grace by which he believed that he miraculously retained within himself the Eucharistic Species from one Communion to the next, and so he lived in an ever-deepening union with Jesus.

Jesus seeks living hearts. He wants to dwell within us in a dynamic, living way; acting in and through us, transforming us more and more every day. That is why some of the saints have said that they spent half their day in thanksgiving for having received Holy Communion and the other half in preparation for the next day's Communion. They wanted to live a continually and constantly Eucharistic life.

We may not always perceive this growth — and there's a good reason for this. A runner who keeps looking over his shoulder to see where he is in relation to others will soon lose his stride. The mountain climber can look down only when she has arrived at a safe resting place. A soldier does not stop in the midst of battle to admire his progress. If we were to see our success clearly all the time, it would be very easy for us to succumb to the sin of pride and to misjudge how far we still have to go. And so the Lord may allow us to perceive our own progress only dimly precisely so that we can progress all the more; then at the right time, in God's time, He will reveal to us just how much we have grown in the spiritual life and increased our love for Him and for our neighbor. Our guardian angel knows this as he journeys by our side and will offer us the encouragement we require.

Our model in this is always our Blessed Lady, who, by her humility, crushes the head of Satan. Through her wholehearted trust in God's plan and in His love, Mary advances the Kingdom in a most remarkable way in each one of us. She always kept her eyes on her Son, which allowed her to notice the needs of all whom He loved — just as she noticed the lack of wine at the wedding feast of Cana before anyone else. Now, from her place in Heaven, she sees all our needs even before we do. When we turn to the Blessed

Mother in our prayers, we find in her a teacher, a defender against evil, and a mother whose arms and heart are always open to us. The angels who are the Virgin's servants rush to our side when we remain at her side.

A wonderful example of this care may be found in a prayer that comes down to us from Blessed Louis-Edouard Cestac (1801–1868), a great apostle among the poor and the cofounder, with his sister, of the Congregation of Servants of Mary. Though he spoke of the prayer's origin as if it were given to some pious person he knew, it was determined in the course of his beatification that he had been the favored soul to whom it had been entrusted. On January 13, 1864, Father Cestac was suddenly struck with what he called "a ray of divine clarity." He saw demons spread out over the earth, ravaging God's people and creation. At the same time, he turned in spirit toward the Holy Virgin. Our Lady told him that the time had come to invoke her as Queen of the Angels and to ask Her to send the holy legions to combat and to overthrow the powers of Hell.

"My Mother," the priest asked, "you who are so good, could you not send them without our having to ask?" "No," replied the Holy Virgin. "Prayer is a condition set by God Himself in order to obtain graces." "Well then! My Mother," he replied, "would you teach me yourself how we must pray to you?" And he received from the most Holy Virgin the prayer August Queen:

August Queen of the Heavens, heavenly sovereign of the angels, thou who from the beginning received from God the power and the mission to crush the head of Satan, we humbly beseech thee to send your holy legions, so that under thy command and through thy power, they may pursue the demons and combat them everywhere, suppress their boldness, and drive them back into the abyss.

Who is like God? O good and tender Mother, thou will always be our love and hope! O divine Mother, send thy holy angels to defend me and to drive far away from me the cruel enemy. Holy angels and archangels, defend us, guard us. Amen.

This prayer has been translated into many languages and was circulated for almost a hundred years. Then it seemed to fall into disuse. It would be very helpful for us to use it frequently, even daily.

Guardians for Our Journey to Paradise

The role of the guardian angel begins with conception and continues to our death. The angel is our faithful companion; even if we fall into serious sin, the angel does not leave us, but continues to try to inspire us to turn back to God. He may do this interiorly by speaking to our heart, or he may do this through the assistance of other people and the circumstances of our lives, especially if we've become hardened to inspiration.

The angels never give up. And so their care is a model for us of the love that *we* should show to those who have fallen away from the Faith, given up the practice of the sacraments, or otherwise turned away from God. Angels are completely faithful, and so they inspire us to be faithful, too. In his famous poetic meditation "The Dream of Gerontius," Blessed Cardinal John Henry Newman, who had a lifelong fascination with and devotion to the angels, attributes these words to an angel who had just completed his mission as guardian:

How should ethereal natures comprehend
A thing made up of spirit and of clay,
Were we not task'd to nurse it and to tend,
Link'd one to one throughout its mortal day,

More than the Seraph in his height of place,
The Angel-guardian knows and loves the ransom'd race.[97]

Our guardian angels' duties and responsibilities encompass all
the aspects of human life — our spiritual lives, our temporal lives,
our physical and mental well-being — as well as all the other souls
with whom we relate on a regular basis. It is believed that the
guardian angels receive graces from the higher choirs of angels so
that they might shed light on us, give us strength from God, and
increase faith, hope, and charity in our hearts — in short, so that
from the depths of our souls we can respond to God with total
confidence and love in daily life.

Our response to the angels' guardianship is threefold. First,
we have to be *interiorly silent* in order to hear them. As we have
discussed earlier, in our world where there is so much noise, so
many voices clamoring for our attention and our allegiance, that
we have to learn to discern the voice of God and the voice of the
angel who encourages us. When we practice this interior silence,
then we can *listen*. We can listen to the words the angel speaks
and so *obey* his commands. *Silence, listening, obedience:* This is how
we honor and cooperate with the angels so that we can engage in
the mission of the Church.

St. Bernard of Clairvaux and St. Aloysius Gonzaga wrote about
the importance of reverence, honor, and trust in our relationship
with the angels. In other words, we are called to an intimate life
of friendship with the holy angels — particularly with our guardian
angels, who are with us always. Our angels' whole desire is to see
in us the presence of Christ — the beauties and the perfections
of God Made Man. Friends want what is best for each other. Our
angels want us to be totally transformed in Christ.

[97] John Henry Newman, "The Dream of Gerontius" in *Prayers, Verses, and Devotions* (San Francisco: Ignatius Press, 1989), p. 701.

When we pray to the angels, we must remember that the most important things we can ask for are faith and love. These are prayers that God always answers. He wants our faith to grow. So every day we should pray very simply, "Lord, I believe. Increase my faith." And we can pray for an increase of love for God and neighbor. "Lord, I love You. Show me how to love You more. I want to love You in deeds and not just in words. I want to love You in the mystery of Your Cross and in all the crosses of daily life. Strip away all my selfishness and hardness of heart. Open my heart to You and all whom You love."

When we stop to think about it, everything else is secondary and negotiable. The circumstances of our lives may be very favorable, or the cross may loom large in our eyes and weigh upon our hearts. But if we have faith in God, if we have love for God and for our neighbor, if we accept the will of God in our daily life, then everything is made easy for us. Everything becomes possible. And so to ask our angels to pray with us for these gifts is the most important thing of all.

The angels live out their guardianship in so many ways. In my life as a priest, I've witnessed on many occasions real evidence of the presence of the holy angels, especially when caring for the sick and the dying as a hospital chaplain. I was once attending to a man who was not a Catholic but whose first wife had always been very serious about the Faith; even after their marriage came to an end, she never stopped praying for her husband. He had promised her that he would be baptized before he died, which she never forgot. Her life was difficult after he left her, but she persevered in her trust in God as she raised her children with her own deep faith.

When her husband developed cancer, his second companion left him and he was alone. But his faithful wife came to his side and watched over him in the hospital, even bringing their now-adult children to be reconciled with him. She did all in her power to bring comfort to his last days and to encourage him to a better relationship with God. But still he refused Baptism. I went to visit him regularly, but I had no success either. But she said to me, "Father, I'm praying to his guardian angel and to my guardian angel. I'm sure he will be baptized."

One Sunday morning I stopped, by chance, to visit the man. I asked once more, "Will you be baptized and accept the grace of Christ? You know that the Lord has been calling for you all these years, and you've seen the evidence of His love in the faithfulness and devotion of your good wife." The man answered, "Yes. Father, I know what I've done; I know how I've lived. I'm sorry for everything, and I ask the Lord's forgiveness. I want to be baptized."

I began to prepare the oils and the holy water for Baptism. But as I was about to begin the ritual, unmistakably I heard a voice within my mind that said, "*NOW!*" And so without any further delay I took the water in a small medicine cup, poured it on the man's forehead saying the words, "I baptize you in the name of the Father and of the Son and of the Holy Spirit." And before I could say "Amen," he died. There was no distress; he simply closed his eyes and was gone. He had gone home to God. His nurses and his family were amazed by this, but what I remember most is the look in his wife's eyes. With his last breath he had accepted the grace that his wife had implored for him for so many years. Her faith and goodness, fire-tried by years of suffering, had grown so strong that it broke down all his interior resistance and called down the infinite love of God Made Man.

Over and over again in caring for the dying and speaking to them about Heaven, I have experienced how the mention of the angels brought consolation and peace, even to those who had been far away from the Church. In many cases, the holy angels have remained fixed in their minds and hearts—a figure first known in childhood, a devotion learned at their mothers' knee, present in their lives as protectors even when they were far from God. But it was clear from conversations I had with those suffering men and women that the angels were always directing them back to the Lord and to the sacraments—back to the life of grace.

It's very important for us to pray for those who are sick and dying, that their guardian angels might be given the power, strength, and grace to enlighten these suffering souls and to bring them to Christ. Sometimes, the angels seem to prod the memory, bringing back into mind the faith and goodness of family members or friends long forgotten, which still touches a dying person's heart. Sometimes, it is the memory of an occasion when a sick person was saved from danger or embarrassment in an inexplicable manner. The reflections brought on by illness allow a person to consider God's presence in those life-changing moments.

In other cases, the words of a (human) friend or a gesture of kindness seem to be endowed with a significance that even a dying person cannot explain. "Why is she so good to me?" "Why does he care so much?" "If that man believes in God and his kindness is a reflection of his faith, perhaps I can believe too?" In these cases, sometimes the faith of one friend provides the bridge that brings the soul to God. Experience has taught me that when that begins to happen, I should invoke the angels to form a bridge of their own, strengthening the faith and witness of religious friends and family members so that by believing in their goodness, a dying patient can be prepared by actual graces to desire and to receive the grace of supernatural faith. I ask the friends to do the same thing, and especially to beg the angels to help them say the right words at the right time.

St. Philip Neri once told St. Camillus de Lellis, founder of the nursing order of Ministers of the Sick, that he had seen angels prompting the "right words" spoken by Camillan priests at the bedsides of the dying. The angels endowed the priests' words with a special gentleness and wisdom. Likewise, the angels can help the sick and the dying to find in Our Lord's sufferings meaning and significance for their own pain, leading them to grow in grace and love so that they might enter Heaven rejoicing with the companionship of the very angels who had been their lifelong protectors.

In our world today, more than ever, we need to trust in God's plan for us right to the end. In so many places, the push for euthanasia and physician-assisted suicide, increasingly called "Medical Assistance in Dying," has deceived many people into believing that a "good death" is one that we control, choose, and create according to our will, not God's will.

But this is not a death like Christ's, who went to the Cross in obedience to His Father's will; Christ offered His life in atonement for our sins. Our own death, however it may come to each of us, has that same dimension of atonement to it. That is why the saints and pious souls prepare themselves for death by accepting in advance whatever form of death may come, knowing that it is only a passage to eternal life.

Our angels are by our side in order to help us to accept the separations that are part of dying and to complete the spiritual and personal tasks that are part of making our dying an example and a final testimony of love for our family and friends. They assist in preparing us to receive the sacraments with the greatest possible effect and to lift away obstacles to our exchanging with those closest to us the final signs of love that transcend words.

Every year on October 2, the feast of the guardian angels, I offer a Mass asking that the guardian angels of all my parishioners might be strengthened in their charge so that minds and hearts might be open to God's love. And in speaking especially to doctors, nurses, and those who care for sick loved ones at home, I always remind them of the presence of the angels. St. John of God, another great founder of a nursing community, often saw the angels come to the aid of sick poor people, working by the side of his Brothers and providing truly practical assistance. One day, the archangel Raphael, in the form of a young man, appeared with a large basket of freshly baked bread in his arms to feed the hungry patients. St. John then heard the archangel say to him, "My brother, we form one single Order together, because these are men who, clothed in poor garb, are equal to the angels." If all Catholic health-care professionals would only realize this, the Church's mission to the sick would be immeasurably strengthened; and if all the family members and friends who are quietly, generously, and sacrificially caring for loved ones at home knew this, how encouraged and renewed they would be!

We can call upon the angels to bring their peace and serenity into situations of sorrow and pain very simply by praying the Holy, Holy, Holy of the Mass. As we pray that prayer, we ask the angels to fill us with the praise of God. Imagine the universe filled with angels, the stewards of the cosmos, and think of them shouting from one star to another, "Holy! holy! holy! is the Lord God of hosts." "Hosts," after all, is our translation of the Latin *sabaoth*, which refers to angelic armies. So when we pray the Sanctus, we are invoking battalions of angels.

This beautiful prayer of the Mass continues, echoing the joy-filled shouts of the crowds when Jesus entered Jerusalem on Palm Sunday: "Blessed is he who comes in the name of the Lord." (Mt. 21:9) If we stop to ponder those words, we realize that in our lives the angels bear the name of the Lord to us so that, in turn, you and I might bring the name, presence, and power of Jesus into the lives of others. We are truly blessed because we have been given this mission as Catholics to go forth in the name of the Lord, to cooperate with Him in the work of salvation, and to stand by the side of the angels accomplishing the will of God, building up the Church and bearing to others the graces that Jesus has won for us by His passion and death.

Adorers

Prayer with the angels leads us to a deeper spirit of adoration. And adoration, as we have said, is the angels' primary duty. Every angel adores the Lord from the very depths of his being.

The essence of the angels' happiness consists of four things: *seeing God* face to face, *loving Him* with the very love that He has for Himself, *possessing Him* in the joy of this love, and *participating in God's life* for eternity. But the marvel is that not only do the angels possess these four perfections of happiness, but these same perfections are meant for you and me. This will be the life of Heaven for each one of us. When we go to Heaven, faith will be replaced by sight; hope will be replaced by possession; and charity, the love with which God loves Himself, will be shared with us and continue to increase in us without end for all eternity.

The life we will have in Paradise is beyond all words. That's why descriptions of Heaven often speak in terms that may seem strange and even childlike to us — streets paved with gold, angels in long white robes, and so forth. How can we express the beauty, purity, and power of the presence of God — the order, the harmony, the delight that will be ours when we see the Lord face to face, adoring Him without end in the company of the angels and saints? We cannot. If the streets are paved with gold, our eyes must be dazzled when we try to raise them higher.

We begin this life of the blessed here on earth by our worship of the Triune God, and especially through personal adoration of Jesus in the Most Blessed Sacrament, an adoration that fills our hearts with delight. Adoring Jesus exposed in the monstrance is our "face time" with the Lord; we gaze upon Him and He gazes back at us. The time that we spend with the Lord, particularly in His Eucharistic presence, is a time that actually makes us more like Christ, since the final model of our adoration is always Jesus Himself, who is the Adorer of His Father in spirit and in truth.

In nineteenth-century France, Blessed Marie of Jesus Deluil-Martiny founded a community of cloistered sisters, the Daughters of the Heart of Jesus, dedicated to adoration of the Blessed Sacrament. The sisters have a truly remarkable religious life. Each day they pray for priests celebrating Mass around the world, uniting themselves to every offering of the Holy Sacrifice. They stand spiritually with the Blessed Mother as she stood at Calvary, accepting and lifting up the Eternal Son's offering. They pray the Seven Last Words of Jesus on the Cross seven times a day and offer to the Eternal Father the blood and water that poured forth from His pierced side as the "Most Precious Offering" that they or we can make. And they chant the Magnificat three times each day, uniting their thanksgiving to that of the whole Church, in union with the angels on high.

Before founding this community, Marie of Jesus had several experiences in prayer in which the Lord inspired her to undertake such a task. On one occasion, she heard Jesus said to her, "Do you know what it really is to adore? I AM the one who truly adores. I adore My Father in Spirit and in truth. I AM Sovereign Beauty." Remembering these words and pondering their meaning reminds us that all the prayers and worship of the Church are offered to the Trinity by means of the Son, "through Our Lord Jesus Christ," Who is the Mediator between heaven and earth. Our prayer is itself His gift.

So when we make a Holy Hour before the Blessed Sacrament, we might well begin with an Act of Humility or an Act of Contrition—some act of truthful and trustful submission to God, which also expresses our wonder and awe. When we ask for His help in this way, we become aware of our total dependence on Him. And so our prayer becomes the rich and beautiful expression of a soul united to the Creator, the Redeemer, the Sanctifier—the Most Holy Trinity.

The angels' adoration is the most perfect expression of their union with God. They are overflowing with delight in God as they contemplate His infinite love. As they walk by our side as guardian angels, their whole desire is to communicate the beauty of their praise to us, if we are open to them. Father Mark Daniel Kirby, OSB, expresses something of this "delighted praise" in a meditation about our angelic companion:

> His greatest joy — perhaps you have already guessed it — is when he accompanies me to the altar to offer the Holy Sacrifice. There he becomes absolutely radiant. He stands, like a deacon, at my side. He is completely at home in the liturgy of the Church, and he knows it inside out. He sings with understanding, he bows profoundly, he teaches me how I am to conduct myself in the presence of the Thrice Holy God.
>
> At the moment of the Consecration, he becomes all luminous: beautiful with an indescribable beauty. I feel him trembling with joy next to me. And then he becomes utterly silent; he becomes like a flame of adoration. At this moment he is never alone. All his confrères arrive and sometimes, just sometimes, one feels, but ever so slightly, the hushed movement of wings of light. They arrive, all of them together, to surround the altar and then, they adore, they adore, they adore.
>
> For him Mass is never too long. Holy Mass is what he loves most on this earth of ours: Holy Mass, and then adoration of the Blessed Sacrament. He is always directing me towards the tabernacle.[98]

---

[98] "My Friend," Vultus Christi, http://vultuschristi.org/index.php/2017/10/my-friend/.

If we are called to adoration in imitation of Jesus, we must re-member that the Christ who *answered freely* will give us the grace to do so as well. The Savior answered His Father's call, giving Himself totally, with His will, His intellect, and His body. He offered them "for us and for our salvation," and continues to renew that offer-ing at the altar each day. His complete and total gift calls forth a total self-giving in return. That is also the kind of adoration we practice. Our adoration of God must be a free act, an act of free and generous love. It must also become an ever more complete action, involving all that we are.

To our adoration we bring our *mind* or *intellect* so that we can ponder the truths of Jesus and the mysteries of our Faith, enrich-ing our soul with heavenly light. We bring to our adoration our *free will* so that we may make sincere acts of hope and of love. We put all our trust in the Lord and in His power to sanctify and to save us, keeping in our *memory* His many deeds of mercy and love.

And we bring to our adoration our body as well, because we are human persons, not angelic ones. Our body, too, expresses our adoration as we kneel, fold our hands, and bow our heads or cross ourselves. These are all physical expressions of our total surrender to the Lord as we say to Him:

> Here I am Lord. I come to do Your will. I come to adore
> You in the Most Blessed Sacrament. I come to discover the
> will of Your Father for me. Make me silent within, so that
> I may hear you and obey Your word. Send me, Lord. Make
> me ready to fulfill Your mission and in ways great and small.
> Teach me to love You today.

The Angel of Peace who appeared to the children of Fatima knelt and then prostrated himself as he adored the Blessed Sac-rament during the second apparition. Many people imitate that gesture when they repeat the words of that prayer, not only in adoration but also in expiation for the many sins of irreverence and sacrilege committed against the Blessed Sacrament. It is a gesture of humility in the face of Mystery, just as the Magi prostrated themselves in adoration before they offered the Christ Child their gifts (Matt. 2:11).

When the burdens of age and illness have taken away not just our health and strength, but even the ability to care for ourselves without assistance, we still have the gift of our free will to accept our own brokenness and to offer it with the broken body of Christ Crucified to our Heavenly Father. We can adore Him from the depths of our own distinctly human poverty, that of illness and age—the one poverty in which every human person comes to share—and offer ourselves in all our interior freedom to Him. That is a spiritual privilege in which even the angels cannot share.

AFTERWORD

——————— ✤ ———————

In concluding this book of meditations about the angels, I would like to offer you a final thought from my friend, Father Mark Daniel Kirby, OSB:

> One thing is certain. We need the angels. God created the angels for the praise of His glory and for our salvation; that is, to participate in His work of bringing us to wholeness, to peace, and to life everlasting in His presence. The angels are sent to us to comfort us in the hour of trial and affliction. Saint Luke, the evangelist most sensitive to angelic interventions, relates that an angel was sent to console Jesus during His agony in the Garden (Luke 22:43).
>
> The angels are sent to bring us the healing of heavenly medicine, and the brightness of God's deifying light. The angels are sent before every advent of the Word, to dispose our hearts and unstop our ears. The angels are sent before Christ, our Priest and our Victim, present in the offering of His Body and of His Blood. The angels are sent to bear our prayers up to heaven and to descend to us, laden with

heavenly blessings. The angels protect us in all our ways. They do all of these things gladly, joyfully, and unhesitatingly in obedience to the command of God.

We cannot do without the holy angels. We need the comfort of their presence, the healing ministry of their hands and the beauty of the praise that ceaselessly they offer to God.[99]

May your reverent love and friendship with the holy angels draw you into an ever-deeper, loving union with God the Holy Trinity and Mary Our Immaculate Mother and Mediatrix!

[99] Dom Mark Daniel Kirby, OSB. "Quis resistet Sancti Michaelis gladio?" Thursday, September 29, 2016. Retrieved from: http://vultuschristi.org/?s=quis+resistet

LITANY OF HUMILITY

✛

O Jesus meek and humble of heart, *Hear me*.
From the desire of being esteemed, *Deliver me, Jesus*.
From the desire of being loved, *Deliver me, Jesus*.
From the desire of being extolled, *Deliver me, Jesus*.
From the desire of being honored, *Deliver me, Jesus*.
From the desire of being praised, *Deliver me, Jesus*.
From the desire of being preferred to others, *Deliver
    me, Jesus*.
From the desire of being consulted, *Deliver me, Jesus*.
From the desire of being approved, *Deliver me, Jesus*.
From the fear of being humiliated, *Deliver me, Jesus*.
From the fear of being despised, *Deliver me, Jesus*.
From the fear of suffering rebukes, *Deliver me, Jesus*.
From the fear of being calumniated, *Deliver me,
    Jesus*.
From the fear of being forgotten, *Deliver me, Jesus*.
From the fear of being ridiculed, *Deliver me, Jesus*.

HIS ANGELS AT OUR SIDE

From the fear of being wronged, *Deliver me, Jesus.*
From the fear of being suspected, *Deliver me, Jesus.*
That others may be loved more than I,
    Jesus, grant me the grace to desire it.
That others may be esteemed more than I,
    Jesus, grant me the grace to desire it.
That in the opinion of the world, others may
    increase, and I may decrease,
    Jesus, grant me the grace to desire it.
That others may be chosen and I set aside,
    Jesus, grant me the grace to desire it.
That others may be praised and I unnoticed,
    Jesus, grant me the grace to desire it.
That others may be preferred to me in everything,
    Jesus, grant me the grace to desire it.
That others may become holier than I, provided that
    I become as holy as I should,
    Jesus, grant me the grace to desire it.

— *Rafael Cardinal Merry del Val*

ABOUT THE AUTHOR

✤

Father John G. Horgan is a priest of the Archdiocese of Vancouver in British Columbia, Canada, and the pastor of St. Pius X parish. A native of Cambridge, Massachusetts, he graduated from Harvard, as well as the Angelicum in Rome, before being ordained by St. John Paul II in 1986. He has lectured and consulted on questions of moral theology and health-care ethics in Canada and in the United States.

Father has had a lifelong interest in the angels and saints and was credentialed through the Vatican's special training course for those involved in the process of "saint-making" in 1997. He has served as a vice-postulator for the cause of Blessed Marie of Jesus Deluil-Martiny and has advised on several other causes.

Father John has been involved with EWTN Global Catholic Network since the early 1990s; he made several appearances with Mother Angelica and has hosted two television series.